W9-BJB-442

Praise for
Tom Koulopoulos and *Cloud Surfing*

"*Cloud Surfing* artfully captures the first major megatrend of our century and shows us a world where hyperconnectivity is the new norm. The extraordinary access to new connections that the cloud enables will have a profound effect on how we scale our businesses and manage our people, processes, and technology." — Andy Zynga, CEO, NineSigma

"*Cloud Surfing* is this year's must-read! Reading it is like walking from room to room of an amazing building. As Tom turns on the light in each room, vague outlines pop into clear definition, revealing a dazzling array of new possibilities. This book reveals an entirely new future, one that goes far beyond the Internet and globalization."
— John Mariotti, CEO of The Enterprise Group and
award-winning author of *The Complexity Crisis*

"The cloud, much like mobile technologies, represents the future of business. If you're running a business today—and encountering barriers to innovation and scaling—*Cloud Surfing* is a much-needed resource. Tom Koulopoulos' enthusiasm for the subject is palpable in this book."
— Chuck Martin, author of *The Third Screen* and other best-selling
business books and CEO, Mobile Future Institute

"Tom Koulopoulos is the prognosticator of cloud-based computing, and *Cloud Surfing* is his crystal ball! Here he has truly captured the implications of the cloud and the way it is transforming the way we work, live, and learn. His insights into growing accessibility and the collaborative power of real-time connectivity to information and resources is an exciting and invigorating journey."
—David DeHaven, Dean, School of Info
Systems/Technology Kaplan University

"Tom does it once again with his new book *Cloud Surfing*. Entertaining, educational, and a perspective changer."

— Carlos Dominguez, Senior Vice President,
Cisco Systems and "The Tech Nowist"

"Cloud computing often sounds like a marketing gimmick for IT managers looking to save money on their server farm. In this insightful book, Koulopoulos shows us why that perception is wrong. He lays out a compelling case for what cloud computing is, how it is changing our lives today, and what we can expect in the future—as our access to information, personal relationships, and the businesses we run are transformed in the cloud."   —Myers Dupuy, President CBANC

Cloud Surfing

THOMAS M. KOULOPOULOS

bibliomotion
books + media

First published by Bibliomotion, Inc.

33 Manchester Road
Brookline, MA 02446
Tel: 617- 934- 2427
www.bibliomotion.com

Copyright © 2012 by Thomas M. Koulopoulos

All rights reserved. No part of this publication may be reproduced in any manner whatsoever without written permission from the publisher, except in the case of brief quotations embodied in critical articles or reviews.

Printed in the United States of America

ISBN 978-1-93713409-9

Library of Congress Control Number: 2012933937

Contents

To Mia and Adam, surfers of a brave new generation,
whose dreams will redefine our world.

In Memory of Maria 1934–2011

From Automating the Old to Enabling the New

Since the 1950s, information technology has been slowly changing how we live and work. But we are about to experience a more dramatic and accelerated change. As this book will describe, the connectivity technology now offers will affect not just how we work, but how we behave—maybe even how we think.

The first applications of information technology were simple: just automate a company's accounting processes. At about the same time, very big computers—ones that filled whole rooms—were starting to solve complex science and engineering problems. But it wasn't until the introduction of the ATM, the "automatic teller machine," that information technology directly touched the lives of most people.

The introduction of ATMs was carefully managed. First developed by Citibank, ATMs were placed in the outer lobby of banks. A Citibank executive told me that the bank was initially uncertain as to how customers would engage with the technology. So a group of executives stood behind a column in the outer lobby of one of the branches to watch customer reactions. One of the first customers was an elderly woman who checked her bank account balance using the ATM, then went inside the bank to withdraw some cash, then quickly returned to the ATM to see if her account balance had been adjusted. At that point, the Citibank executives knew that they had a winner.

How primitive this now seems, as today hundreds, if not thousands, of new applications become available to consumers each day. Technology is generally seen and experienced as a force for good, but that has not always been the case.

When Mike Hammer and I published the original *Reengineering* book in 1992, we saw the world of business frozen in complexity, technology, and outdated business processes. Simple work took too much time to perform and cost too much. We had studied an insurance company that was taking twenty-four days to issue a simple policy and invoice. Why? Because the work went through sixteen different departments, each highly automated but not well connected. Our favorite expression became "obliterate, don't automate." We didn't want companies to automate old business processes. We wanted companies to focus on rethinking work processes first, then apply technology.

We even argued that work could be redesigned without the help of information technology. But I would not make that argument today. The role of information technology is dramatically different than what it was in 1992. The Internet became the first major change agent, making technology so ubiquitous that it is now the great enabler of process change. You have to look no further than how this book is produced and sold to see how the Internet has changed a whole industry.

It would not be an overstatement to say that the Internet has changed our lives and work. But this process of change has just begun. The confluence of the cloud—the ultimate computing utility—with the connectivity provided by mobile devices and the ubiquity of the Internet will deliver radical change in many places.

Recently, I sat in a three-day conference on innovation in education. The most inspiring presentation described how children in undeveloped countries now access textbooks that sit in the cloud through their cellphones—the most common form of mobile device. Education in these countries now looks more advanced that in so-called developed countries.

You are about to experience in ***Cloud Surfing*** how much change the cloud and "hyperconnectivity" will enable. People are coming together as they have never before. Businesses need no longer be constrained. The cloud provides them with unlimited capacity. Work will change. Behaviors will change. We will have more choice in our lives. With technology, the future is now.

—Jim Champy, co-author of *Reengineering the Corporation*

Acknowledgments

One of the most gratifying and humbling aspects of writing a book is the opportunity to remind yourself of how much you rely on the help of others.

Books begin with ideas, which are incredibly convincing while they reside solely in the author's head. But ideas only come to life with collaboration. I was very fortunate to have an extraordinary team that helped me to think through the many pieces of this book as well as the long process of bringing them together. If this book, and the ideas it contains, hit a chord with readers it is because of these amazing people.

The idea for *Cloud Surfing* began over three years ago in conversations with Erika Heilman, prior to her co-founding Bibliomotion. At first the idea seemed much too far ahead of the market. Undaunted Erika spent the better part of those three years working with me to refine the message of *Cloud Surfing* numerous times. Without her emotional and intellectual commitment to the project I doubt it would ever have progressed beyond the kernel of an idea I started with. Her enthusiasm was the fuel I needed to realize my ambition.

Erika and her partner at Bibliomotion, Jill Friedlander, are bravely innovating the relationship between publisher and author in ways that are long overdue. Simply put, they have spoiled me rotten by setting a new bar for what an author's experience should be. Along with publicist Barbara Henricks , social guru Rusty Shelton, production pro Jill

Schoenhaut, and copy editor Susan Lauzau the Bibliomotion team brings more firepower to publishing than most major publishing houses many times their size, but also maintains the intimacy that all authors crave.

My literary agent John Willig has been an incredible ally, a consistent advocate and source of encouragement throughout. With me now for eight of my nine books, John is my touchstone. His voice of reason and sharp sensibility are always my first stop. John not only gets the publishing business and its dramatic evolution but also has a deep passion for the value of big ideas—even if they start as very small ones. As important, John has been a good friend whose counsel and advice are always at the ready to help this author navigate both publishing and life's travails—and few are the authors for whom the two are not often intertwined.

Early on, as *Cloud Surfing* was taking shape, I was also lucky enough to enlist the opinions and insights of Erin Rodat-Savla, a long-time colleague who graciously volunteered her time to kickstart *Cloud Surfing*. Erin is one of the best mental sparring partners I've come across. Her quick wit and thoughtful energy were just what I needed to get things rolling by turning rough ideas into conversations, mind maps, and case studies. It was after these early conversations with Erin that I realized the true extent of the Cloud's reach and impact.

My sincere thanks also to all of the cloud pioneers who agreed to be interviewed and who provided valuable case studies, including; Rob Wrubel, David Dehaven, Myers Dupuy, Mark Woodward, Andy Zynga, Maynard Webb, Lukas Biewald, and Carlos Dominguez. These are the folks who are doing the heavy lifting and are building the future of the cloud.

I owe an especially large debt of gratitude to my many clients who are constantly teaching me how innovation happens not only in the cloud but also in the trenches. I'm fortunate to be able to see the future from the vantage point of these bold pioneers. And, of course, there is the tremendous energy and learning I get from my audiences every time I step up on stage to deliver a keynote, as well as my brilliant students at Bentley

University. While I may be the "hired talent" or the "professor" I am also a *very* lucky student—there is nothing like a room of a few thousand professionals or, for that matter, thirty always-on, graduate students to keep you humble, honest, and sharp.

Then there is my friend and mentor for nearly two decades, Jim Champy, who was gracious enough to provide the Foreword for *Cloud Surfing*, and whose guidance has helped me chart my own career. Jim is that rare breed of person who can help you to frame nearly *any* challenge as an opportunity. Something we all need more of.

As *Cloud Surfing* was being written my mother, an incredibly strong, beautiful, talented, and vibrant woman, passed away after a long illness. Although I'm not sure she ever fully understood what I did for a living, it did not stop her from being my greatest cheerleader. While her passing was hard enough, it was followed by even greater swells that tossed me about and could easily have capsized me, along with the book, were it not for a handful of close friends and family who kept me upright. It seems a silly effort on my part to even attempt to thank them in these short sentences. However, I've come to realize that true friendship rarely requires as many words of thanks to be spoken as it does words of frustration to be heard. To these dear friends, especially Juergen, Mike, my brother Nick, Andreas, Giota, Joe, Dad, Deb, Harry, Steve, Eliot and my aspiring muse KT, thank you for your love, kindness, honesty, and friendship.

Finally, my gratitude and the largest measure of my love to the two greatest sources of inspiration I could have ever hoped for, my children Mia and Adam. Through their eyes the world remains for me a place of fascination, wonder, and hope. Whatever challenges I may face, ambitions I may have, or future I may imagine, it all pales in comparison to the joy you have brought into my life and the motivation you give me to occasionally pull my own head out of the clouds.

Hyperconnected

To those who reach for the clouds, the few who make it
and the many more who fall back to earth trying: you are all
builders of a brave new future.

Nearly fifteen years ago I happened to be sponsoring a large event in San Diego on the future of technology and knowledge work. I'd invited dozens of speakers, including the late Peter Drucker, economist Paul Romer, and management guru Tom Peters. All of them were talking about the evolution of technology.

As the organizer, I didn't have the luxury of sitting in on every session and hearing all the predictions being made, but one session stands out in my mind. It was a small breakout session set up for about forty people, yet the room was overflowing. Attendees were lined up at the back of the room, standing shoulder to shoulder. A colleague asked me to walk over and see if I could gently herd a few people to another session to ease the crowding. But when I got to the overflowing room I was curious, and I nudged my way in to see what all the buzz was about. What I saw and heard over the next few minutes changed my view of the future in what has to be the single most profound insight of my entire career.

A pair of technologists from the Stanford Research Institute (SRI) were describing their view of the future of the Internet. This occurred at a time when we barely understood the near-term impact of the Internet. Just as many people were wondering if it was a fad as were claiming it was a revolutionary phenomenon.

The image the two technologists used to illustrate the Internet of tomorrow was a large cloud. In this cloud, they claimed, would exist a nearly infinite number of possible connections, resources, capabilities, skills, and ideas, which they called "objects." It was, as they described it, the ultimate free market, where people could instantly access, purchase, and apply the resources of the world to solve almost any problem.

These objects would float around in the cloud, available to anyone who needed them. Many objects would have no owners, belonging to everyone and free to use, while others would be complex objects that could be purchased or rented for single use. But what was most spectacular about their vision was that this cloud would not have any geographical center. It would not be housed on any one machine, server, or desktop, and would not be the property of a single company or even a coalition or cartel of companies. The cloud belonged to humankind.

In 1999, to call this far-fetched was an understatement. It was beyond far-fetched, it was pure science fiction, and the term *lunatic fringe* would have been a more fitting descriptor for those who subscribed to it. Yet the session on the cloud drew people to it like bugs to halogen.

For some reason, the utopian view of that cloud never left me. I tried to apply it to the Internet as it evolved and kept looking for ways to use it to describe how technology and the world's use of it was changing. But the fit always seemed forced, somewhat contrived, and stretched beyond the boundaries of believability—at least until very recently.

When companies such as Salesforce.com began espousing the benefit of the cloud, while longtime players in hardware and software such as Oracle—and more specifically its visionary founder Larry Ellison (who coincidentally was an early investor in Salesforce.com)—started bashing it as old wine in new bottles, it finally struck me that we had arrived at the starting line of a journey into the cloud.

It's a journey that has in many ways been obvious from the outset of computing, and in fact from the earliest days of wired communication. Just as Leonardo da Vinci could have told you that a flying machine needed wings with camber and surface area to support flight but could not create an engine to power it, we have understood the virtues of surfing the cloud but have lacked the engines to do it. The changes to society wrought by the cloud, like those that came with the evolution of aircraft, will be much more profound than any of us are able to predict.

However, this book is not just about the new engines that are creating the cloud; more importantly, it's about the behaviors that are shaping both the cloud and humanity in what I believe is the most powerful synergy ever to sweep the face of the earth.

As we will see throughout this book, the early indicators of these changes in behavior are everywhere. Some are subtle changes, such as the way we build relationships through social media; others are dramatic changes, such as the formation of real-time value chains that morph to anticipate and adapt to changing consumer behaviors before consumers even know those behaviors exist.

We're living in what I call a hyperconnected world, a complex and interrelated global network of economic, social, political, and individual interests. In some ways we are already seeing the impact of hyperconnectivity in the way the cloud is being used to shape social and political agendas as well as business.

Hyperconnected

If you were asked to identify the single greatest phenomenon contributing to global growth, prosperity, and social and political change over the past two hundred years, what would you choose? Perhaps you think it's the acceleration of technology, or maybe that it's improvements in health care, pharmaceuticals, transportation, telecommunications, globalization, or education. Yet one phenomenon underlies all of these changes, and it is the same one that will allow us to keep pace with increasing rates of uncertainty and complexity in the future. It is the dramatic increase in connections.

This is not just an increase in person-to-person connections, such as those created through telecommunications or social media such as

Human & Machine Connections

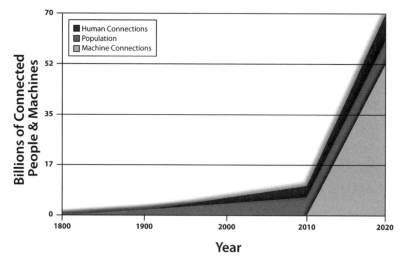

FIGURE I-1 While the number of connections between people is increasing as the population increases, from five billion connections in 2011 to a projected seven billion in 2020, the number of machine-to-machine connections dwarfs this, projected to grow from one hundred million in 2011 to fifty billion by 2020. A simple tally of the number of people-to-people connections, machine-to-machine connections, and people-to-machine connections will likely reach seventy billion by 2020. Coincidentally, this approaches the hundred billion neurons in the human brain. Keep in mind that even the 70 billion connections shown here are extremely conservative since it assumes only one connection from each category person-to-person (population), person-to-machine (human connections), and machine-to-machine (machine connections). The reality will be orders of magnitude higher, with the potential for 4,900,000,000,000,000,000,000 connections.

e-mail, Facebook, or Twitter; it is an increase in connections between virtually every machine, device, process, and person. There exists an intricate and immensely complex mesh of unimagined scale and reach that we have only just begun to appreciate.

Until now, what we have experienced are increases in connections that are separate, localized, and segregated. But what if all of these segregated connections were suddenly part of a single, interconnected whole that worked in harmony? Today that strikes chords of fear in most of us as we imagine the threat that such a coordinated body of information could pose to our security, identity, and intellectual property.

For example, imagine that all the information about you—your personal history, data about your behaviors and experiences, and your communications, whether by phone, e-mail, chat, or social networks—was combined in a way that captured the essence of who you are and what you do, and even what you might do. What if all of this information was connected, and was reliably and instantly available? Frightening? Of course it would be, in the context of today's world, which is the equivalent of the World Wild West when it comes to the way these connections are handled, or, more to the point, mishandled.

But what if the context changed? What if this chaos were tamed in such a way that it offered a nearly unlimited amount of value, both to you as an individual and to businesses? What if all the fears you have today about the way in which the Internet can create risk were eliminated, while all the ways that the Internet creates value were increased? What if there were new opportunities for you to work in ways that are financially, professionally, and personally more satisfying? What would that tomorrow look like and how would you surf this vast tsunami of connections to get the most out of them, rather than be swept away by them?

Answering these questions is the broad ambition of this book. But a discussion of this magnitude involves more than the image of a network of computers that can be used in the same way as an electric utility.

While we'll start by using that idea as a springboard, the larger agenda for this book involves looking at a variety of forces that are driving fundamental changes in behavior for individuals, businesses, and nations.

An Agenda for This Book

This book covers a great deal of territory so it's best to start with a broad scoping of the topics we will cover in each chapter. While the order of the chapters has a natural flow and each builds on ideas in previous chapters, it's not critical that you read the book from front to back. Once you've made it through the first two chapters, feel free to rummage about. To help in your journey, here's a brief synopsis of each chapter.

We'll start in chapter 1 by defining the cloud and separating it from the idea of a simple network of computers, a mistake often made by those who feel the cloud is nothing more than a marketing ploy that repackages mainframe computing time-sharing models popular in the 1960s and 1970s. Then we'll look at some of the basic shifts in behavior that will occur as the information technology industry moves to a business model that extracts value based on behavioral patterns and influence rather than one based on devices. This is a shift that will make consumers and user experience the ultimate products around which businesses will innovate.

In chapter 2 we'll talk about the evolution of economic models for the cloud, describing three distinct ways in which the cloud will deliver value over time. Then we'll look at how the socioeconomic global climate is creating a perfect storm for the advent and fast adoption of the cloud. Most prominent among these socioeconomic models will be the critical importance of "time to community" as a metric of cloud-based value creation.

Chapter 3 considers how the tremendous onslaught of data, analytics, connections, and overall complexity of the cloud can be harnessed by using a "pull-driven" framework of personalization that allows users to cut through the noise factor inherent in a hyperconnected world.

From there we'll move to a discussion of transparency, security, and trust in chapter 4. Here, we'll cover a broad swath of issues, including the ability to travel in time across the cloud's perfect memory, dispelling current myths around security in the cloud. We'll also take a closer look at how personalization creates more opportunities to track and understand behavior, the creation of cloud-based personas, and, ultimately, the importance of managing our reputations and brand in the cloud.

In chapter 5 we'll bring into focus the importance of mobility in the cloud and position it as the "killer app" for dealing with the challenges of living and doing business in real time.

Having discussed in the first half of the book how the cloud will alter many of our fundamental behaviors, in chapter 6 we take on the topic of how innovation will accelerate in the cloud, examining what I call first-, second-, third-, and fourth-derivative innovation. In addition, we'll look at the expanded role of open innovation as it is facilitated by idea platforms such as NineSigma and we'll introduce the notion of cloudsourcing as a way to mobilize the fast-growing global pool of talent.

Chapter 7 builds on this innovation capability by describing some of the ways in which commerce will be altered to better align investment, value, and risk. We'll also look at the topic of achieving scale within the cloud—especially the critical role small business will play—as well as the promise the cloud holds for future national and global prosperity.

Chapter 8 furthers the discussion of cloudsourcing as a sophisticated means of not only outsourcing work but creating a new type of elastic organization that can deal more adeptly with changing market needs, volatile patterns of demand, and the prevalence of uncertainty in the marketplace.

As we bring the book to a close in chapter 9, we'll look at what may be the most ambitious undertaking in the cloud, that of using it to educate people in an entirely different way. We'll examine its role in both traditional education and as a tool for educating people in the developing nations of the world, where the bulk of tomorrow's workers will come from.

Finally, in the Afterword, we'll push the envelope to look at some of the far-reaching implications the cloud will have on how we will work, live, and play.

As you read through each of these chapters, keep in mind that what we are attempting to define with the metaphor of the cloud is a tectonic shift in the way we look at many of the basic precepts we have used to build business, politics, and society. Because of the expansive nature of this agenda, our efforts here can only be considered the beginning of the dialogue. But the beginning is, in many ways, half of the whole that establishes an understanding to guide us through what will likely be a hundred years of change to come.

Welcome to the cloud.

1

Defining the Cloud

We are all hungry and thirsty for concrete images.
—*Salvador Dalí*

History is written in the collective images that we share as a civilization. Jack Schmidt created one of those images. Schmidt had a rare moment with nothing else to do on December 7, 1972, as he floated about in zero gravity with his Hasselblad camera in his hand. On a lark, he turned to face the retreating Earth as *Apollo 17*, the last manned mission to the moon, was leaving Earth's orbit for its 250,000-mile journey. The image he saw through the viewfinder was serendipitous: he quickly framed the shot and took the picture, one of thousands taken during the Apollo space program. Yet it is that image that has inspired generations and is arguably the most widely distributed photograph in the history of humankind: the blue marble.

The image of the world floating in its singular beauty against a backdrop of infinite blackness forever changed the way we perceive ourselves. Seeing in literal terms that we are so small, so connected to each other, and yet so very alone in the cosmos—that was the moment when the idea of globalization became real.

In the decades since, we've talked about being green, the global village, the flat world. Whatever your favored phrase, its genesis was somehow spawned by that single image. Images have power: they become symbols for ideas, simplifying the complex for all to understand. Change needs a billboard to broadcast its message, a meme that acts as a container for its many parts.

So what image will define us as we move forward in the twenty-first century? What symbol will suggest our future world? Many come to mind; perhaps the image is an upside-down globe with Asia on top or a picture of melting icecaps and rising seas. When I think about how we will deal with the many challenges that face us, one image stands out as a metaphor for the way we will work, live, and play. It's the image of an amorphous swirling chaos of nearly infinite connections of people, machines, and technology that cross all known boundaries; it's the image of myriad forces in a constant state of flux, disruptive, powerful beyond measure, and nearly impossible to harness—yet.

It is the image of the cloud.

Defining the Cloud

So what is the cloud? Let's keep it simple for now: the cloud creates intelligence through connections.

But before we go any further with what the cloud is, let's talk about what the cloud is not.

First of all, the cloud is not a synonym for the Internet. While the cloud relies on the Internet as one method of connecting people, machines, and information, it extends well beyond the Internet to mobile devices, sensors, radio, satellite, and other forms of connective technology. A simple way to compare the cloud and the Internet is to think in terms of evolution.

The Internet is single-cell amoebas, plankton, and the most rudimentary forms of life that crawled out of the primordial soup. The cloud, however, is complex forms of life, with brains and nervous systems that can sense and respond autonomously to the world around them, even to very complicated and unpredictable situations.

If you think back to the vast increase in the number of connections shown in the introduction (figure I-1), there is a significance to the total number of connections projected for 2020, seventy billion. The human mind is estimated to have between fifty billion and two hundred billion neurons, with most experts agreeing that there are about a hundred billion. The coincidence is more than just interesting. While I'm not claiming that the cloud will be as intelligent as a human, at least not by 2020, the dramatic increase in the number of connections certainly points to how radically different living and working in the cloud will be as compared with the Internet.

Because the cloud is constantly changing and evolving, it's tough to pin down an accurate definition for long, but for our purposes we'll use the following: *the cloud is an evolving, intelligent, infinitely scalable, always available, real-time collection of technology, content, and human resources that can be accessed as and when needed.* That's a mouthful, so let's break it down into each of the cloud's major parts. We'll talk much more about all of these throughout the book, but a basic foundation at this point is critical, especially if you are just learning about the cloud.

The cloud is:

- Evolving and intelligent
- Infinitely scalable
- Always available in real time
- An integration of technology, content, and human resources

Evolving and Intelligent

The cloud is not just a network of connected computers and storage devices, what is often called *cloud computing.* That's only the foundation that the cloud is built on. The intelligence in the cloud allows it to have an awareness of and an ability to instantly connect to the correct technology, content, and human resources that best meet your needs. For example, if you want to use the cloud to do sophisticated work on a project involving chemistry, the cloud knows about your preferences and capabilities and matches you with the software, hardware, and people best suited to the specific task. This is the sort of cloud that the researchers at SRI, whom I mentioned earlier, described in 1999.

The cloud is also constantly evolving to take the shape of the organizational, social, and political context that it inhabits. In the same way that intelligent life evolved to adapt to a changing ecosystem, the cloud will evolve as our needs and the complexity of our problems evolve.

Infinitely Scalable

The cloud grows as your needs grow. This is often referred to as *elasticity*, meaning that you use the cloud, and invest in it, based on the needs you have at any given moment, rather than being required to buy excess capacity and resources in anticipation of growth.

A great example of the cloud's scalability is Animoto, a company we will talk about in more depth later in the book. Animoto is a cloud-based multimedia solution for people who want to create high-quality, MTV-like video montages for professional or personal use. Because Animoto works in real time with video, graphics, and some pretty amazing artificial intelligence, it requires a great deal of computing horsepower.

When its founders first launched the company they expected that fifty computer servers would handle the peak load of demand that users would place on the system (servers are computers that run the applications and do all of the processing for an application). However, within three days the demand had outstripped their wildest dreams and they ended up needing thirty-five hundred servers! I'll do the math for you: that's seventy times more capacity than they had projected. The good news for Animoto was that they didn't need to buy any of the extra capacity beforehand. As demand increased and users paid more for higher-quality videos, the cloud Animoto used scaled in real time.

This last point, aligning value and risk, is an important one that we will stress repeatedly throughout the book. *By scaling to actual success rather than trying to predict the success of your offering, you significantly alter the relationship between risk and investment by capping your downside while leaving the upside unlimited.*

This is equivalent to a manufacturer not having to invest in workers, plant, and equipment unless consumers actually bought the product. Here is an even better example that really boils this principle down to its essence: What if I told you that you could play games in a casino and only place your bet if you won? I'm not claiming that every bet you place in the cloud will be a winner, but the degree to which people and companies can now experiment with new ideas and innovations increases radically due to the reduction in risk that the cloud offers.

Always Available in Real Time

The cloud is a global resource for both technology and people. Because of that, the resources you need to get virtually any work done are available around the clock. There are no national borders or time zones in the cloud. While the notion of having work follow the sun is not new to large, multinational companies, small and midsize businesses have not had this opportunity in the past. The costs required to set up a multinational operation, from hiring talent to contracting to escrow of funds, have historically been prohibitive for small and midsize businesses. All of the tasks associated with a global business can now be done in the cloud through platforms that act as intermediaries for technology and human resources. Resources include large companies such as Amazon, with its cloud computing and storage solutions as well as its human resource solution, Mechanical Turk. Another example is LiveOps, a company that provides on-demand talent in the cloud to small and medium-sized businesses that want to run lean by using a small core of employees and then adding staff as needed, without the overhead associated with carrying that talent when it's not needed.

Technology, Content, and Human Resources

When most people think of the cloud today they think of computers and data storage, also known as datacenters. These are large, factory-like warehouses of computers and data storage that can be leased to users through the Internet. Many companies, such as Dell, Amazon, Google, Microsoft, and HP, are providing these sorts of outsourced cloud computing capabilities.

These same companies also provide services and solutions, which include everything from software to contract employees who perform a particular business process (customer support, for instance).

The Adolescent Cloud

But *cloud computing* is just the early form of the cloud, what we'll call the *adolescent cloud*. The adolescent cloud is still very much a work in progress that acts as a bridge between the current state of the Internet and the cloud that we will be describing throughout the book. To keep things simple, when I talk about the cloud I'm including the adolescent cloud. So you may find yourself saying, "Hey that sounds a lot like the way the Internet works today." You're right, but when you find yourself thinking that way I'll try to help you stretch your imagination into the future.

Whether it's the adolescent cloud or the ultimate evolution of the cloud, the cloud we'll be talking about is much more than hardware, software, and services. The cloud includes not only the basic foundation and plumbing for a business but also many of the resources that it might need, from content to marketing to people. For example, companies such as Threadless provide aspiring T-shirt designers with the ability to submit and vote on each other's designs. Winning designers are then compensated and their T-shirts are sold at Threadless.com. Other companies, such as iStockPhoto and 123RF.com, allow aspiring photographers to upload their pictures and sell them to individuals and companies looking for stock photography. These are not just technology examples; they are new business models.

While some of the human part of the cloud is included—in the pools of talent provided by traditional outsourcing companies such as Dell—it also includes a much larger, more organic, and more diverse set of resources ranging from myriad smaller software applications (think of apps for your smartphone) to individuals who act as part-time or full-time talent in the cloud.

When we consider all of these dynamics of the cloud, there are ultimately two questions that we need to answer in order to apply the cloud to our lives and to business. The first is, how will the cloud change the business models of organizations, namely those trying to compete for cloud-based services? The second question is, how will the market change its behaviors and expectations based on what the cloud can offer?

The answer to each of these questions depends in large part on the time frame we choose. In the near term, let's say the next two to three years, much of the cloud's evolution will be in hybrid combinations of local or onsite hardware and software along with cloud-based solutions.

If we think of the onsite software and hardware as part of a closed system, meaning that it is proprietary and not easily, if at all, connected with the cloud, we can still see forces that are moving these closed systems to more open environments. For example, many companies are relying on outsourcing solutions, which force them to open their internal systems to third parties. Since these third parties are often global partners, the connection between the proprietary closed systems and the outsourced solution may well be through a public or private cloud. By *public cloud*, we mean a cloud that is protected from intrusion but is accessed through the public Internet. A private cloud is closed to all but member participants.

The difference really is a matter of how well physical and software-based security protects access to the cloud and defines what is required to be a member of the cloud. A public cloud, such as Elance or oDesk, is easy to access and gain membership to, and is therefore a likely resource for a small- to medium-sized business that does not want to invest in computers, applications, and storage. Companies like E2open, on the other hand, use large private clouds that have strict criteria for membership and access.

Other examples, such as Salesforce.com, have created public clouds that host applications that businesses can use as needed and that they pay for by the dose. All you need to do to access the applications and store your data in the cloud is to buy an online membership. In other words, rather than buying expensive software applications that need to run on the company's computers, you can buy access to applications and storage for your data on computers owned and maintained by Salesforce.com.

Alternatively, larger or regulated companies may opt for a private cloud, which has hard criteria, may vet members, and requires greater adherence to specific policies and legal requirements. The hardware for these private clouds may also be dedicated to the needs of the members rather than being shared with users of other private or public clouds. This is also referred to as a virtualized environment, because it breaks up the process of computing among multiple servers in multiple geographic locations.

Keep in mind that what I'm describing here is just the tip of the technical aspect of cloud computing. The number of variations on public and private clouds—how resources such as physical computers, servers, software, data, and processes are shared or isolated—is nearly infinite. You will likely hear terms such as *tenant, multi-tenant, virtual servers, virtual machines, shared databases and schemas, data isolation,* and many others bantered about as though they were clearly understood by anyone dabbling in the cloud. In fact, the specifics of how a cloud architecture is built and protected is an issue of prime concern for the builders of these environments. But I'm not trying to give you an education on the mechanics of cloud computing technology, just as I wouldn't try to teach you structural engineering to help you design a house. A basic understanding is all we're going to get into, and it's all we need.

For all of the types of cloud architecture we've covered (and for those we haven't), there are economic forces that will drive private and public clouds toward convergence in the longer term, which we'll define as five to ten years. For companies investing in private clouds, there are still higher costs involved with maintaining something that is not ultimately part of the core competency of the organization. As hardware prices continue to fall, economies of scale will develop in the cloud that will make it very difficult to justify a private cloud.

On the other hand, small and medium-sized businesses will increasingly find it easier to procure talent in the cloud, what we'll call *cloudsourcing*. The larger the cloud, the more efficient the free market dynamic of the cloud will be and, as we'll see in chapter 7, the lower the risk in employing talent will become.

What this ultimate cloud, shown in the upper right quadrant of figure 1-1, will look like is still anyone's guess. But the business models that will make it attractive and push it along are already starting to emerge. One of these is the power of the cloud to shift value from simply lowering the cost of technology to capturing data about behavior.

It's the Data, Not the Device

The greatest long-term value of the cloud, and the reason that companies such as Amazon, Apple, and Google are rushing to claim their turf in the cloud, has to do with the behavioral insight the cloud can deliver about its users.

What is propelling the cloud more than any other single force is the continued drop in the cost of cloud computing and the continued increase in the value of data in the cloud about how we behave.

Progression from Traditional Onsite Software & Hardware to the Cloud

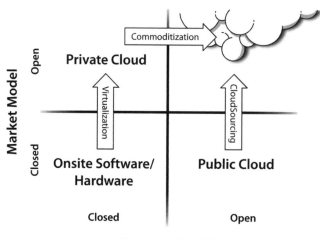

Business Model

FIGURE 1-1 The progression from traditional onsite software and hardware to the cloud will consist of numerous near-term and long-term shifts through both private and public clouds. Private clouds will be used in cases where businesses perceive higher security in closed business models that prevent the compromise of sensitive information. While this still allows businesses to address new market needs within existing business models it will prevent the movement to new more radically innovative business models. Alternatively, public clouds are already being used for new business models to address existing market needs, for example outsourcing certain tasks through human clouds such as Elance. Long term, however, public and private clouds will merge into one cloud with the ability to both protect sensitive information and adapt quickly to new market needs and new business models.

The reason Google gives away as much technology as it does, allowing you to store vast amounts of data on its servers—for example Gmail and YouTube—and to communicate through its devices—for example Android-powered smartphones—is that the data it is capturing about your behaviors, interests, and patterns is infinitely more valuable than any amount of hardware and software they could sell.

For example, if you have used Gmail, you are all too familiar with the ads from third parties that appear in your free Gmail account trying to pitch products and services that are relevant to the content of your e-mail. You might say, "Well that's a fair trade-off. They give me free technology and I give them a little info on who I am." But that information is not limited to who you are. If I send an e-mail to your Gmail account from my private, non-Gmail server, it still gets analyzed by Google. So now Google knows not only about you, which you have tacitly agreed to, but also about me and anyone else you communicate with via e-mail. The same is true of your buying habits on Amazon or iTunes as well as all of the data about how you use the devices that connect you to the cloud, such as your smartphone.

But let's not limit ourselves to a discussion about content and data. We can easily extend this idea to other realms. For example, General Motors is currently enabling cars equipped with its OnStar service with what's called GM-RelayRide, a service that allows owners to put their cars in the cloud! The idea is based on the fact that an average driver uses his car only two hours a day. With GM's new RelayRide, an owner could integrate his car with a cloud-based fractional rental capability that makes his car available for short-term, hourly rentals. With six million OnStar subscribers and another nine million OnStar-equipped vehicles, GM has a wealth of data about driver behaviors and patterns. Based on these behaviors, RelayRide coordinates matches of car owners and renters, maximizing the use of the car, subsidizing its owner, and providing a high level of convenience for renters.[1]

In this new cloud-based reality, the product is no longer what is being sold, whether it's an item or a service—instead the product is *you*. You have become the most valuable single product that anyone can own or trade. When I say *you*, I am of course referring to the data about who you are, what you do, when you do it, and even why you do it. The repercussions of sharing this data are well beyond anything we can even begin to fathom today, but part of our journey throughout this book will be to delve into the possibilities it creates.

This data grab is one of the least understood but most substantial shifts in the way technology providers will justify and build their business models in the cloud, and it is the primary reason that the move to a single, unified cloud will create the greatest change in the way we do business.

Breaking Free of Terra Firma

So if the cloud is such an incredible new way to do business, why isn't it a no-brainer for every business? After all, what business wouldn't want to reduce its risk and increase its ability to scale, grow, and innovate?

The answer is simply that we've built much of our view of computing around existing ideas of how we should work and how we should build our organizations based on a theory of resource constraints. In a resource-constrained scenario, where computing and human resources have a fixed price and limited supply, we have to optimize our organizations for the best results given the resources available. But what if we tweaked three of these constraints, namely, price, talent, and time?

For the sake of stretching our imagination, let's say that the price of computing was reduced to net zero (I'll explain net zero in just a bit), talent became virtually unlimited and near zero (again, hold on for an explanation of the terminology), and time latency was effectively collapsed to absolute zero?

A net-zero cost means that you are only paying for something if it is generating an immediate return. Recall the earlier case of Animoto, where the company only bought cloud computing power as consumers bought its video service. In this model, you never spend more than you make; therefore the net cost is always zero.

Near-zero cost for talent means that you can employ people to solve problems for you without paying them until a suitable and acceptable solution is developed. You still pay for the solution, but not until you accept that it is the solution you are looking for. We'll see examples of this in cloudsourcing companies such as InnoCentive, NineSigma, and OpenIDEO. There is still (usually) a price to be paid, but there is no risk of paying someone to develop a solution if one cannot be developed. We call this near zero because just having an acceptable idea or solution does not mean that the implementation of the idea will generate adequate revenues to cover its cost.

The absolute-zero latency of time results from the immediate ability of the cloud to connect you with hardware, software, and human resources. While it's a bit premature in the adolescent cloud to refer to absolute-zero latency, this is exactly where the cloud is heading.

The negation of risk is a pretty radical claim that hardly fits the model of business we operate within today, which is a highly structured model where we have to buy infrastructure, employ people, and spend significant time searching for and putting both in place.

This current highly structured approach to building a business is a significant hindrance in fast-paced markets. It narrows our field of vision and limits our options by establishing high hurdles for investment in new enterprises and ideas. These basic barriers to entry allow incumbents

FIGURE 1-2

Net zero	You pay for a solution only if it is generating an immediate return. For example, you only purchase computing power and storage when and if needed.
Near zero	You pay people to solve problems for you only if a suitable and acceptable solution is developed. For example, you post a problem on Innocentive.com and select one of the submitted solutions to receive an award.
Absolute zero	This is the absence of any latency in time that results from the immediate ability of the cloud to connect you with hardware, software, and human resources.

with less than ideal products and services to stay in business. Most of all, these constraints set our expectations for what is possible and what is not based on business assumptions and plans that have to be fairly convincing. I've repeatedly seen this sort of structure stifle innovation in large and small companies. In short, you need to justify delving into the unknown by fully anticipating the financial impact of the unknown. That's clearly a foolish exercise. I call this the terra firma approach to innovation in the area of terra ingonita, the part of antique maps that would be labeled "Here be Dragons," to illustrate the fear in venturing into the unknown. Maps were useless when you ventured into terra incognita, as are the financial tools we use to venture into the future. We try to explain the future based on our understanding of the past. It's convenient and rational but it doesn't work. The future is not simply a continuation of the past.

What's truly amazing is how quickly we develop blinders about the right way to approach a problem and what is feasible. We soon abandon the creativity needed to view the problem in a new light when we are forced to deal with only the known variables of a market. Because of these hurdles, we easily convince ourselves that no amount of creativity can solve familiar problems. It's why we doubt the radical nature of innovation. Whether it's the radio, the telephone, the lightbulb, the Internet, the iPod, or the cloud, we are absolutely oblivious to the impact innovations can and will have on us and the extent to which they will change the way we experience the world. The reality is that none of these innovations could be justified based on the conservative model of doing business; they all required thinking about the market in a new way. The same can be said about the cloud.

When familiar patterns of business are disrupted through radical innovation, it seems that the disruption always comes from the most unlikely candidates for change. As though only a virgin set of eyes, untainted by the knowledge of what will not work, are foolish enough to see the opportunity change can cause.

While we are surrounded by unlikely successes, we never cease to be amazed by them. Amazon redefines the way books are bought and sold; Google redefines the way we learn; Apple redefines the way we experience music. In each case, an outsider that stood no rational chance against the incumbents overtook them by light years. Like an amnesiac with no long-term memory, we remain awe-struck by the phenomenon, no matter how many times we experience it.

In today's world, the level of complexity, the speed of change in markets, and the sheer magnitude of the problems we are dealing with demand that we break free of the terra firma approach that has so severely limited how we justify investment in, and fundamentally collaborate to solve problems. Otherwise, we are quickly going to find ourselves the victims of complexity rather than its masters.

So what does this have to do with the cloud? It's simple. The cloud represents the consummate disruptor to structure and traditional models of justification and experimentation. It's a pervasive social and economic network that will soon connect and define more of the world than any other political, social, or economic organization, yet we are still looking at it primarily as a way to cut costs.

The cloud is the first megatrend of the twenty-first century. It's a trend so large that it defines the way we will address virtually every other challenge we will face for the next thousand years. It's a place where we will all live, work, and play in the twenty-first century. It's where nearly thirty-five million people already work. It's where your kids are when they dive into online play. It's where you meet and make friends in social networks and where you are likely to find your spouse. It's where companies go to find the next big idea and where political campaigns will be won and lost.

But when most people think of the cloud they form it into the same patterns they are accustomed to seeing. To many, the cloud is synonymous with the Internet. To others it's just another form of distributed computing, where storage and computer power is purchased from utilities such as Amazon, Microsoft, IBM, or Google.

That's not the way I want you to look at the cloud. Throughout this book we will define the cloud as not simply technology, but as a mechanism for change to our most fundamental assumptions about the way we conduct business and interact with each other.

It's not easy to envision the cloud in this new context. We just aren't wired as human beings to understand what we have not experienced.

Breaking Free

A wonderful exercise in the challenge of breaking free of known patterns, which I've conducted with tens of thousands of people, is nothing more than a sophisticated Rubin Vase—an image that oscillates between a perfectly symmetrical dark vase and two white faces.

My version shows a short animation of a silhouetted girl spinning, which you can easily find on the web. I play the video clip continuously and then I ask viewers to tell me if they see the girl spinning clockwise or counterclockwise. Half see her spinning clockwise and half see her spinning counterclockwise. It's what comes next that's startling.

Fewer than 15 percent of observers can change her direction. The rest of us are just stuck. Once we pick a pattern there is little we can do to change it, even when we know the pattern exists only in our mind.

Thomas Kuhn understood this phenomenon intimately. In his timeless book *The Structure of Scientific Revolution,* he explained in painful detail the fortresses we build to defend patterns of the past as sacred. The greater the revolution, the higher and thicker the walls of these fortresses.

That's absolutely the case with the cloud.

Cloud Context

In its most powerful form the cloud is a new context for business and society. The cloud is at the same time the enabler of terrorism and its antidote. It is the underlying driver of the destabilizing shift in power from the industrialized world to the developing world and also the mechanism by which the entire world will develop a new equilibrium over the next hundred years. In fact, the cloud isn't about any one technology. E-mail, instant messaging, social networking, cloud computing, and crowdsourcing are all small pieces of the cloud. They may make it easier to define how parts of the cloud work, but they don't define how it behaves. Nor do they get to the heart of how *we* will behave, and it's the behavior of this new world order that we most need to understand.

First, we need to appreciate that the cloud is a game changer in that it redefines so many rules about the way we interact and run our businesses. It isn't a trend or a fad. This is the evolution of a new intelligence whose structures and patterns, for just about everything, will challenge our notion of the familiar.

Second, don't confuse the cloud with the Internet. The Internet is just a collection of connections. It is no more relevant to the cloud than phone service is to how you build a business or an economy. You may need phones to run a business, but you don't build your business model around them.

For instance, think about how the cloud alters the process of viral marketing, changing the most basic tenets of how markets are influenced by new products and ideas. Viral marketing leverages the cloud as a built-in platform for influencing mass markets with near-zero investment, from YouTube videos that have launched sensations, such as teen singer Justin Bieber, to social media campaigns that locked in the youth vote for Barack Obama, whose YouTube videos had more than 80 million views. However, using viral marketing is not new; Orson Welles used it very effectively in 1938 to wreak havoc and cause outrage among listeners who thought they had been manipulated by Columbia Broadcasting's "The War of the Worlds" radio episode. However, Welles had a platform available to very few, Columbia Broadcasting. If you wanted to market in the twentieth century, you had no choice but to pay for a platform. If you intend to market your products in the cloud, the notion of paying for a platform becomes meaningless. The platform already exists. What's important is how you can create influence in the cloud. This shift from platform to influence is perhaps one of the most profound shifts in marketing, and one that many companies and individuals are only just starting to grasp.

You Can't Plow a Cloud

The shift from platform to influence leads to one of the most interesting implications of the cloud. The power of your message is determined not by the scale of your platform (i.e., your subscribers, viewers, and listeners), but by the scope of your influencers' networks. In other words, a single blog has the potential impact of the largest company's multimillion dollar PR program. These influencers are fast becoming one of the most sought-after assets in the cloud. What constitutes an influencer is still more art than science, but cloud influence is already being ranked by companies such as Klout, PeerIndex, and HubSpot's Grader.

The importance of influence has to do with the fact that in the cloud all communications are weighed by the value of their ultimate influence on the individual. That's a difficult concept to appreciate fully. *Think of it this way: traditional marketing is like plowing snow, and the larger your plow the more snow you can move. If you want to influence people using this model then you buy a Super Bowl ad for a million dollars.* This is the way Apple launched the Macintosh in its 1984 halftime Super Bowl add. However, if you try to plow through a cloud you're wasting time. Clouds don't plow well. In fact, people in the cloud respond negatively to this sort of traditional approach and see it as manipulative and disingenuous. To move a rain cloud, you need to cause every single molecule of water to move individually so that the cloud can move collectively. The same applies to the cloud we are talking about. Influence means moving individual people toward your brand, product, or service based on trust in a third party, a party that is more likely to move them than you ever would be. You can think of this as a form of endorsement, but these influencers are not like the Michael Jordans of the world. The value they get is not from you but from their reputation, which is built on trust and integrity.

One of the most profound examples of this shift in the way we use influence to create social momentum is the firestorm of unrest that ignited during 2011 in what has become known as the Arab Spring. During a nine-month period, starting in Tunisia in January of 2011, protestors organized themselves using cell phones and social media to demonstrate and protest. This was a grassroots uprising that ultimately toppled the governments of Tunisia, Libya, and Egypt, as well as disrupting nearly all countries across the Middle East.

The movement in Tunisia, called Takriz, has surprisingly deep roots in online organization, having first started using the Internet in 1998 for communications. One of the movement's founders, Ben Ali Foetus, was a hacker who decided to hack the Internet in order to get around the exorbitantly high usage rates charged by the Tunisian government.

But the Arab Spring's long-term influence has extended far beyond the Middle East, to countries across Europe and the United States. During the fall of 2011, protestors started to organize themselves around what has been termed the *Occupy* movement. Occupy started with an "occupation" of Wall Street in September of 2011 and spread across the country to more than two hundred cities. Groups gathered in cities to protest a broad spectrum of social inequity, with concerns ranging from the greed of large corporations to government policies and taxes that favor wealthy citizens and companies, to the failings of capitalism in general. Their goal was simply to disrupt and gain attention for an effuse cause. In many ways, the Arab Spring, and its offshoot Occupy movement, are the first cloud-based attempts at experimenting with the power of social media and influence to create entities that can at the very least disrupt existing social, commercial, and political institutions, and, at best, completely subvert and overcome them.

Protests are clearly not a new phenomenon. However, this particular wave of social media–enabled movements is heavily dependent on the ability of participants to connect quickly through technology and to effectively wreak havoc on government and commerce by mobilizing on a scale that would otherwise require substantial investment in organization.

While the Arab Spring may have been a bellwether for social networking–enabled demonstration, the roots of mobile-based protests date back to the 2000 national political conventions, when protesters used mobile phones to swarm like bees, evading police. The problem was so great that, days before the Republican National Convention, John Sellers, who at the time led the Ruckus Society and was a primary influencer of a vast network of demonstrators, was arrested by authorities preemptively and charged with a range of misdemeanors, including, for the first time in history, the use of a cell phone as an "instrument of crime." Sellers was held on bail of one million U.S. dollars, an extraordinary amount of money for the alleged crime.

In a similar move, Middle Eastern countries took drastic measures to stifle protesters' ability to communicate by shutting down their national Internet, posting bogus protests to popular blogs, and then waiting in anticipation to apprehend protesters. The efforts were ultimately of little use but they vividly illustrated both the power and the reliance we have on connectivity in today's communities.

We need to understand the tremendous power of these hyperconnected groups in the cloud to mobilize popular opinion in a way that can significantly alter the course of politics and business, for the better or for the worse. The Occupy movement marks a turning point in the way that dissatisfied communities can disrupt the status quo. While the early stages of the Occupy movement may well subside, I would not be too quick to discount it as nothing more than a group of students with too much time on their hands.

When we talk about Joseph Schumpeter's views on the future of capitalism (in chapter 7) we will look at the theory of creative destruction, which is reflected in the Occupy movement, and contains the seeds of what, in Schumpeter's view, could lead to the fall of capitalism. Even though Schumpeter could not have foreseen the advent of the cloud and the role it would play, his theory of "creative destruction" is frighteningly similar to the way in which the cloud could theoretically influence the course of world events to topple capitalism. Alternatively—and from the point of view I espouse—the cloud could be responsible for creating an entirely new dimension of opportunity for entrepreneurs and innovators, one that pushes capitalism into a new orbit.

This subtle but profound shift in the behavior of hyperconnected groups in the cloud is going to influence everything about our lives. It will determine how individuals work, as well as why and for how long we will work. It will define how organizations hire, build teams, partner, form alliances, compete, and go to market. The cloud will determine the nature of the classroom, along with how we teach and the role education takes in building knowledge and careers. For nations and economies, it will define the balance of power and trade that has always been at the heart of global stability or, as is often the case, instability.

Tapping the Other 90 Percent

As we've already established, the cloud is an evolving phenomenon. Consider that there are seven billion people on the planet, yet only five hundred million even remotely qualify as knowledge workers—that is, people who make a living based on the use of their minds rather than their muscle. Eighty percent of the world's inhabitants still make less than ten U.S. dollars per day. And, lest we believe the Internet is somehow changing all of this overnight, only 1.7 billion, just over 25 percent, have 24/7 access to an Internet connection.

Imagine running your company with just 25 percent of your employees talking to each other. Yet that's precisely what we are doing on a global scale. Despite all of the talk about the flattening of the world, jobs moving offshore to developing economies, and increases in productivity brought on by technology and the Internet, we are still in the dark ages when it comes to employing the world's talent. In other words, we are still using plows to move ideas.

The fact is that all of the innovation and achievement we have experienced until now has involved a ridiculously small fraction of humanity's potential. Research and development, education, and access to the resources needed to develop and exploit ideas have been closely held assets. This phenomenon is reminiscent of the factoid about how we humans use less than 10 percent of our brains. The cloud is about tapping into the other 90 percent.

Describing the full impact that the cloud will have on this equation would be tantamount to explaining the effects of e-publishing to a thirteenth-century monk hand-illustrating the *Nuremberg Chronicle*.

The good news is that we do have some sense of the near-term changes and are already seeing the impact of the cloud. Investments in higher education, health care, and the Internet are creating a workforce unlike any other in the history of humankind, with the potential to be amazingly connected across social and national boundaries. These are workers who will live longer, work longer, and play longer. And that workforce is not only growing in real terms, as population increases, but it's growing exponentially in terms of its ability to reconnect itself in whatever manner is needed to solve the problems of the moment.

Don't lose sight of the power of connections. This is not just about having more smart and educated people. It's about having more of these people connected to each other. We put a lot of our hopes into the notion that the more people who are on the web, the more ideas will flow from it. Perhaps, just maybe, one of those ideas will solve our problems. Casey Mulligan, a well-known Chicago economist, has even proposed that we need to grow the world population to increase the odds of that happening![2]

The cloud is not about throwing more brains at the problem. That's an interesting idea, but it's linear.

The cloud is exponential in itsimpact; it has a multiplier effect that goes well beyond the power of any collection of individual skills. What we lack is not brains but the ability to connect them.

We need to stop playing dice with our future and start leveraging the power of this wealth of ideas. This means putting in place the processes that innovation needs in order to thrive. We need to go beyond the fundamentals of an Innovation Zone, which I talked about in my previous book, to build a global Innovation Factory that will produce an engine for connecting, driving, and developing new ideas through hypercollaboration.

In many ways, there is an amazing parallel between the hyperconnectivity of the cloud and the advancements that took place during the early part of the twentieth century, many of which began as experiments in small business and collaboration. Globally, there was an amazing rush of upstarts, which leveraged one another. In large part, it's the reason that there is so much contention around the ownership of twentieth-century inventions like the internal combustion engine, radio, telephone, and television.

Ideas flowed freely in the early days of patents, resulting in one of the most prosperous periods in history. We put in place the political, organizational, legal, and educational cornerstones to scale this era of invention; we protected intellectual property and formalized methods for teaming and partnering. The model worked for the problems and challenges of that day and age. But it no longer works for today's complex problems.

In addition, the cloud is increasingly made up of an aging demographic in developed countries, which creates a talent pool of free agents that will radically alter the notion of retirement by working long past traditional boundaries of "old age." It's proven that as workers age, the likelihood of their becoming free agents increases; while 25 percent of those under fifty years of age are working as free agents, the rate increases to 40 percent of those workers over age fifty.

This just adds to the ocean of entrepreneurs that will flood the market and challenge all of our notions of work and employment, creating an amorphous human cloud that is always available and on demand to solve the world's greatest problems. But this will only occur if it is empowered and enabled beyond the sort of hopeful serendipity that Mulligan talks about.

How does this pool of talent contribute to the cloud? Well, as much as we'd like to believe that we can each understand our own domain of expertise better than anyone else, the greatest ideas rarely come from the places we most expect them, large companies and labs. Sure, discovery may be facilitated by the scale of large players, but that is not where most discovery starts. Instead, big ideas come from outliers.

It's counterintuitive, but the biggest companies today started in times of economic recession. They were strapped for cash and they were extreme outliers. Yet they altered markets and social behavior. What is it about the lack of resources and capital that is so essential to creating fertile soil for good ideas to grow and thrive?

Companies Started During Economic Recessions or Depressions

1876	General Electric	1975	Microsoft
1931	Allstate	1976	Apple Computer
1939	HP	1980	CNN
1954	Burger King	1981	MTV
1955	McDonalds	1992	Clif Bar
1957	Hyatt Hotels and Resorts	2000	Method
1973	FedEx		

In large part, creativity thrives in difficult circumstances because these situations foster collaboration and networking, creating connections between like minds and similarly impassioned people who have far less to lose than incumbents. Think of it this way: in times of crisis and uncertainty we instinctively migrate toward a tighter bond of community. This is when we network best, enhancing the likelihood of our success. It's why sites such as LinkedIn became so popular among professionals during the economic downturn. In fact, LinkedIn had been around for almost a decade before it reached critical mass during the recession of 2008.

What if we could sustain this level of innovative capability and collaboration?

That is exactly what's happening, as social networking in the cloud is altering the way we work. We are raising the bar for what constitutes normal communication and community to a new high-water mark. The impact of this is just starting to make its way into how we do business. While many people discount social networks as the province of distracted youth and out-of-work professionals, the ability of these networks to scale is incredibly powerful, giving them a reach much greater than that of many large companies. The formation of these virtual groups in the cloud is rampant and constant. Cloud employment is already topping $100 million in annual revenues through human clouds such as Elance, oDesk, Live/Work, InnoCentive, NineSigma, and others. In these human clouds, problem solvers reconstitute themselves around work as and where they are needed. The result is an inversion of the power structure, from power based on organized scale to power based on disorganized networks and individuals.

The cloud is the foundation of all of this connectivity.

2
Cloud Economics

So it's time to roll the dice for two reasons,
economics and for the future...

—*Bill Parcells*

One of the best ways to understand the current and future value of the cloud is to look at the three distinct value propositions that exist for it. To make this straightforward, I like to think of it as a series of courses in *cloud economics*, which covers everything from the basics of cutting costs to the more advanced proposition of aligning risk and value.

Let's start with Cloud Economics 101, cutting costs.

Cloud Economics 101

When I was a youngster, my father once sat me down at the kitchen table with a half-filled glass of water. Looking at it, he asked me that age-old question, "So, Tom, is the glass half full or half empty?" My father, an engineer by training, had a way of springing these sorts of questions on me without warning. But this time I was prepared. Thinking that this was a test of my basic outlook on life, I responded with an affirmative, "Half full, of course!"

"No," said Dad, "it's not half full.

"Hmm," I thought to myself. Perhaps Dad is expecting the more practical answer that speaks of possibility rather than naïve optimism.

"Well, I guess it's half empty," I said with a little less self-assurance.

"No, Tom, it's not half empty either."

Now I was completely confused. What other state might the glass be in? Was it just under or over half empty or half full?

Dad looked at me with a hint of a smile and uttered a proclamation that only the mind of an engineer could grasp. "The glass," he said, with a big pause, "is the wrong size."

The most fundamental value proposition of the cloud, and the one that has brought it to center stage, is that we have been using the wrong-size glass for our computing problems. In an effort to save money, individuals and small companies buy glasses that are far too small to accommodate growth and success. Large, established companies must buy enormous excess capacity to accommodate peak loads and unpredictable demand. In both cases, technology is being used incredibly ineffectively or inefficiently.

Cloud computing solves the dilemma by allowing us to buy a glass that scales as needed. This is the utility model of cloud computing. As with electricity to your home, you pay as you use it. The utility deals with the issues of peak load, infrastructure, and delivery. You just worry about turning the switch on.

This simple proposition has huge value for many companies but is especially advantageous for smaller and midsize businesses that can't play the "what if" game when it comes to guessing how much computing power they will need. It's also a far more secure model for these businesses, half of which don't even bother to back up their data.

When Amazon and Google talk about elastic computing capability, it is this cost-cutting aspect of the cloud that they are addressing. But that is just the beginning. The next level of benefit inherent in the cloud is the acceleration of value creation.

Cloud Economics 201

One of the challenges throughout the era of information systems has been that of building applications that address the majority of needs of all users but that can also be customized to address the specific needs of individual organizations. While these are often touted as 80 percent solutions, meaning that 80 percent of the functionality needed is already built into the application, anyone who has deployed or purchased a software solution knows that the last 20 percent of the solution ends up costing many times the cost of the first 80 percent.

I recall being introduced to this reality during my first job out of college as an application developer for early accounting systems. I worked for a small company and part of my role was to call on CFOs to convince them that a computer-based accounting system made sense. It's funny to think back on a time when you had to make a case for computerized accounting, but it wasn't that long ago. It was 1981, and I had graduated from university with two degrees, one in accountancy and the other in computer information systems. My employer must have thought they hit the jackpot. After all, who better to convince a CFO of the benefits computer systems can bring to the tedium of accounting than an accountant with a technology background? Yet the obstacles I faced were surprisingly difficult to overcome.

The objection raised by nearly every CFO or VP of finance I encountered was that there was no way an automated system could ever replicate their chart of accounts, the list of accounts and subcategories of accounts that make up a company's accounting system. A complex chart of accounts is not only a very long list, it is also an extensively categorized list, with many levels of nesting, similar to a very detailed table of contents.

It's laughable today to think that something so easy any novice spreadsheet user could easily accomplish it was such an obstacle thirty years ago. It's even funnier to think that each of these accountants felt that his chart of accounts was so special. While the specific low-level account names might have differed, the template and mechanics were all identical.

Yet, as computer-based accounting and business systems began to take hold, customization ran rampant. As a result, for every dollar of software sold in the 1980s and 1990s, ten to twelve dollars worth of services would be purchased in order to develop the high levels of customization that users perceived they needed. So much for an 80 percent solution! This ultimately resulted in some of the most costly and complex applications available today, enterprise resource planning, or ERPs. ERP applications from companies such as SAP and Oracle were notorious for requiring not only very high investment in software but also incredible investment in an endless stream of services and maintenance. Even apparently simple upgrades from one version of the software to the next were fraught with problems.

For many large companies this sort of expense was the only way to develop an application that addressed the many nuances of their internal business systems and processes. However, this same model of information system can be an overwhelming burden for the vast majority of businesses, which are better off investing in their core competencies rather than in technology. Until recently, the alternatives for these companies have been to outsource technology, which can still be costly, or to rely on off-the-shelf desktop software, which is not customizable.

The cloud changes the rules of this game. Companies such as Salesforce.com are developing cloud-based applications that can be used without onsite hardware or software, but which can be customized as required if a customer wants to use a private cloud. This category of software has become known as software as a service, or SaaS.

Because a company is only purchasing the capability it needs, SaaS represents cost savings, but its benefits go beyond that. SaaS also accelerates the organization's ability to create value because the company can focus its resources on its own core competency rather than diluting resources by investing in in-house IT.

Both Cloud Economics 101 and 201 make perfect sense and create measurable value in cost savings and recaptured resources that can be focused on core business, but they still leave out the final, and greatest, long-term benefit of the cloud, the ability to align value with risk.

Cloud Economics 301

The greatest challenge in launching any new business or idea is aligning potential value with potential risk and resources. For example, if you decide to create an online store that sells car parts you will need to make decisions about how much to invest in your supply chain, inventory, distribution channels, website/store, computer systems, and software. All of these decisions will require a certain amount of investment and therefore risk. As with any business, part of what you will need to determine is how much risk is acceptable before your business generates a return on your investment.

If we were to chart the relationship of value to investment and risk, we would see a band of projected investment and return over time that forms the sort of funnel function in Figure 2.1.

Figure 2.1 illustrates a fundamental precept of business, namely that the greater the investment you make, the greater the potential downside as well as the higher the potential return you can expect. There is nothing uncommon or surprising about this type of analysis. If your business success rises above the top edge of the funnel, you will be pleasantly surprised and may invest even more in building the business. If, on the other hand, your results fall below the bottom edge of the funnel, you will have to decide if you want to continue with the business or assume greater risk and stick out the initial losses.

But what if we were able to change this model by capping the downside risk and allowing for an unlimited upside, with no requirement for up-front investment. That sounds too good to be true, and it was, before the cloud. But as we'll see in chapter 2, the cloud allows you to purchase resources, capacity, and capability in real time, if and when you need them. What this means is that you can scale your infrastructure, people,

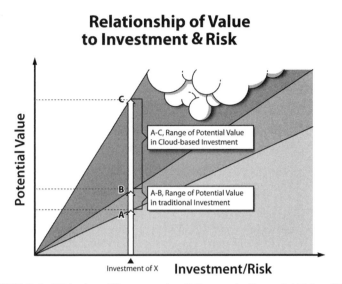

FIGURE 2-1 This chart illustrates the difference in Potential Value (Y Axis) given an Investment and Risk (X Axis). In this case for an investment of X a traditional business model will provide a return in the range from A-B. However, in a cloud-based business model the same investment has a much higher potential value, A-C, since the initial investment need only be adequate to prove the model works. From there investing to scale the business model is commensurate with the value realized.

and computer systems in direct proportion to your success. This reduces, and in some cases eliminates, risk while preserving the upside.

By aligning risk and value in this way, the cloud alters the economics of experimentation and innovation by virtually eliminating the risk involved in unsuccessful ventures and ideas.

The Perfect Storm

While the ideas in the three models of cloud economics have only recently become options for business, the concept of the cloud dates back to 1961, when computer scientist John McCarthy first described computing that would be delivered the same way that a power utility delivers electricity.

The term *cloud,* however, is a relatively new addition to the technology and business lexicon. The first attempt to protect the term goes back to 1997, when NetCentric attempted to trademark "cloud computing," an effort it abandoned in 1999. Then, in 2001, the *New York Times* ran an article about Microsoft's early Internet venture, Hailstorm, in which the term *cloud computing* appeared.[1] But it wasn't until 2006, when Salesforce.com, one of the major players in the field, and Eric Schmidt, then CEO of Google, referred to software as a service (SaaS), as a form of cloud computing[2], that the term began to take hold.

When I first heard the term used by researchers at the Stanford Research Institute in the late 1990s, I was drawn to the metaphor of the cloud not only because of the technology implications but also because of the way the vision of a computing cloud closely aligned to the way clouds operate in nature, in a fascinating state of dynamic disequilibrium. In physical clouds, water molecules are suspended in a constant tug-of-war, always in flux yet also always working together.

Not to go too far down the path of this metaphor, but the clouds we see floating above us are formed of tenuous relationships between separate but temporarily aligned partners. As anyone who has flown through fluffy cumulus clouds can attest, they are filled with violent currents that are rapid and unpredictable; in their ultimate form, cumulo nimbus clouds, which form violent thunderstorms, are among the most powerful and destructive forces in nature. Tiny water droplets with near zero potential for harm on their own can be nature's most ferocious element when combined, especially when combined quickly!

That visual depiction of small, seemingly inconsequential particles joining to make a great force resonated with me because it so closely resembles the economic move toward highly distributed organizations and globally interconnected businesses and people that are creating the power behind the change in today's world as a direct result of the ability to create massive connections.

The same is true of the economics of the cloud we're talking about in this book. The cloud is unpredictable but also unstoppable. It can shape itself to accommodate virtually any situation. Because of the rapid growth in interdependency and connectivity over the past fifty years, we have been navigating directly into the midst of a perfect social and economic global storm in which four weather fronts are converging to create the cloud we are talking about. This convergence is bringing about a sea change in the way we work and create economic value.

These trends are the cornerstones of the current demand for cloud-based business models and the economic drivers that are pushing us into the cloud.

The Perfect Storm
- Placeless work
- Ageless work
- Weightless work
- Complex work

Placeless Work

The growth of the Internet and worldwide investments in higher education have created a global innovation factory that is seething with new ideas and opportunities for collaboration.

This is especially true of a global economy that is in turmoil, creating new markets and educated workers but at the same time experiencing record unemployment. Marketplaces for knowledge workers such as Elance, LiveOps, and Amazon's Mechanical Turk are all providing work to people around the globe. At the same time, idea markets such as Inno-Centive and NineSigma are connecting problems to solutions without regard for location or even formal qualifications.

Ideas are taking shape in the least likely places and with the least likely people. There is no assembly line in this factory of ideas. Work and knowledge know no physical boundaries, traveling freely to where they are most needed. Never before have so many people joined to build so much value based purely on their ambition, energy, and intellect. We are experiencing a democratization of ideas without historic precedent and with little sense for how profound the shift may be.

Ageless Work—Increased Work-Life Expectancy

A radically changing demographic for work has emerged. Populations across the world, in virtually every major geography, have a work-life expectancy that is increasing faster than life expectancy, with the two likely to become one and the same in the near future. I often joke that at this rate we will continue working long after we are dead. I'll explain toward the end of the book why that may not be as outrageous as it sounds.

When you consider how many of an economy's social programs and health care services an aging demographic requires, working further into what was once considered the age of retirement not only alleviates this problem but also creates a degree of continuity and mentorship that has been impossible to achieve in the past.

People are living longer and working longer than at any other time in human history, and yet our organizational and social systems are ill equipped to deal with this inevitability. Within the next fifty years, it is likely that in any single organization we will find five generations collaborating and working side by side. This penta-generational mash-up is often seen as divisive and abrasive, yet it may also provide some of the greatest fuel for innovation we have ever experienced because of the richness and diversity of ideas that different generations of workers bring to the table.

Weightless Work—Extreme Availability

The world's talent has never been so available across economies that are increasingly tied to one another. In this new, interconnected global economy, not only do work and value flow instantly, but they are as ubiquitous as electricity and phone service. We can plug into work and workers as easily as we turn on a television and surf channels. Work has become weightless, moving without friction to wherever a need exists.

Thinking of innovation as a national or a corporate agenda in this context is as unlikely to work as believing that carbon emissions can be controlled by having a handful of countries go green.

The reality is that we live in an entangled, intereliant world where only the tireless power of a global innovation agenda will provide long-term stability and the solutions to our problems.

There exists a limitless workforce of innovators in the cloud, ready to attack any challenge.

Complex Work—Complexity Surrounds Us

One of the greatest challenges to every business and individual is the dramatic increase in the complexity of work. In organizations, that complexity shows up on computer desktops littered with applications that don't work with each other, a deluge of information sources, rampant growth in policies and procedures, increased regulations and compliance obligations, and unceasing change.

At the same time, employees are tasked with being faster, more accurate, and more efficient. It's a tightrope walk for even the most adept high-wire performers. In this pressure-cooker environment, dealing with complexity is not an option but a necessary core competency.

Buffeted by these winds of change, we need to relearn what it means to build successful careers and businesses. Simply put, we have created a world rich in invention, collaboration, and ideas. We know more, share more, and spend more on creativity than ever before, yet our capacity to grow our ideas is still in the dark ages. All this is happening at a time when we desperately need to build solutions to global problems that include pandemics, climate change, energy scarcity, and food insecurity, which create massive challenges, given our current approaches.

This broad-based context of global socioeconomic challenges is not separate and distinct from the way we run our businesses. The rising tide of complexity and the uncertainty it generates has a long-term impact on planning, especially as it applies to the coordination of tasks among global partners. I was recently speaking with the CEO of a large and very successful global company, and he said, "The challenge I face is not planning for next year or the year after. We have enough cash on hand to weather just about any storm. What keeps me up at night is how to make sure that our entire value chain, including business partners, suppliers, distributors, and customers survives the storm." His point was simple: in today's economy no one stands alone. The survival of one company or industry is intimately tied to the survival of others. Like a team of mountain climbers tethered to one another, our ascent into the cloud is not a solo climb. Success is based on a level of collaboration and community that we are just beginning to appreciate.

Time to Community

On the Mediterranean coast of Turkey, some five hundred kilometers from Ankara, lies the ancient city of Ephesus. Built in 1000 BCE, Ephesus is one of the most extraordinary excavations of an ancient city. Its mosaic-lined streets, twenty-thousand-seat stadium, and grand city plan are a magnificent testimonial to the art and science of ancient civilization.

As visitors walk down the main boulevard of Ephesus, they encounter what is perhaps the most impressive sight in the city, the striking three-story library of Celsus. The library towers over the city center, a reminder that the inhabitants of this metropolis were as hungry for and as protective of knowledge as anyone in today's wired world. Ephesus forces you to ask yourself whether we, three thousand years later, are fundamentally any different; you are left fumbling for an answer.

What has changed radically from the days of Ephesus to today's community in the cloud is the foundation upon which all of society is built: time to community. *Time to community* is the time required to build a community of similar social and/or commercial interests. That time interval has been steadily decreasing throughout history, often with extraordinary implications. However, from Gutenberg to Google, it's not just the scale and speed of community that has changed but also *the way* in which we form community.

Fast-forward from Ephesus to the present day. As this book is being written, social media has reached a frenetic pace of activity. Facebook is approaching one billion users and is growing at a pace that, if unabated, would equal world population in the next five years.

Lest you chalk up all of that growth to high school and college students who have nothing better to do with their time, note that the largest demographic of Facebook users is between thirty-five and fifty-four years old, and the greatest increase in percentage growth is in the fifty-five and older age group.[3]

Redefining Time

At 9 PM on Christmas Eve in 1906, Reginald Aubrey Fessenden changed the meaning of community forever at Brant Rock Station in Massachusetts. It was there that Fessenden transmitted the first wireless radio transmission consisting of more than mere dots and dashes.

An ocean away, a handful of passengers on ships in the middle of the Atlantic were, for the first time in human existence, connected in real time to the intimate sounds of another human being beyond the reach of his voice. Christmas wishes and a few lines of scripture set to the tune of "O Holy Night" played on a violin heralded the era of electronic community.

The metronome of our lives is governed primarily by our ability to make connections. The number of connections and the frequency with which we use them defines the way we perceive time. More connections make time seem shorter and our decisions feel rushed. Fewer connections make time's passing seem slower and our decisions feel much more complete.

A simple analogy is the way we behave when it comes to telecommunications today when compared with our behavior just a few decades ago. If you're like most people, it's likely that you've found yourself in situations where you are juggling multiple conversations at once. Perhaps that means being on e-mail while also using Skype, talking on a cell phone, texting, searching on Google, and socializing on Facebook. For my sixteen-year-old daughter this is commonplace. There is rarely a time of day when she is not using at least two or three modes of communication simultaneously. According to Nielsen, nearly 57 percent of us use the Internet while watching TV. In my household, it's not unusual for me to be sitting in the living room with my son and daughter channel surfing on the large-screen TV while we are all also surfing the web or using a cell phone. In other words, there may be seven to nine screens in use in one room with three people.

A Kaiser Family Foundation report[4] on simultaneous use of media showed that eight- to eighteen-year-old children consume, on average, seven hours per day of media while multitasking and absorb about ten hours of media from their various electronic devices. But that's conservative when compared with a study from Dr. Harry Rosen, professor at California State University who contends that the total number of hours sixteen- to eighteen-year-olds spend consuming media is twenty hours per day, when you total all of their streams of media, while baby boomers tap out at five hours of cumulative media intake daily.

As much as I try to operate even in that relatively pitiful baby boomer mode of multitasking, it is still maddening to me. My behavior is fundamentally single-threaded. I like connecting with one person or a group of people in unison on a single topic rather than trying to slice my brain's bandwidth into many small conversations.

This trend toward electronic multitasking is not just a matter of perception. In fact, if you plot the increase in time spent communicating electronically with the length of each individual conversation, you find that the two are moving in completely opposite directions, with total time communicating going up just as fast as average time for each communication goes down. Like it or not, we are all being forced to perform this time-slicing juggling act just to keep up with each other.

We can chalk much of this up to the often-touted Moore's law, which, simply stated, tells us that computing speed and storage densities double, relative to cost, every eighteen to twenty-four months.[5] But that is just an empirical metric. It doesn't tell us much about how these increases also change the way we behave in the cloud.

The real dynamic driving behavior is the number of people and machines that are connected to one another. At the time of this writing, there are more than five billion cellular phone numbers in service. That does not mean that five-sevenths of the world's population has a cell phone. As many as half of those cell numbers are for machines, everything from gas station pumps to ATMs to point-of-sale terminals. It is the rate at which these connections are increasing that ultimately causes the cloud to impact behavior.

If you're still having a tough time tying the notion of time-based decisions with the pervasiveness of these connections, then consider the explosion of QR (Quick Response) codes in the past few years. A QR code works much like a bar code, but it has the capacity to store from ten to nearly five thousand alphanumeric characters about a particular product, service, or other piece of information. QR codes can be read by most smartphones, providing users with near-instant access to everything from information about a restaurant's menu, location, and ratings to an augmented-reality application that overlays data about a product onto its image. Say you are at a department store and want to purchase a flat-panel TV but are not sure about the reviews that model has gotten from other buyers. You can just point your smartphone camera at the QR code and bring up the reviews on Epinions.com, glance over the reviews, and make a decision on the spot.

But why stop there? You could easily get information about not only consumer items but businesses and people. Scan my QR code and you instantly know not only who I am but most of what I've done in my professional and personal life. I know what you're thinking: "But I don't have or want a QR code!" Fair enough. I can understand your reluctance, but is it a reluctance based in perception or fact? If I want to dig, I may well get a great deal of the same information about you but I'll also get some irrelevant or outright incorrect information. Would you prefer that I get everything and try to sort out truth from falsehood, or that I get an authoritative description of you?

The profound competitive realities associated with the arrival of full-blown time-based competition are still only dawning on most businesses today. Those businesses that have yet to grasp the importance of this key trend are reminiscent of the early twentieth-century railroad companies that failed to understand the effect that automobiles and planes would have on transportation. While the market passes them by, the slow-movers become stuck on metaphorical rails, unable to change their speed or direction due to the outdated tracks they have laid by the mile. It's downright funny to see companies like Circuit City, which had done an extraordinary job of positioning itself as *the* big box technology hardware store, try to keep up with technology but nearly implode by their ineptness. What Circuit City did not understand was that its core competency as a big box store was not in its selection but rather in its experience. In its heyday, the store was a bastion of learning for consumers. Floor staff were not primarily salespeople but technology sherpas who helped customers understand new technology. As the company grew, two dynamics worked against it. First, consumers became much more educated about the technologies they were buying, and second, Circuit City started cutting costs by moving from highly educated floor staff to salespeople. The result was the pure commoditization of its services. Customers could not justify the time it took to go to a store for something they could get online with even better service provided by peer reviews. The result for Circuit City was the shuttering of its brick-and-mortar stores altogether, with a fallback to its relatively frail online presence.

At the same time stores such as BestBuy and Radio Shack have made inroads by leveraging the value of time by giving customers a one-stop shop for comparing and purchasing one of the most complex and fast-changing consumer buying decision, cell phones. By bringing together all of the major cell phones carriers under one roof, they streamline the experience of buying by allowing one-stop comparisons of plans and devices. This sort of focus on minimizing the time consumers spend comparing the plethora of complex options will only increase in value as the complexity of real and virtual goods continues to increase.

Don't kid yourself. Although the fundamental rules of commerce have remained essentially the same throughout history, the changes in consumerism that will take place over the next decade will radically alter the expectation of lag time, whether your business is high tech or low tech.

A basic ability to create value through the connections we have available at an accelerating rate is critical to a complex series of interactions, and soon it will simply be impossible to catch up if you are not already exploiting the cloud.

The formation of the cloud is in direct response to this. With little or no lag time in transactions, both buyers and sellers have become ever more conscious of time as the principle metric of success. Consumers already take for granted the ability to find information on goods and services at the click of a mouse. This attitudinal shift is not going to retreat, and it is this shift of time-based expectations that, more than anything else, will bring the cloud to center stage.

In a demand-driven market where customers configure their own products and services, the luxury of response time is eliminated. In its place, the cloud creates a synchronous and almost instantaneously responsive market.

Engineers describe a machine that works efficiently as being frictionless, meaning that it is free of obstacles that prevent it from running optimally. Part of what I hope you will take away from this book is an understanding of how the cloud is moving us closer to a frictionless economy, one that will become the defining construct for all business in this millennium. I know it's a bit of a stretch to envision that given all of the friction in today's economy, but it is precisely because of these challenges to traditional business models, the near catastrophic global economic crisis we are facing, and the dramatic generational shift in social networking that we need to radically rethink the way in which we operate as individuals, businesses, and governments.

One final item, along these same lines, before we embark on the rest of our journey into the cloud: the economics of the cloud are intimately connected to the movement toward social networking and what I like to call the social economy. Trying to separate the two is foolish, because so much of the cloud is based on human connections and interactions that are facilitated by the cloud.

Here are five ways the social economy is redefining us and how we do business in the cloud:

1. Social influence is where the value is: social marketing is all about influence. Take *The Huffington Post* as an example. Adeptly using the notion of a "network of influencers," Arianna Huffington was able to give new meaning to the term *socialite* and cash in on a $300 million windfall by selling her six-year-old news aggregator to AOL. The Huffington Post was the ultimate cloud influencer, with more than nine thousand bloggers who provided its content. It's also worth noting that an uncompensated writer has filed a class-action suit on behalf of the site's unpaid bloggers for $105 million, since they have been writing for free and received none

of the windfall. Like I said, we're *redefining* the rules of business—not that we've *redefined*, them!

2. Social transparency: social business requires transparency, something that can be difficult for many companies to accept. Consider how often you try to protect and conceal the inner workings of your organization from the marketplace, customers, and partners. What if most of that information could no longer be concealed? Take a lesson from Jonathan Schwartz, who was CEO of Sun Microsystems before its acquisition by Oracle. Schwartz's blog was open to any and all—it wasn't always pretty but it was open, and it set the tone for the transparency of the entire organization.

3. Social time: social business is real time. The immediacy and always-on nature of customers requires a reciprocal approach on the part of every business. In the cloud, customers will judge your company by how quickly you respond to their needs, complaints, and behaviors. Take, for example, Comcast, which, like most cable companies, is still seen by many as the "cable repair guy who wants you to define a two-hour window within which you will patiently wait for service. Which makes it all the more surprising that they have put in place a Twitter handle, @comcastcares, which is monitored in real time for customer concerns and complaints. At least I have someone to talk to while I wait for the cable guy.

4. Social meaning: your brand is only as powerful as it is clear in what it represents. I buy Apple, in part because it's a better computer. But I also buy Apple because it says something about who I am. What does your brand say about who I am (notice I said "I" not "you")? What value does it bring to *my* life?

The era of customer loyalty is over. In the cloud, you need to create a brand that respects my values and supports them.

5. Social experience: even hard-goods manufacturers such as BMW are learning that experience is social as they move the experience of driving to mobile devices such as iPods, with apps that not only work with their products but also redefine the notion of a driving experience, in and out of the car by connecting your car's systems, your driving behaviors, and even your interests, for example, what kinds of shops, restaurants, or leisure activities you favor on long weekends so that BMW can send you an itinerary with suggested routes, stops, and activities for the coming weekend.

This same principle applies to simpler products, especially commoditized products that are difficult to differentiate. While the product may not be distinguishable from others like it, the experience of buying or using it can be. In the cloud, these experiences are richer and far more personal, because they rely on your persona, or online representation of self, something we talk about more in chapter 3.

Part of the anxiety about being so openly exposed in the cloud comes from the challenge of managing your reputation or brand. The fact that your reputation can be so easily influenced by others and your identity so easily compromised is the cause of a fair amount of concern in moving to the cloud, where your personal details and organizational image exist primarily, if not exclusively, in the cloud. We'll look at this in greater depth later, but for now keep in mind that most forms of commerce today require that you give up a bit of yourself to gain some convenience.

Ultimately, the cloud is our best hope of evolving our organizations to a point where we can keep pace with the tremendous degree of creativity and innovation that will be required of us in the years and decades to come.

Here is the good news: if you're using any of the products we've covered then you are already in the cloud. The volatility and uncertainty of the world are only increasing. The winds of change are already at a Category 4; the storm warning has been sounded. The only question that remains is whether you will run for shelter to the structures you are familiar with or build the structures of the future.

3

Complexity in the Cloud ▲

Out of intense complexities intense simplicities emerge.

—*Winston Churchill*

Although the time we live in is arguably the most complex in human history, at least we have the advantage of using powerful technology to manage this complexity. During World War II, battlefield status and strategy was managed using strings and pushpins on a wall map. If you want to appreciate the challenge of complexity, I'd suggest a visit to the Cabinet War Rooms in the underground central London bunker from which Winston Churchill and his generals managed the war effort. Yet there was one technology without which the outcome of WWII may have been entirely different.

During the Battle of Britain, in the spring and summer of 1940, England's Royal Air Force was outnumbered by a factor of four to one and its planes were technologically inferior to those of the German Luftwaffe. If you were to wager on the obvious, Britain did not stand a chance. But thanks to a network of twenty-one long-range radar stations (constructed, in no small degree, at Churchill's urging), the R.A.F. knew *when* and *where* enemy planes were coming from. With this advantage, British pilots could lie in wait for German planes and then attack. Thanks to the efficient coordination between radar operators at Fighter Command and the R.A.F. pilots, the tables were turned and Germany's air offensive was stymied. In September 1940, Hitler called off "Operation Sea Lion," his planned invasion of Great Britain. Praising the R.A.F. pilots in a speech before the House of Commons, Churchill noted, "Never in the field of human conflict was so much owed by so many to so few." Radar has made pivotal contributions to so much of military and civil transportation since that time.

At its core, radar is nothing more than a means of separating important signals from unimportant ones, what engineers call filtering out noise. Modern transportation would simply have been impossible without radar. The accuracy needed to handle the volume, complexity, and speed of air traffic and the ability to foresee and predict weather patterns and conditions was essential to the modern age. But as air traffic increased, even radar was not enough. Satellite Global Positioning Systems (GPS) and onboard collision avoidance also had to be woven into the fabric of aviation to handle greater complexity and risk. Ultimately, GPS technology, which was intended for very few, became part of the everyday travel experience for anyone with a cell phone.

The Sensory Cloud

The vast array of sensors and networks that we take for granted in predicting weather patterns and planning our daily work and leisure activities is in many ways an apt analogy for the similarly pervasive means of navigating through the complexity of the connections of the future. In the world as we know it today, there are a multitude of connections to sensors that record our public and private actions and activities. Take, for example, video surveillance cameras. In London there are more than five hundred thousand such cameras recording activity 24/7, and there are about ten times that number throughout the United Kingdom. The Chinese government has launched the Golden Shield project, which promises to have millions of cameras installed, along with compiling a database of every person in China, 1.3 billion people at the time of this writing.

By contrast, there are far fewer surveillance cameras in New York City, which has fewer than ten thousand cameras. However, targeted applications of surveillance cameras are being used throughout the United States. The U.S. Department of Homeland Security has installed 358 real-time video cameras on buses in San Francisco. These cameras are not just capturing images but can also track eye movements, perform facial recognition, and even bathe you in scatter X-rays to see under clothing. In Washington, D.C., high-crime neighborhoods are using a system called ShotSpotter, which uses a combination of cameras and microphones to identify the location and number of gunshots fired. Other companies, such as Skybox Security, are planning to deploy a constellation of from twelve to twenty-four satellites that will provide on-demand pictures of any point on Earth down to one meter resolution, a limit imposed by the government for national security and privacy reasons. However, unlike present-day satellite imaging, which can take days to deliver an image, Skybox provides deep analytics with the image that can help to make sense of patterns and trends emerging from the formation of crowds, traffic patterns, and other complex movements of people or machines.

As if that were not enough, there is also a wealth of data being mined from your cellular devices, which can be used to record your movements and activity. Add to this aerial surveillance, satellite surveillance, GPS, RFID, and data mining surveillance of your commercial or consumer transactions, and things start to get interesting. But numbers do not tell the entire story.

We are creating a sensor-based society that would have made George Orwell absolutely cringe. It is not just the sheer number of cameras and sensors but their connections to one another that allows for real-time action. In the case of ShotSpotter, police will receive notification of gun-fire even before the first 911 calls start to come in.

While the consequences of the cloud on our personal liberties is some-thing we need to be concerned about as these pools of now-disconnected information are brought together, we need to also recognize the tremen-dous benefits that such aggregated information might offer.

Let's take the use of surveillance cameras in London as an example. In 1993, the news of the abduction, torture, and murder of three-year-old James Patrick Bulger provided a gruesome example of how ineffectual surveillance can be if it is not connected in real time to social networks. James was abducted from the New Strand shopping center in London by a pair of ten-year-old boys. The abduction was seen on the CCTV (closed-circuit television) used in the shopping center. However, the heartbreak-ing part of this story is that by some accounts more than fifty bystanders saw James and his abductors during the course of the day. In fact, James was even taken to a pet store by his abductors, who were thrown out because of their behavior. Some of the bystanders who saw James crying and bruised on his head from an injury even questioned the boys, who made up various stories about who they were and where they were going. Yet all of these numerous interactions did nothing to save James.

I bring up this sad case because it speaks volumes about the way in which life in the cloud will contrast starkly with life before the cloud. What if the CCTV footage was available to James's mother? What if one of the fifty bystanders who saw James had texted or tweeted the inter-action to a local authority? What if the ten-year-olds had cell phones that could have been pinpointed at the time of abduction by linking the CCTV footage to their location and identities? What if face recognition software could have been used? I know all of these "what ifs" are sheer speculation, but the exercise raises the question of what might be pos-sible in the cloud. I also understand full well that it paints a frightening picture of what the world might look like and how intensely we might be observed in the future.

Separating the Signal from the Noise

Before you recoil in horror at this new picture of reality and the nearly complete loss of any anonymity, stop and think about how much more identifiable and traceable you are today than you were just ten years ago. If you are anything like me, and if you're reading this book that's a fair comparison, then you spend your life tethered to devices and tracked by sensors already. If I want to find out where you are and what you are doing, it doesn't take much more than basic access to the Internet. My point is that we are giving away personal liberty, and have been for some time, in exchange for convenience and value. This does not mean that we should not fight zealously to protect our privacy, but that we should also fight zealously for value in exchange for giving any part of it away. In the cloud, that struggle will be vastly more profound than it is today.

In the meantime, as we move toward the connected cloud, the deluge of information we already have available to us has resulted in what can only be termed *global attention deficit disorder*. It could well be claimed that capturing your attention, as a brand, company, blogger, entertainer, or individual, and retaining it, is now the single most valuable and contested asset of most companies and the key to inferring meaning from all of this disconnected data.

In his book *The Age of Spiritual Machines*, Ray Kurzweil describes how a heightened level of frenetic activity is changing the very nature of time. Significant events in our lives are paced so closely together that they are becoming indistinguishable from one another. Societal, political, and technological shifts of a transformational nature used to occur a few times in one's lifetime. We have seen that time frame collapse from a lifetime to a decade, then to years, months, and days.

Psychologists have long known that as the "noise" around us increases our filtering mechanisms also increase—this is a basic survival skill. It is what scientists refer to as signal-to-noise ratios. It is the same principle that SETI (the Search for Extraterrestrial Intelligence) uses to sniff out intelligent life in space by scanning the chaotic radio noise of the cosmos for a discernible pattern of intelligence. As the background noise of our world increases, we need to become better at identifying relatively weaker and weaker signals. Yet filtering without accompanying focus can be a dangerous proposition, the equivalent of blinders on a raging plow horse. That's especially true of the potential to use the sensor-based capability we are building in ways that have obvious negative consequences for law-abiding citizens. In other words, how do we separate the well-intentioned use of sensors to capture the illicit activity of criminals from the capture of activities of law-abiding citizens? Today we do not fingerprint everyone just to capture the few that will be involved in criminal acts, because we believe in the right of privacy for all citizens until they are suspected of conducting a crime. A sensor-based society turns this ideal on its head.

The Uncertainty Principle

Compounding the volume and velocity of information that we are capturing are increasingly shorter windows in which to make decisions. We are weaving the web of our lives ever tighter by dedicating smaller and smaller intervals of attention to each task and responsibility. It's what I call the Uncertainty Principle:

> *As the volume of opportunity increases, the time to act on each individual opportunity decreases proportionately.*

This phenomenon is something you are likely experiencing firsthand. Today it seems we all have more to do and less time in which to do it.

Consider, for example, that the average length of a phone call has dropped from about nine minutes in 1985 to less than a minute today. At the same time, the number of minutes billed has skyrocketed from two billion in 1985 to over one hundred billion in 2010, and that's not

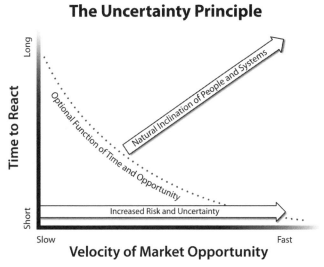

FIGURE 3-1 The uncertainty principle: as uncertainty and the velocity of market opportunity increase, the time to react decreases.

counting the two hundred billion unbilled minutes used yearly on Skype alone.

For us as individuals, this new way of life has not been a gradual change but a sudden shock. It wasn't that long ago that we associated distinct places and times with working, family life, and personal leisure. An eight-hour workday, Monday through Friday, was the norm; evenings and weekends were off limits for work—they were devoted to family and leisure.

Some time ago, AT&T ran a series of television ads that made the assertion "YOU WILL." The ads showed a futuristic view of the world that included being able to stream movies to your home or computer, sending a fax from the beach, conducting a video conference call with anyone around the world from your hotel room, sharing documents and images on tablet computers, and tucking your child in for the night from a video-enabled telephone booth. I often play those ads for people and ask them, "In what year do you think these were first aired?" Most people

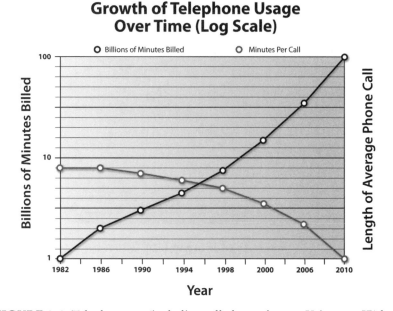

FIGURE 3-2 Telephone use (including cell phones, but not Voice over IP) has increased at an accelerating rate over the past thirty years, from 1 billion minutes used in 1982 to 100 billion in 2010. At the same time, however, the length of the average phone call has decreased from nearly 10 minutes to under one minute. The trend illustrates how we are relying on more communications of shorter and shorter duration.

respond with the early 1980s or even the 1970s. Amazingly, it was less than two decades ago, in 1993! We are shocked that what we believed then to be on the bleeding edge has so quickly become a normal, even indispensable, way of life, and we chuckle at the fact that AT&T brought none of this technology to market. Rather, these innovations were introduced by companies that either didn't exist when the ads aired, such as Netflix, or those that had no place in that future view, such as Apple.

With the advent of the Internet, cellular communications, e-mail, social media, wireless network access, and portable smart mobile devices, we have been thrust in a very short period of time into a constantly connected mode for which we have little preparation.

The lines of demarcation between the compartments of our lives have become increasingly vague. Technology links us to work anytime, anywhere. Productivity increases, yet it comes at the high cost of lost privacy, downtime, and necessary disconnection.

From an organizational standpoint, the same uncertainty principle seems to apply.

Value chains are becoming far more intertwined, but also far more susceptible to global disruption as they become more intereliant on global partnerships.

All of this creates a level of complexity that makes the coordination of commerce critical but also a highly fragile activity. We've built an incredibly powerful global machine for business, when things work well and uninterrupted. But a single act of terror, natural disaster, or economic crisis can quickly bring commerce to a halt. In fact a recent study by fmglobal.com of 600 global financial executives identified supply-chain risk as their greatest concern. It's as though we built a superhighway that can support unlimited speeds and then put traffic lights at every on/off-ramp.

So what can be done? How can the cloud help companies and workers maintain their sanity and mitigate risk? Answering these questions today, while we are thrashing about in the midst of all this chaos, is a monumental challenge. But there are glimpses of hope that may provide role models for the future.

Let's go back to our R.A.F. example from the start of the chapter. The key benefit in using radar was its ability to find meaning in noise. If you have ever used or seen someone use a metal detector, the kind that many people use on the beach to find valuable objects left behind in the sand, you probably have an idea of how this works. What's interesting about both radar and metal detectors is that they need to be tuned in to what you are looking for. In other words, if you tune them too broadly everything starts to show up as meaningful; if you tune them too finely you will miss most of what has value and come up with only the largest objects.

This process of tuning in to the right frequency is essential whenever you are looking for something. What if we could tune our view of the cloud in such a way that we had a personalized view of only those things that had meaning to us? That's the power of pull.

The Power of Pull

One of the most basic problems that the cloud addresses, and one which has plagued organizations throughout the industrial era, is that of highly specialized but isolated workers. Simply put, increasing specialization in complex organizations and societies tends to isolate us from one another, making our knowledge of what others do in the same organization or process scant, or perhaps even nonexistent. This is at the heart of the complexity that stifles innovation.

Think of the problems that plague health care, where a patient's medical records, history, and numerous prescribed pharmaceuticals are represented in an incredibly disconnected set of sources and managed by different health care professionals in different places.

If an increase in the number of connections is an essential attribute of the cloud, you have to wonder whether we are going to be exacerbating our current problems through even further specialization. The answer is: absolutely not. In fact, the cloud is a direct antidote to this systemic challenge, which faces everyone and every industry, for two reasons.

First, when two people's respective tasks are separated by several days, they are less likely to understand the impact of each other's work than if the tasks were separated by seconds, minutes, or hours. Why? In a word, *iteration*. Iteration is a fancy word for the dialogue that occurs when you are negotiating a process that requires complex interactions and where the decisions are not immediately apparent.

For example, think of a negotiation on a large contract. The back and forth of iteration is a necessary aspect of arriving at a correct and timely decision. However, the longer it takes to iterate a task, the more difficult it is to maintain the continuity of the discussion. As a result, the task's integrity suffers and it becomes harder to come up with the best results. In other words, if it takes two days to get a response to a question rather than two seconds, you are either less likely to ask the question or you are more likely to get an answer that does not directly address the question. By the same token, you are less likely to understand or change a process if you are removed from it by significant intervals of time.

The cloud closes the time intervals by eliminating the inherent transfer times in routing not only information but also work from one person to another. Keep in mind that this is not a problem that can be solved by a communications network alone, any more than it was solved by the evolution from paper memos to e-mail. Electrons may travel at the speed of light, but work and people do not. The Internet and the current concept of cloud-based computing (what we've called the adolescent cloud), where computing power and storage are used as needed, is only the most basic value proposition of the cloud.

If you don't believe that this is more than a problem of how quickly we can transmit and access information, ask yourself this question: When did I last read my e-mail? If it was 30 minutes ago, then you could say that the e-mail messages waiting for you have taken 30 minutes to get from their sender to you, although the actual message probably took mere nanoseconds to be delivered. "But, wait a minute," you're saying. "I have a smartphone, and my e-mail gets to me immediately." Your smartphone may indeed notify you that work needs to be done, but does your smartphone provide all the tools you need to do the work? It probably doesn't, and that is true for most work delivered electronically, because much of the information—and the applications that we need to act on that information—exists on specific localized devices.

The underlying problem is that complex work rarely exists in isolation. Work on the contract negotiation I was just using as an example may require links to other supporting documents or to regulations or to people with specific knowledge. As communication travels through the cloud rather than to and from point-to-point proprietary systems, the cloud is able to connect all of the information, people, and resources we need to act on the information.

While smartphones such as BlackBerry, Androids, and iPhones have alleviated some of the problem by allowing on-the-go pickup of e-mail, they fail to provide a true platform for work because they do not have the ability to instantly make all of the necessary connections. In many cases, lack of screen real estate prevents viewers from being able to see the complexity of the work. But that's just the start. There are three parts to this problem.

The first is that we have focused for too long on the delivery of *information* and *not* the delivery of *work*. Work, by its definition, is not delivered— it is orchestrated and performed. No matter how fast the information assembly line runs, the work will always end up waiting unless the right tools, resources, and people connect it with the performer of the work.

For a business to achieve the elusive goal of intimacy—that is, the ability to quickly act on work and not just to transport information—it must go beyond the delivery and networking of information alone and consider instead the way the work is performed and how it can bring together the tools and resources needed to do the work. Delivering the information alone is like sending parts down an assembly line without sending the instructions, expertise, and tools needed to assemble the parts.

To use a simple example, imagine a setting where the work includes analyzing large-format documents for engineering, high-resolution x-rays or images, large sets of documents for a financial transaction, or comprehensive volumes of regulations and procedures. In all of these instances, and many others, the key is analyzing, not just transferring, the information. It's why we spend so much time printing information once we get it and then litter our physical desktops with documents, which we need to somehow organize and assimilate. It's not that we need the physical artifact in order to do the work but instead that information systems have been built around the central character of the document or the information rather than the work. Work is about coordinating and organizing documents and information. When documents and information are contained in myriad applications, systems, and sources, which do not work together, it's the human being that ends up being the superglue to hold all of this disparate information together and give it context. But even once we have organized the information we still need to pass it on to a colleague or customer. This lack of an ability to transfer work as an object with all of its pieces of information, resources, and tools is also the reason that you might end up being transferred to three customer service agents, describing your problem three times. It's also why a visit to the emergency room requires that you explain your symptoms to each nurse and doctor who comes to your bedside. The doctor may have all of the data but she does not have the story or history that forms the critical context for the data.

Working the Cloud

Part of the difficulty we have in envisioning how work will get done in the cloud is that the devices we use to perform most work are not devices that support the full spectrum of work. Just putting data into the cloud and pushing it back out again does very little to alleviate this problem— if anything, it compounds the problem by creating access to even more information with even less context

The second limitation of most of the mechanisms we use today to transfer work is that the applications needed to get the work done are also tied to specific devices and locations. If I'm sending e-mail, almost any device will do, from a cell phone to a PC, but if I'm working on a complex budget with colleagues around the world I need to define a specific time zone, use a specific application, collaborate and share information in a specific environment, and have available all of the supporting documentation needed to make decisions.

The third, and most challenging, limitation is that today most work is pushed out to us rather than pulled in *by us*. In the push model, hard rules define who the work goes to. We live in a push-driven world, where information is sent to us constantly. Think about the way you work and live. E-mails, phone calls, news, media, and product and service ads are primarily pushed out to you whether you ask for them or not. If you look at how much time you spend sifting through all of this noise, you will undoubtedly find that a large chunk of your day is spent acting as a complex radio telescope separating the background noise of the universe from the signals that have meaning. Each time the phone rings, an e-mail arrives in your inbox, or you open up a magazine or book, you are adding yet one more channel of potential noise to an already crowded radio dial.

Am I suggesting that there is no need for push? Absolutely not! I've stumbled upon many serendipitous circumstances, people, products, and bits of useful information that I would never have known to ask for. Push provides a level of serendipity to our life that can create value. But is a haphazard approach to life and work the only approach, or is it just the only one we know? The question is not how to eliminate push but how to minimize and filter it.

That's the idea behind the pull model. In the pull model, you exist in the cloud as a series of interests, behaviors, skills, capabilities, competencies, preferences, and connections. All of these create a persona for you that defines what's uniquely important to you.

The pull model is not entirely new. In one form or another, we've been using it for as long as there have been sources of information to cull from. In fact, you can set aside the discussion of information in the modern-day sense and apply the notion of pull to our perceptions of the world around us. We filter out what we feel is irrelevant based on what we are looking for, like we do with the *I Spy* children's books, which show pictures of objects crowded on a page, among which you need to find a few well-hidden items.

An even better illustration is a very funny collection of videos that has gone viral on the Internet, and that prove this point in a most amusing way. There are many variations of the video, but nearly all start by asking the viewer to count how many times a group of people, usually six to ten, pass a large ball back and forth among themselves. The short video then shows the group passing the ball back and forth. As you watch intently, counting every pass of the ball, you are focusing entirely on the activity that you have chosen to see; you are in pull mode and nothing that is pushed at you will get through your acutely tuned filter. All else is eliminated from your visual and mental frame.

The proof comes when, at the end of the video, you are asked not to identify the number of times the ball was passed but instead to describe the person in the gorilla suit who was moving in the background of the video nearly the entire time that the team was passing the ball. Most people are incredulous at this point. What gorilla? You would swear that there was absolutely no such thing in the video. Yet when you play the video a second time you do indeed see the gorilla moving slowly, gesturing wildly behind the people you were focusing on but nonetheless in clear view. Yet you missed it completely! Your reaction is one of dumbfounded amazement. How could you possibly have missed a guy in a gorilla suit? Easy. You put in place a pull model that was finely tuned to a specific purpose and process: follow the ball! Your task was clear and you were not going to be fooled by any trickery or sleight of hand. Yet you missed something so large, absurd, and overwhelmingly out of place. Congratulations, you are human!

Our survival is keenly dependent on using a pull model, whether we are cave-dwelling predators identifying prey or businesspeople spotting market opportunities. But that innate capacity to filter is being tested beyond its intended level of endurance. We're so bombarded by push-driven information that we have already exceeded our ability to make sense of the data we have available, and yet we've barely begun to experience the extent of push overload. In the cloud, this will get infinitely worse, not only because of the sheer amount of information but also because of the number of people who will be participating in the cloud as creators of content.

We underestimate the degree to which we are both educating and bringing on board new citizens of the cloud. Even the most generous estimates place the number of active Internet users at about two billion. If you consider that world population is currently approaching seven billion and will be closing in on ten billion in the next decade, where it may well be capped due to fundamental resource constraints, this still leaves five to eight billion people who may come online, a fivefold increase in raw population numbers but a staggering 100,000,000,000,000,000,000 potential connections among humans. And this is not counting the additional fifty billion connections due to devices, sensors, and machines. Using today's technology and behaviors to deal with this number of connections is a fundamentally flawed plan.

Surfing this magnificent tsunami of opportunities and complexity will require pull-driven models that are difficult to even conceive of today. However, one type of pull model that uses a personalized approach called a portal is already being used, and is evolving as an important way of dealing with the chaos of today's cloud.

The Personal Portal

A portal is a single point of personalized access, and represents a key ally in both finding meaning in and orchestrating the volume of information available in the cloud. With a personalized portal, you can create one place where all of the disparate information, people, processes, and applications you need to do your job, make a decision, and collaborate with others are instantly available in a coordinated and reliable manner.

Portals are not entirely new. Some of the simplest examples are Internet destinations such as Yahoo!, which have been providing users with the ability to aggregate various feeds from proprietary and third-party services to create a personal web page with weather, stock market data, news, and mail at a single point of access. While these portals may help in organizing basic publicly available sources of information, they do little to integrate other proprietary sources, such as your personal banking, financial and insurance data, work-related activities, health and medical records, or the other information you need access to. In these areas there are other portals, such as Mint and Manilla, which act as aggregators of financial data, including bank accounts, brokerage accounts, credit card balances, mortgages, and loans. But these only provide windows into your transactions and balances; they integrate the way you can view the information but not the underlying applications (the software that manages the information) that manipulate it.

Portals were originally nothing more than search engines. The initial value proposition was simple: no one could hope to find anything in the vastness of the web through "conventional" means, so offering a full-text index of the web provided a great leap forward and a chance to take advantage of the new hyperlinking capabilities built into web protocols.

Portals soon morphed from search engines to "navigation sites," which became the term used to describe the functions available in early portals such as Excite, Infoseek, Yahoo!, and Lycos. While it was assumed that search engine users could navigate around through a raw associative "web" of "links," it soon became evident that developing professional research skills in order to find information was not high on the average user's list of priorities. So, to address user frustration and reduce the average "search time" for relevant information, these navigation sites added the function of categorization—filtering popular sites and documents into preconfigured groups by their content (sports, news, finance, etc.), which is still what you see today if you go to Yahoo.com

These sites not only provide search functionality and a library of categorized content, they also offer access to "communities of interest" (for example, Yahoo!'s financial community), real-time chat options, personalization of content by user-specification, and direct access to specialized functions (shopping networks, auctions, online trading sites, etc.).

Although all of this happened well in advance of the cloud as we know it today, it laid the foundation for a core principle of how we navigate the cloud, establishing that there should be a single point of access from which to make connections for all of our information needs: news, shopping, browsing, and social networking. Until now, that utopian view of a single point of access has been elusive. We are surrounded by computer devices that each offer a portal toward a particular aspect of our lives. My laptop is great for writing, my smartphone is great for texting, my iPad is great for e-mail, my GoDaddy server is great for web hosting, my home server is great for graphics and multimedia, my AppleTV is great for entertainment, my GPS is great for travel, and the list goes on. I have more gadgets for more uses than I could ever have contemplated a decade ago. I feel like the frequent flyer who opens up a copy of the SkyMall catalog, that bastion of useless inventiveness, only to find things I absolutely never knew I could not live without.

The reason for all of this disparity is that there is no single technology driving each of the individual information sources you need access to. Instead, *you* become the superglue that connects all of these systems. It's an element of complexity that has far exceeded the bounds of reasonability, which is why most of us end up with a dozen windows open on our desktops at any given time as we try to make sense of our lives and our work. As an analogy, imagine that every time you went from your bank to your brokerage house to your supermarket to your gas station you had to use a different language to communicate. In many ways, that is exactly what we are doing today with personal and professional use of our desktop, corporate, and Internet applications.

In the cloud, personalized portals become a two-way street with well-defined and standardized mechanisms to communicate with each other so that you can not only view aggregated information but also act on it. Every one of your sources of information and applications exists as an object that can be connected and which can talk to the others.

This coordinated view of the cloud also brings into the conversation the notion of how you identify what is relevant to you, your interests, and your work without creating tunnel vision that limits your ability to see new opportunities and threats.

So what might these new cloud-based opportunities and threats look like? Once all of this information about you is aggregated and archived the biggest challenge that we will face is creating a cloud that we can trust to protect not only our identities but also to provide greater value in exchange for the transparency it will create in our lives.

4

Truth in the Cloud

Security isn't something that you buy,
it's something you do.

—*Mark Mellis*

In 2000 I joined the board of directors of a small start-up company with a very big ambition. The company had developed a software program that captured the activity and all the changes that occurred on a website or on multiple sites, and then allowed the user to go back and forth in time to view the website as it had been at any point in the past.

Imagine, for example, being able to go to a company site and slide a handle at the bottom of the screen to view exactly what the company's website looked like on any given date and time. Imagine doing the same for an individual's website.[1] The software could also track an unlimited number of connections to associated websites and information sources. What you ended up with was a perfect history of the Internet. Granted, the Internet was much smaller and simpler then, but there was no reason that the approach could not have scaled with the increase in storage and computing power over the past decade.

We had some major corporate clients who were very interested in being able to do this for their own websites but also for competitive purposes. In fact, one of our most interesting prospects was a large government intelligence agency that wanted to do this to track large portions of the Internet. If you think that this is still the stuff of fiction, you're wrong.

The Internet has become a vast library of historical artifacts, the likes of which we have never before encountered. We have at our fingertips the potential for a near-perfect collective memory and historical record. But the constant churn of the Internet makes it a stream into which you can never step twice. Constantly changing in unimaginably complex networks of connections and vast content, the ebb and flow of the Internet is unlike anything we have experienced as a society. According to tech guru Yuri Milner, more content is being created every two days on the Internet than had been created from the dawn of civilization through 2003.

Until very recently, capturing all of this change in a way that makes it possible to move back and forth in time has required an imaginary time machine. There has been no way to automatically create a complete history, because so much web content comes from proprietary databases and content management systems; for example, the content of *The New York Times* can be searched, but only through the portal provided by *The New York Times*.

As the content and linkages of the Internet change, they are lost. We cannot roll back to a particular event, date, or time and view the millions of web pages as they existed at that moment and every subsequent moment to the present because the information is owned by a particular party and it is often located behind a firewall[2] of some sort. Even if we could access this information, the applications used to manage it are often proprietary. It's difficult enough to do this with a single website much less with the millions of websites that exist. Or can we?

What if you could record every instance of the past and use it not only to surf the past but even to predict the future?

Amazingly, Isaac Asimov coined a term for precisely this sort of capability as early as 1950. He called it *psychohistory*, the ability to predict the future based on huge amounts of accumulated data about behaviors of the past. You can't do this with the Internet but you can with the cloud. Think of it this way: the cloud is to the Internet what the moving picture was to photography. Rather than capturing a single instant in time, the cloud is capturing a continuous stream of history, connections, business, society, behaviors, and every nuance of our individual lives, our businesses, and the interactions between them, as well as the global community we have formed. You can see the embryo of that stream already in sites such as Internet Archive (archive.org), which catalogs more than 150 billion web pages since 1996 on an ongoing basis. But Internet Archive provides snapshots in time of individual websites, not the ability to roll back to any point in time across multiple websites and their content.

Facebook has embarked on a similar endeavor through its Timeline offering, which allows you to build a surfable history of your Facebook activities and applications. The difference, in the case of Timeline, from what I've been describing, is that Facebook allows you to highlight the events that you feel are important rather than capturing all of your activity. Facebook is also only one facet of your digital identity. However, some industry watchdogs are concerned about the way that the company handles privacy and user information. Facebook admitted to tracking 750 million users' activities and the websites they visited even when they were logged out of Facebook. While the company claimed this was a technical blunder, it nonetheless illustrates the ability of the cloud to capture an amazingly telling history of behavior and interests.

While Facebook's approach is still part of the adolescent cloud, the implications of this capability as it matures are nothing short of mind-blowing. Imagine being able to roll back the clock and get an absolutely precise historical record of everything from the weather and stock markets to the evolution of major sociopolitical trends. As the web reflects an increasingly complete view of the world, this becomes a time tunnel into the past.

One of my first exposures to this power of the cloud came in a dramatic trademark infringement case I was involved with. A trademark I owned was being used by another company, and it had refused to cease and desist in its use of my mark. After years of drawn-out legal battles and hundreds of thousands of dollars spent by each side trying to defend its use of the trademark, we were closing in on the even costlier court battle. As I talked to my lawyers about what they needed to nail down the case, it came up that part of the challenge was showing in clearly understandable terms how the infringement had been carried out over time. The infringing company claimed that its use had little to do with the way my company had used the trademark.

Through extensive discovery—the process by which lawyers find evidence to prove their case—my lawyers had pieced together ads and images of the way the trademark had been used. When I saw this portfolio of the trademark's use, it struck me that what was missing was a single cohesive story of bad behavior. Sure, the pieces of the case illustrated by the various images of ads and clippings of text from periodicals showed a somewhat convincing argument, but it was far from crystal clear. I wanted there to be no doubt as to the clear intent and long-term history of infringement.

At that time, Internet Archive was barely known, yet it had been collecting data on websites for nearly a decade. In fact, I was shocked to see images of our own website as it had evolved over the past decade from its very first crude format. In a matter of minutes I had pieced together a decade-long story of infringement of our trademark that was amazingly clear and comprehensive. Proud of myself, I brought it to my lawyers. Keep in mind that these lawyers were partners in a very large, heavy-hitting LA firm that practiced only trademark and patent infringement. Yet they had no idea Internet Archive even existed. That simple discovery contributed to a substantial out-of-court settlement. I didn't know it then, but I was indeed cloud surfing back in time.

Now take that story and extrapolate. The example I just provided applies not only to legal issues and to business, but to our personal lives as well. The trail of breadcrumbs we leave in the cloud is indisputable and unforgettable. Our lives are being documented in vivid detail, and we will forever be captives to this record. Frightening? Perhaps, if you think of it in terms of just *your* history being out there. But what happens in a generation's time, when everyone's history is out there? Do you see how the playing field is suddenly level? When our lives and our businesses become this transparent, it redefines the very nature of honesty and trust.

But let's not stop there. While there is no doubt that the cloud will first be engaged as a tool for legal purposes (note the growing role of e-mail in corporate and public litigation), it will also give us a much more reliable facility for understanding decisions in context.

The U.S. government has just such a program already in place under an agency called IARPA (Intelligence Advanced Research Projects Activity). The mission of IARPA is to tap into the tremendous data available through all forms of communication and to analyze how the trends and behaviors that emerge from this data may help to project events in the future.

Why is the cloud able to do this so much better than the Internet? For the same reason that Google is able to tap into your cloud-based e-mail and use your conversations to recommend products and services. As information moves to the cloud, the metadata—the data about your data—becomes extremely easy to capture and use. This metadata is an easily missed byproduct of the cloud and yet it represents an incredible asset to whoever owns it, especially if it can be mined in such a way as to infer trends and behaviors over time.

With this sort of history available at our fingertips, might we be able to go beyond surfing the cloud retrospectively to apply prior experiences to future outcomes? Granted, the past will never offer a 100 percent accurate rendering of the future. But it will certainly help us to hedge our bets. The difficulty we have today in believing that this is possible is that until now we have used disconnected pieces of history and woefully incomplete context to determine how past behaviors and actions impact the future.

Here's an analogy that makes this concept easier to understand. Until now we have made projections and predictions about the future of the stock market based on publicly available information. This is typically empirical data about how the market behaves based on an incomplete image of why it behaves the way it does. But let's say that the cloud could piece together all of the myriad disconnected actions and activities that surround this empirical data. Today we call that insider trading if it is based on information that is not generally known and available outside a company's key executives and decision makers—by definition of fair practice and law, insider information cannot be used as the basis for buying or selling stocks.

What if the cloud was able to make market predictions by using sophisticated semantics and metadata? (*Metadata* is another term used to describe information about information that is not immediately obvious or would require far too much effort to infer, given today's Internet.) What is insider information versus generally available information? Again, I'm not claiming a 100 percent accurate set of connections or predictions. Instead, let's just say that what we today consider connections that constitute insider information will incrementally become more generally available. It's tough to comprehend exactly how that will play out but it's not tough to accept that it will have an impact.

The key here is that you are not digging for these connections and you do not have to speculate about the possible context of a particular event. Instead, the cloud is doing this for you. At the very least, it challenges everything we know about how the past influences the future.

While initially this will not change the basic rules of commerce, it will dramatically change our ability to form connections faster in a much more complex world. Of course, the first thing that comes to mind is just how secure all of this data is when it's in the cloud. While there may be benefits to being able to surf the cloud over time, the risk of having my data and my company's data in the cloud seems reason enough to be concerned.

The Myth of Security

With every major economic or social shift there seems to be a central myth to be dispelled. In the case of the cloud, the central theme to be exorcised is that our personal and organizational security will be compromised more than it is in its current form.

We tend to measure risk in the cloud based on an illusory benchmark of zero risk without the cloud, instead of comparing it to the actual risk we currently have to contend with on the Internet. Identity theft and corporate intrusions are commonplace in today's model of computing and Internet use. It seems intuitive that the more information about us that is out in the cloud the likelier it is that our identities can be manipulated, stolen, or otherwise put at risk. It also follows that intellectual property about products, services, and patents may be similarly compromised. We should have no illusions here. Cybercrime is already estimated to be a one trillion dollar global business.[3]

However, we have even more to worry about in the way we use physical devices to store our data and applications locally. According to a study by the Phenom Institute, more than twelve thousand laptops are lost or stolen every week at U.S. airports! The study further shows that:

- Only 33 percent of those laptops are recovered
- 53 percent of business travelers surveyed carry sensitive corporate information on their laptops
- 65 percent of those who carry confidential information have not taken steps to protect it while traveling
- 42 percent of respondents say they do not back up their data

This is hardly a secure model for personal or corporate data, but it's a statistic that takes most people by surprise and one that is seldom used when talking about the benefits of the cloud. The point is that if we are to measure risk, we need to do so based on where we are today and how much safer we could be.

So how can a cloud-based model offer greater security? First, it's important to understand that being in the cloud does not equate to simply putting data on the Internet. When looking at the security of the Internet compared with the cloud, the analogy might be to claim that cars are safer than aircraft. The fear of hurtling through the sky five miles above the ground is much easier to comprehend than that of driving on a road where you can pull over any time. Yet, the annual risk of the average American dying in a commercial aircraft incident is only one in eleven million, compared with a one in five thousand chance of being killed in or by an automobile. The numbers clearly do not support the perception of risk. But for those who are terrified of flying, the fear is not to be dismissed so easily.

As is the case with our analogy of airplanes and cars, the rules that apply to the cloud are vastly different from those that we apply to localized computing.

The Myth of Control

As with the comparison of aircraft to automobiles, comparing the cloud to the Internet is fundamentally flawed. The first flaw is that the perceived risk is not about the numbers but about the fear inherent in loss of control. When you are behind the wheel of an automobile, you have the perception of control over your fate. The same is not true when you are sitting in a machine that uses some invisible force and myriad complex technologies to defy the laws of gravity. The cloud, incorrectly, implies a loss of control, because ultimately everything you own, from your applications and documents to your data and e-mail, all exists somewhere else. However, the "somewhere else" is a heavily monitored, fortified, and secure array of computers that are built with the objective of securing data with multiple layers of physical and cyber security. Ultimately that security translates into increased control over your data since it is far more likely to be reliably available.

The second flaw that skews perception is the fact that when people are killed in airplanes they are rarely alone. A few hundred people killed in a single plane crash will get far more attention than a few hundred people killed separately each day in automobiles, even if a few hundred die every single day of the year in cars as opposed to one day every few years in an airplane. The same applies to the cloud. We hear of incidents where thousands of identities are stolen in a single breach of a corporate firewall while thousands of laptops, many of which have data about many more thousands of individuals, are lost or stolen every week in airports alone.

The third flaw that makes cloud and Internet comparisons inaccurate is that they differ in users' awareness of how secure their information is. The ability to track and address breaches and compromised security is far greater in the cloud than it is for any localized computing environment, especially in the case of an individual or a small business, which has not only limited resources and sophistication with which to track a breach but also has far less discipline surrounding the basic security of data. For example, in the same Phenom Institute study we discussed earlier it was found that fewer than half of all laptops are backed up or secured in any manner, for instance by using encryption. To use our airplane analogy again, this is sort of like comparing the precision and reliability of a commercial airline with that of a crop duster, which, coincidentally, is not even required by the FAA to have an onboard radio!

The fourth flaw is that most people have a perception of the cloud as an uncontrolled and amorphous entity. You might think that this is no more an obstacle than the Internet faced initially, but the Internet had a more concrete presence, namely the web, the graphical interface used to access the Internet. Websites made the Internet tangible in a very visible and personal way. However, unlike the Internet, which you can experience and see as a website, and unlike a laptop, which you can touch, see, and hear, the cloud comes across as an abstract concept. Like the theory of gravity, we get that it is but have no idea *how* it works.

People often ask questions such as, So where does the cloud exist? This is sort of like asking, Where does electricity exist?

It is certainly in your home, it's in a lightbulb and the outlet on the wall, but it's also located in every part of the transmission system, starting with the turbines, solar panels, or windmills that create it. Asking where it is has no real meaning. What counts instead is the question, Is it there when I need it?

The final flaw in how we perceive the cloud's role is in the way we will use applications, or the programs that perform the work for our personal and professional tasks. Today, these applications are mostly local applications, meaning that they exist in one place that may be on a laptop, a server, or a remote computer connected to us by a network such as the Internet. Many current descriptions of the cloud simply put more of these applications on a remote server. For example, Microsoft and Google both have suites of applications for word processing, spreadsheets, and graphics that they host or run on remote computers so that you do not need to install the applications on your local computer. The same is true of Salesforce.com and Animoto, which we covered earlier. The apparent advantage of this is that you never need to buy the application or have to worry about having the latest version. While that's a benefit, it is not the long-term objective of cloud-based providers of these applications.

In the short term, you might rent cloud applications to reduce the cost of buying and maintaining them. This is the model popularized by Salesforce .com, a pioneer in the move of enterprise applications to the cloud.

But the greater play over the long term is in giving away the applications, as Google does. Why would a company like Google give an application away when it has a strong precedent of value that other vendors are charging for? Because your use of the application conveys knowledge to the owner, allowing them to better understand your behaviors and interests. This knowledge can be translated into endless opportunities to market other products and services to you.

Trading on Behavior

To better understand the marketing opportunities inherent in the cloud, take as an example Gmail, Google's web-based e-mail service, which has more than two hundred million users. (Other examples of web-based e-mail include Yahoo! and Hotmail, each of which has more than three hundred million users.) When you use Gmail, the service tracks the specific words in your e-mail correspondence in order to target specific ads from paying advertisers that may apply to you. As a user of Gmail you immediately start to notice two things. The first is that your Gmail includes a sidebar with ads from a variety of sponsors with items that are anywhere from spot on to just plain comical. For instance, I was recently using my Gmail to comfort a friend going through a traumatic divorce. Immediately, I began noticing sponsored ads for not only divorce attorneys but also for books about how to win back your spouse, gadgets for eavesdropping on their communications, and, of course, for dating sites! The more these web-based e-mail providers know about you, the more opportunities they have to target market to you and to connect you with other resources in the cloud.

The second way this behavioral information can be used is by creating what are called content network ads, which appear on websites that have nothing to do with Gmail. In my case, I started getting ads on multiple sites for the same list of providers, even when the site had nothing to do with personal relationships. At first, the sensation you get is one of an Orwellian reality where somebody is looking over your shoulder to see what you have been doing. This sort of broad syndication of your persona can take on multiple dimensions based on your many interests and, as a result, can appear very haphazard. Why, you wonder, am I seeing ads for dating sites when I look up new tires for my sedan—and worse yet, what if my spouse sees these ads coming up on my laptop? It feels like a clinical trial that I haven't volunteered for.

But this approach is web-based. It is not cloud-based.

In the cloud, this capability can be used to build a more complete version of your persona by correlating behavioral data from far more complex applications that provide an even greater understanding of your patterns of use. The reason is that in the cloud, all of your desktop, web-based, and enterprise applications are subject to the same level of analysis, especially if they are all owned by one cloud provider, such as Amazon or Google.

When you consider how much of your life you spend in front of a computer screen sharing the most intimate details of your life and business you start to get a sense of how valuable these trends can be. They are also threatening. What's especially interesting about this approach to tracking behaviors is that it is all driven by automated algorithms that are able to do the tracking and targeting through what is known as meta-tagging. A meta-tag is a way to identify your preferences without divulging your identity, as the matchmaking is happening entirely based on words, phrases, and language. The meta-tags become not just part of who you are, they also cluster you into communities of like interests that can represent new markets.

But let's not limit ourselves to a cloud that resides only on the Internet. Think for a moment about which device is closest to your person for the greatest length of time each day, day in and day out. Right, your cell or smartphone. One of the largest predictors of your behaviors is your use of a cell phone, especially one enabled to track your movements as well as online activities. Providers such as Verizon are already using cell phones to track and predict traffic patterns so that you can get real-time information about road conditions and delays.

However, this is just the tip of the iceberg. We can use our cell phones to take pictures, scan 3D barcodes, pay for services, board an airplane, and, of course, to define our social network. This warehouse of data, which combines geographical, consumer, and network patterns, is one of the gold mines being tapped by providers of mobile technology. Aha! Now you see why Google is so keen to build and acquire mobile technology.

Now, take that basic mechanism of tracking and tagging and apply it on the broadest possible scale so that all of the applications you use—professional, enterprise, mobile, local—are in the cloud and can communicate with each other not only to track your current preferences but also to predict your future behaviors. You're starting to get a picture of how powerful the cloud can be.

Meet Your Cloud Persona

Not that long ago, I carried a stack of business cards with me wherever I went. No more. Just use any search engine; I don't care how you spell Koulopoulos, you'll find me. There is value in that, but there is also a price to be paid for being so connected, for being everywhere, and it's not clear exactly how steep that price will be. Welcome to the cloud, a boomtown with apparently limitless boundaries, opportunities, and risks, where your persona is the new currency.

Your persona is more than just who you are on social networking sites such as Facebook and LinkedIn. Your persona is a combination of your interests, data, documents, networks, behaviors, and virtually anything else that enables you to interact with the cloud.

Protecting personas in the cloud is something that we are just starting to come to grips with. The implications range from protecting your brand and image to warding against outright identity theft. While much of the focus today is on limiting access to private data, such as financial or medical records for individuals, or sensitive corporate data for companies, there is an even bigger problem to consider, that of reputation.

While a security breach can be costly, it can almost always be detected and ultimately corrected. But a tarnished reputation is nowhere near as easy to recover from. This is certainly as true in the cloud as it is outside the cloud.

One of the most dramatic examples of brand damage came with the 1982 poisoning of seven people in greater Chicago as the result of cyanide-laced Extra Strength Tylenol capsules. Although the capsules had been tampered with by a third party and Johnson & Johnson (Tylenol's makers) mobilized a costly PR campaign and recalled more than thirty million bottles of the drug, it still cost the company more than $100 million and caused a drop in market share from 35 percent to just 8 percent. Despite this, Johnson & Johnson set a new precedent for crisis management by being proactive and not only putting in place corrective advertising but developing new technologies to prevent tampering with over-the-counter drugs. Due to Johnson & Johnson's measures, Tylenol regained market share in only a year. Still, it was a blow to the brand that could have ended the product line.

I bring up Tylenol specifically to point out that reputation management is not just about preventing a malicious or unintended attack on a brand. Companies and individuals have to be able to also quickly respond to attacks on their reputation. In 1982, well before the Internet, Chicago police cruisers were dispatched to drive through neighborhoods with bullhorns and loudspeakers announcing that Tylenol products should be avoided. In the cloud, mechanisms for protecting your reputation are far more sophisticated but the premise is very much the same; be proactive in protecting yourself and instantly reactive in correcting misinformation.

There are two things that you need to understand and manage in order to protect your content and also your reputation or brand in the cloud. The first is the short-term solution and the second is the long-term solution.

The Short-Term Solution: Protecting Your Reputation in the Cloud

One of the greatest impacts of the web is that it has made pretty much everyone a critic. People who would have never spoken out about companies, brands, events, or other individuals in the past have been handed a digital megaphone, and their audience, which was previously limited to a close circle of friends, family, and colleagues, is now as broad as their ability to influence through social networks, blogs, and online reviews. Sites such as TripAdvisor.com are flooded with over twenty million reviews for four hundred thousand properties. While the vast majority of these reviews are genuine, there is no doubt that some gaming is going on, whereby a property may post reviews about itself under pseudonyms or disgruntled guests may post especially negative reviews.

While the door to this sort of peer-based review for hotels, companies, and products was opened long before the cloud, through published guides, such as Zagat's, as well as early Internet sites such as TripAdvisor.com and Orbitz, the challenge going forward is that opinions in the cloud do not go away with each new edition of the cloud, since the cloud never forgets.

So what happens when you are on the wrong side of negative, targeted, or outright malicious opinions? Say your company has unwittingly turned out a batch of product that was quickly recalled without incident in the off-line world. In the cloud, the fallout is infinitely more difficult to address and rein in.

Your option in the adolescent cloud is to mount a proactive campaign to protect and rectify your reputation through services such as Reputation.com, a California-based firm that specializes in online reputation management solutions for both individuals and companies. Its lineup includes proactive reputation management, privacy control solutions for social networking, a service to safeguard and remove personal information from the Internet, and protection for false and malicious online attacks.

Founded in 2006 by Michael Fertik, Reputation.com came about after Fertik picked up on the growing cyberbullying trend and the effect it was having on life online and off-line. While working as a court clerk, Fertik started his firm, which was dedicated to protecting Internet privacy by monitoring and managing online reputations.

By filtering through the mass of information generated and published in the cloud, Reputation.com and similar companies, such as Integrity Defenders, step in where traditional PR firms leave off, and for a much smaller fee and time commitment. Individual users can simply enter their full names and e-mail addresses to generate a quick three-point scan that shows their level of vulnerability.

I decided to give it a spin, and I entered my name and e-mail address, then sat back while the site did its thing. Within a minute I had a preliminary assessment of my online reputation, based on my visibility, perception, exposure, and influence. I was pleasantly surprised to see that no immediate threats were lurking on the other side of my computer monitor, in the cloud. The site went on to tell me how I could raise my profile online, using other services such as Klout, which ranks your online influence. Reputation.com also shows how to mitigate future issues associated with Internet privacy, identify theft, and other cloud-based perils.

Removing online data requires a subscription to Reputation.com's MyPrivacy service, which removes your information from sites like Spokeo and PeopleFinders.com, as well as other online databases. Reputation.com also works with the Direct Marketing Association (DMA) to reduce unwanted physical mail by getting you off the mailing lists of more than three thousand companies.[4]

Businesses turn to Reputation.com's souped up offerings, which start with a short quiz that includes questions such as: What do you want to do? (make my private data less visible; suppress negative content); Is there something on the web you don't want people to see (yes or no); What would be most useful to you? (help me establish a basic online presence, help me build a strong online presence, help my business become more visible online).

In addition to managing reputations for individuals and companies, Reputation.com also provides services similar to those from LifeLock and IdentityGuard to protect personal data and keep identities safe from identity theft.

Credit the sheer volume of Internet users, websites, and web-based communications with upping the ante for crooks trying to exploit the cloud's information bank. In 2010 alone there were 407 data breach incidents, 26 million exposed records, and 8.1 million victims of identity theft.[5]

That's a lot of frustrated people and businesses looking for ways to keep their information private, and that's exactly what Reputation.com is banking on. Much more than just cloud identity, the word *reputation* implies a richer understanding of who you are and what you are, and whether you are trustworthy, reliable, faithful, and so on.

The cloud has put all of our information "out there" in a way that no other medium has been able to do, historically. That creates a perception of greater risk in the cloud. But this is not much different than fearing that putting my money in a bank is riskier than stuffing my mattress with it, simply because the money is not in my possession.

The Long-Term Solution: Owning Your Digital Locker

While services such as Reputation.com can help to protect your identity and brand, what about the vast stores of information that you will create in the cloud? In addition to information about yourself, you will also be leaving an incredible trail of schizophrenic activity as you bounce from one service to the next, trying to access your content, including documents, files, photos, and media. Look at where all of this information resides today: you undoubtedly have numerous on- and off-line repositories, from your local computer to physical hard disk backups, online backups, and countless Internet-based services such as Facebook, Twitter, Flickr, Amazon Kindle e-books, and many others.

Whether you realize it or not, by using all of these sites, you're building a digital collection of content that can have dramatic implications in defining you and that will continue to live on long after you are gone.

Your online activities, friends, connections, comments, and dozens of other elements come together to make up your own digital locker—a place in the cloud that stores critical information about your own identity, plus all of the content (or access and links to that content) that you possess.

For the first time in history, the individual lives of ordinary people are being documented, shared with the world, displayed for all to see, and archived for future use. The task of recording history was previously left up to historians, who focused mainly on preserving accounts of the most newsworthy events and individuals, but the cloud pretty much ensures that we will all create an online legacy that will live on for years after we are gone.

However—as we've already discussed—*nothing really ever "goes away" in the cloud.* Your digital locker is no exception to that rule. A digital locker is more than just who you are on social networking sites like Facebook, Twitter, and LinkedIn. It incorporates your interests, personal data, documents, networks, behaviors, and pretty much anything else that identifies you and enables you to interact with, create value, and connect to people, applications, and machines in the cloud.

The question is, where will the digital locker be stored and who will have access to it? As we said in the previous discussion about portals, this information is currently widely dispersed and disconnected, making it difficult to keep straight. The result is an enormously inconvenient and inefficient way to identify yourself. That's a far cry from the notion of a digital locker. But when you think about the benefits of the cloud, such as personalization and pull models, the primary value of a well-defined and protected persona is the ability it has to align your interests within the cloud, so you can find value and value can find you.

One of the interesting aspects of this aggregation of personal information in the cloud is that *much of what constitutes the behaviors and persona that might be stored in your digital locker is not personally constructed by you.* Your social networking and search sites, insurance firms, banks, retailers, and the other entities that you do business with also contribute to the cause. They will have information about your accounts and business transactions in the cloud, and they will analyze your preferences to help them operate and make business decisions. Individuals in your networks also have equal footing; that simple "retweet," post on your Facebook page, or blog comment about your recent accomplishments can result in information that's just as valuable to store in a digital locker.

Yet, one of the current challenges in developing digital lockers lies in the fact that companies you do business with play a major role in the development of your digital persona but *should not* contribute to *your* digital locker. The reason is that a digital locker should be owned by you, and access to its contents should be under your control at all times. Today, that's not always the case. Let's say that a site changes its contract, sells data, and/or denies service without informing the user; what happens to the user's digital information? For example, when Yahoo! purchased eGroups, users were surprised to find that they were locked from their data unless they provided the new owner with a complete profile and agreed to new terms of service. Had the user declined to do so, Yahoo! still owned the data and the correspondence archives.

This has been an ongoing battle in the digital space for some time. In October 2001, various listserv owners were stunned when all of their archives and data were deleted; they were given neither explanation nor any form of recourse, and Yahoo! did not respond to any attempts to contact them. Even an examination of the terms of service offered no explanation, as most of those affected could see no conflict. It was not until a *Washington Post* article was published that these owners even knew why their data had been deleted. Yahoo!, it seems, had declared them terrorists.[6]

The current concern over how companies such as Facebook use data about you, your network, and your behaviors has sparked a counterculture that is looking for ways to bring the value of these vast collections of insights back to their owners—namely, the members who create the content to begin with. Unthink is one of a new breed of social networking sites that promises to emancipate its members by not monetizing its users' personas without their explicit direction. Unthink allows you to specify which brands you want to associate yourself with and then allows those brands to reach out to you directly to benefit from the power of your influence. The edgy *emancipation manifesto* of Unthink plays into the realization that all of this information about what we do in the cloud has value—the question, ultimately, is to whom?

One Version of the Truth

Although it makes sense that you would want to maintain ownership of your digital locker, most of us still shudder at the thought of sharing its contents without strict controls that mitigate the threat of someone stealing our digital identity.

Well, let's stop and think about that for a bit. I'll use the example of Hasan Elahi, an American citizen who was stopped during a routine flight back to the United States by customs agents in Detroit. Unfortunately for Elahi, the Justice Department and the FBI had flagged him because he rented a storage facility in Florida, and they suspected him of using it to warehouse explosives connected to Al Qaeda. Hasan spent the next six months cooperating with U.S. officials, who went so far as to submit Elahi to polygraph tests. Once cleared of any involvement, Elahi was still concerned that he might have to account for his whereabouts in the future.

In an effort to keep an adequate log of what he was doing and avoid further suspicion, Elahi took a rather radical approach. He began documenting his every move and posting it online. As Elahi recounts it in an article published on October 29, 2011, in the *New York Times:*[7]

> My thinking was something like, "You want to watch me? Fine. But I can watch myself better than you can, and I can get a level of detail that you will never have."
>
> In the process of compiling data about myself and supplying it to the F.B.I., I started thinking about what intelligence agents might

not know about me. I created a list of every flight I've ever been on, since birth. For the more recent flights, I noted the exact flight numbers, recorded in my frequent flier accounts, and also photographs of the meals that I ate on each flight, as well as photos of each knife provided by each airline on each flight."

Hasan ended his article by saying that, "Despite the barrage of information about me that is publicly available, I live a surprisingly private and anonymous life."

Hasan Elahi's approach may seem to move the issue of privacy to its extreme resolution, but are we really all that private today? At least Elahi's digital locker, crude and un-user-friendly though it may be, is an authoritative account of who Elahi is—at least according to Elahi. Can you confidently say the same about your online persona? Likely not. The point of a digital locker is that it can be validated, eventually making it the document of record of our lives and creating "one version of the truth," something we will come back to again when we look at commerce in the cloud in chapter 7.

Again, I can sense you shuddering at the thought of such exposure. But that reaction is no different from the reaction you would have received from a person living a hundred years ago had they been presented with the level of transparency and visibility that we are already experiencing today. In many ways, the illusion of privacy and the expectation that we can be found in the cloud carries greater risk than the reality of transparency. The solution is not turning the clock back—we have a 100 percent lousy track record at that. The solution is in managing the future so that the benefits continue to outweigh the risks and costs.

Microsoft's Foray into Digital Lockers

Today, we are far from the reality of a verifiable digital locker. However, one of the earliest examples of a digital locker originated with none other than Microsoft, which launched a service, actually called Digital Locker, as part of Microsoft Marketplace in 2006. Microsoft's Digital Locker was much less ambitious than what we are describing. It was used for purchasing and downloading third-party software titles compatible with Microsoft Windows, so that users could access their purchased software on any computer the software license allowed.

Microsoft introduced the Windows Marketplace Labs website, which featured a beta version of Digital Locker. While Digital Locker offered a more secure online buying experience and gave consumers a single source for storing personal information, including their purchase history and licenses, it did not provide the breadth of purpose that we have been describing. The service simply gave consumers direct access to the sources from which they purchased products, contact information, purchase information, and the license information, all of which was stored in the security of Digital Locker.

The idea behind the service was a good one, but Microsoft shuttered its digital marketplace in August 2009, much to the dismay of the many users who had started to rely on the service. But, like many good ideas that are cultivated prematurely, the concept of a digital locker sat on ice for a few years while the rest of the world caught up with the cloud. Today, the idea of a central repository of all things digital is more conceivable to the average person struggling to manage her identity—or to authorize another to do it—and to manage all of her connections in the cloud, from retail experiences to content to her digital legacy in the cloud. This last item is one of the most interesting aspects of having a digital persona in the cloud.

Living On in the Cloud

As I mentioned earlier in this chapter, your digital locker will absolutely outlive you. Just look around the web for examples of this. Celebrities are logical and obvious starting points in this quest. From Amy Winehouse to

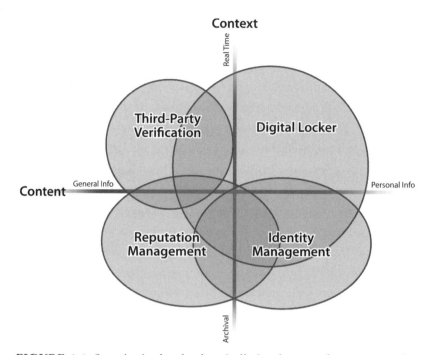

FIGURE 4-1 Security in the cloud typically involves two factors: protecting content and the context of access. Content about you or your company can be generally available, such as opinions and reviews, or personal/private, such as your social security number or financial data. Context of access can be archival, meaning that it involves analysis of existing content, or it can be real time, meaning that content is being created or used in some form of transaction that requires a high level of immediate trust and reliability. In each of the resulting combinations of content and context, a different set of tools and methods needs to be used to provide security.

Michael Jackson to Kurt Cobain (the latter passed away before the word *cloud* was ever connected to technology), the legacy of these stars lives on in the cloud long after they do. And every year on the anniversaries of their deaths and births, these stars almost "come alive" again in the cloud thanks to devoted fans and other contributors.

However, you don't have to be a rock star to have a digital locker that gets attention and outlives you. For example, look at Melissa Waller, who, at the age of thirty-one, was diagnosed with stage IV lung cancer, a devastating diagnosis, especially for Melissa, who had never smoked a cigarette in her life.

For the next two years, Melissa documented all of her treatments, progress, feelings, and emotions on a popular blog that touched everyone who read it. Those readers would interact with her in the cloud and offer their support and well wishes.

Melissa passed away in November 2010, but her legacy lives on as people continue to read about her experiences with the disease, learn what she went through, commiserate with her challenges, and give feedback on her life's story. While tragic, Melissa's story is not unique. Each of our journeys through life is filled with the range of human emotions that we all so desperately want to understand, relate to, and connect to.

What makes a digital locker especially profound is that it authors itself by constantly keeping a rich history of your life experiences as they are expressed in the cloud.

Stop and think about this for a moment. What I'm claiming is that you have lost editorial authority over your life.

How does that strike you? If you're anything like me, you'll recoil in horror. As an author, I'd like nothing more than to narrate my own life's story, and in the process I'd recount it all with complete objectivity—sure!

The value of a digital locker is, in large part, that it can reach a level of objectivity that is impossible to come by without unbiased and independent observation. This ability to track behaviors in the cloud frightens us today because the ownership of these observations is still in the hands of third parties who may not have our best interests in mind. But if the issue of ownership can be resolved, and my claim is that it will be as the cloud evolves, then this objective information can help you find the best possible connections when you most need them, not unlike

Hasan Elahi has. This does not mean that serendipity will not continue to play a role in our lives, only that we will rely a bit less on pure serendipity and a bit more on what I call *architected serendipity,* that is a means by which to create situations in which valuable connections are more likely to happen. In many ways this is exactly the sort of dynamic that is powering the attraction to social networking sites such as Facebook and Twitter.

Still, this new reality is a bit tough to swallow. Take heart; this is very much a generational phobia. When those in the younger generation, who are having their every move and misstep documented in the cloud, are vying for the reins of power in the corporations and institutions of the future, they will all have relatively well-documented pasts to contend with. This fact will surely level the playing field, as everyone's past will be equally observable and equally exposed. Today this is not the case since the tracks left in blog posts and social networks are much more prevalent for a 20-something applying for a new job than they would be for the 50-something hiring manager. Eventually however, even without the advent of digital lockers, we would all be in the same state of behavioral exposure. Digital lockers will not entirely eliminate that phenomenon but they will at least ensure that the information about us has a higher level of accuracy, credibility and rightful ownership than what passes for our digital reputations today. But these digital reputations create another interesting twist in the use of digital lockers, namely, what happens to them when we are gone?

Locker Room Antics

The fact that our digital legacies will live on long after we're gone is an eye-opener for many people. It's something that many of us will want to file in a back corner of our brains along with personal funeral arrangements, epitaphs, and wills. Facing one's own demise isn't easy, but the idea that—like Melissa Waller—you can use the cloud to create a lasting legacy via a digital locker is actually kind of cool.

Tweets about your last 5K race, Facebook wall posts announcing the office holiday party, photos of that Maui sunset, and YouTube videos of your child's college graduation also come into play. Remember that your online persona comprises all of these elements, each of which is worth something to someone, somewhere. In fact, that someone may not even be you. When sixteen-year-old Ajmal-ur-Rahman died in an accident while racing his motorbike in Hyderabad, his grief-stricken friend Shaad Ali Khan turned to a social networking site.

Khan logged on to Facebook and uploaded pictures of himself and Ajmal that were taken when Ajmal had visited his house just a few days before the tragic incident. "Some of us close friends have each other's passwords," Khan said. "We keep sharing memories of Ajmal by updating the page with pictures and various experiences shared together."[8] Khan's actions and the responses they evoked prove the power contained in a collection of status updates, tweets, comments, connections, and networks, all stored in the cloud. Like many others in today's virtual world, this young man is helping someone "live on" in the cloud, even though the subject's physical legacy has come to an end.

Several firms have jumped into the fray to help people manage access to their digital lockers in the event of their untimely demise. Legacy Locker, Asset Lock, Great Goodbye, Vital Lock, and Deathswitch are serving as repositories for passwords, account numbers, data, information, and other tidbits that come together as part of a digital locker. These firms provide a valuable service in that they force people to plan for a future where they may not be around to divulge a password, reveal an account number, or provide a Facebook update.

The services are fairly easy to use and typically require you to register an account, create multiple security questions (just like any other online web application), and divulge your "verifiers," or individuals who can access the account should something happen to you. From there, you identify your online assets by entering website names, usernames, and passwords, and then assign beneficiaries for each of those assets. Much like a bank safe-deposit box, the digital locker will serve as the watchdog for those assets until you or one of your verifiers decides otherwise. As these services evolve they will not only provide secured access to your digital locker but also have in place rules that govern what information can be changed, by whom, and under what conditions.

Not unlike a last will and testament or a trust, digital lockers will have legal stature that carries specific powers and penalties.

Digital lockers expand beyond simple repository status by helping loved ones untangle virtual assets after an individual dies. Laws in the United States and elsewhere are vague on the fate of digital rights to online accounts after death, leading to complications and legal wrangling for survivors who want access to the online services of the deceased. In one highly publicized case, for example, the family of a U.S. Marine killed in Iraq went to court in 2005 after being blocked from getting access to his Yahoo! e-mail account, with the company arguing that it could not release "private" information and that the account was "non-transferable" under its terms of service. (Yahoo! will only provide access with a court order.)[9]

A Reflection of Yourself

Clearly, digital lockers aren't just about storing personal data and preferences in the event of your death. They are also direct reflections of personal interests, behaviors, emotions, likes, and dislikes. A personal portal that resides in the cloud and reflects the various elements that make up your persona is a valuable tool that can be used for many different things. The cloud's longevity and indelibility make the digital locker both a tool and weapon. Knowing only the correct spelling of your name, for example, a first date can check you out before putting too much time into the relationship. A potential employer can get a handle on your interests and behavior. A college admissions officer can examine your social networking activities (if you've made your accounts public) and get a good feel for the "real" you.

The cloud is a two-way street, of course, and you can use the same strategies with your dates, prospective employers, and institutions of higher education. It's also somewhat under your control in that you decide what goes into your locker, what others see, which behaviors you project (no one really needs to use expletives on Twitter or Facebook, for example, and with just a little tweaking of privacy controls, that particular offense can be hidden from public view), and what others see when they Google your name.

We can also use digital lockers to embrace our individual differences or personas. We all have multiple personas that emerge depending on what we are doing (e.g., Facebooking for fun, looking for a soul mate on eHarmony, posting professionally about a work topic, and so forth). Right now, these personas are one big mash-up that doesn't help us utilize the value of the cloud, because it confuses who we are with what our given interests are at any one time. That's where personas come in. They alleviate that problem by helping us to define what aspect of our lives we're currently expressing in the cloud.

As the Internet continues to become an even more ubiquitous part of our daily lives, the use of digital lockers will only grow. So, too, will the need for enhanced security to guard the data we're shifting into the cloud. As more people gain access to more information, you'll want to know that your sensitive data is protected and available only to the people whom you designate. All signs point to these new cloud lockboxes becoming a hot item, as more of us strive to leave behind legacies that go beyond the physical.

Of course, the real value to a digital locker in the short term will be the ability it has to provide you with instant access to all of your information and applications no matter where you are. At the same time your behaviors will be best understood and incorporated into your digital locker through a single ubiquitous device. As we'll see in the next chapter this will result from the link between the cloud and what is fast becoming the killer application for the cloud: mobility.

5

The Mobile Cloud

We are rapidly getting to the point where the single
most important medium that people have is their wireless
device. It's with them every single moment of the day.
It's genuinely the convergence box that everyone has been
talking about for so many years.

Andrew Robertson, chief executive of BBDO

One of the greatest misconceptions about the cloud is that it is primarily intended to create a network for traditional computers, such as PCs and servers, the machines that we connect to when using enterprise or web-based applications and information.

That all changed while we were asleep at the wheel. Since 2010, the number of mobile phone sales has topped that of PC sales. In 2011, the number of mobile phones in the United States exceeded the nation's population. We are already living in a post–PC world, and this is a significant shift in how we will behave and the way the cloud will evolve.

While PCs, laptops, and tablets will continue to play a near-term role in how we perform knowledge work, especially in enterprise settings, the smartphone is the device through which we will most often and most conveniently express our behaviors and through which we will most often connect to the cloud and the cloud to us.

Eric Schmidt, Google's former CEO, once said: "If you don't have a mobile strategy, you don't have a future strategy." The same can be said of the mobile cloud. The future of the cloud is one in which we are able to maintain a constant connection to it. While we could speculate on how that might happen in the not so distant future through implants, the smartphone is the closest thing we have to an implant today. When we are awake, it is always within arm's reach, and for many of us it's just as close when we are not awake. My sixteen-year-old daughter sleeps with her phone on her pillow; mine is on my nightstand. It's a wireless tether to the rest of the world that I panic at the thought of being without.

We have developed a global addiction to the idea of being always on, and some of us judge our own value and that of others by how quickly and adeptly we can use a cell phone to tap into the cloud.

The most striking aspect of the mobile phenomenon is its incredibly fast penetration of the world market. If you look at the history of communication technology prior to the mobile phone, nothing matches the rate at which mobile has been adopted or the sheer number of mobile phones in use, which at the time of this writing tops five billion worldwide. If that number doesn't surprise you, then recall from the Introduction that by 2020 there will be fifty billion machine-to-machine (M2M) connected devices as well. Today there are only one hundred million of these M2M connections. These are devices in your car, home, or office or on your tablet or smartphone, all of which are connected and communicate with one another without the intervention of human beings.

To call this sort of pervasive connectivity a network is accurate, but it downplays its power and intelligence. A network has a series of established nodes and connections that have both identity and purpose. In other words, the Internet, before the cloud, had websites and e-mail addresses that clearly defined the who and the what of each node on the network. For example, *tk@delphigroup.com* defines who I am and *www.tkspeaks.com* defines what I am.

In the cloud, the who and the what are not dependent on any one node, person, or place (think of a URL such as *www.gm.com* as a place). The power of the cloud, and its primary differentiator when compared with the Internet, is its ability to combine these nodes to identify patterns that create new identities. For example, today if I need to find a provider of auto parts I would most likely go to Google, Bing, or Yahoo!, use the search engine, and come up with suppliers of auto parts. The results would be ranked based on sponsored ads and on relevance to my search criteria, that is, whether I specified a certain type of part or automobile in my search. If I'm using a shopping site, a supplier might also be rated by others who have purchased parts from that supplier.

What I'm describing here is the simplest sort of pull-based model, which we talked about in chapter 3. It's better than using the Yellow Pages, but it is a far cry from the cloud-based model.

In the cloud, my search is not for something I know exists, let's say a new set of tires for my car; it also includes past buying preferences from my history of shopping for auto parts, a knowledge of the types of automobiles I own, the mileage of my car taken directly from sensors that record it in real time, the history of the car's maintenance, my current geographic location, the balance in my bank account, the ability I have to afford a certain type of tire, my credit card balances coupled with the companies that accept the credit cards I have, insight into who else in my community is buying tires at the same time, and even a projection of how long I will keep driving my car based on my behaviors and its condition.

So why is this mobile? Well, when you think about nearly everything I just listed, each of these can be inferred from my mobile device, which can be everything from my digital wallet to my navigator to my onboard connection to all of the sensors in my car. As smartphones become able to capture even more behavior, for example through mobile wallet technology such as Google Wallet, this will only increase. Short of an implant, my smartphone is the best single device for capturing all of my personal interactions.

The smartphone will ultimately become my go-to portal into the cloud and will create a pull-driven model that will know me and be able to predict my patterns better than even my partner or spouse.

Advances in smartphone interfaces and the proliferation of apps (over five hundred million at this point and doubling every three months), coupled with the enormous decrease in the cost of smartphones, have empowered us with a wealth of information and computing power at our fingertips. This is as true for us as individuals as it is for enterprise. And in a perverse twist of technology, our most personal devices have also become our most professionally valuable ones. Drawing the line between work and play has never been harder. I chuckle at the sight of moms and dads with their kids at playgrounds, school events, or in line at the amusement park while they are also texting and talking (loudly) to business associates. Then again, it's no less common to see kids at the dinner table texting each other nonstop.

An Architected Serendipity

Perhaps one of the most vivid memories I have of using a smartphone in the cloud came at one of the most difficult times of my life, while my mother was in hospice. Her condition was such that she could not communicate with us at all, but we believed she could still hear us.

At one point, my brother Nick and I were at her bedside, each of us holding her hand and talking to her. Then Nick pulled away to use his iPhone. I didn't think much of it, since we were both spending time with her around the clock and the rest of the world seemed to take little notice that for us life was standing still. That's the funny thing about cell phones: they don't have the ability to filter who, when, and why someone is calling and match that with your mental or physical state at that moment. They are detached, unemotional messengers.

I assumed, as he reached for his phone, that he had a matter of some urgency to take care of. After a few quick swipes and taps, Nick took his phone and placed it on the pillow next to Mom's ear. It took me a few seconds to piece it all together, but then I heard a song in Greek that Mom used to love to dance to. I never expected that. The song itself must be fifty years old, is entirely in Greek, and I wouldn't have had a clue as to where to look for it. Yet in a few seconds Nick was able to find it, download it to his phone, and play it.

Trivial? Yes, compared to how much more we can do with even today's adolescent cloud. Meaningful? Without a doubt.

I bring this example up not to pull at your heartstrings but to make the case that what we are creating in the cloud, even at this early stage, has value. We can make connections in the moment that have repercussions we can't even see yet, as we make our way into this new, hyperconnected world.

In the cloud we are creating an architecture for the unanticipated. In this new architecture we will be measured, as individuals and as organizations, based on how quickly we can bring together solutions in real time. The examples are, of course, not just personal. For the enterprise, the mobile cloud means an ability to manage widely distributed and heterogeneous information systems without having to rely on a multitude of devices and physically disconnected sources of information.

This architected serendipity didn't just happen. It's been evolving for some time and it's important to understand how we got here. Although the smartphone is an evolutionary leap, as with all evolution the path was far from direct and certainly not planned.

A Short History of Applications and Their Demise

At the beginning of the application software era, during the 1970s, we didn't have to worry much about the diversity of platforms, infrastructure, clients, and servers. None of that existed. Information systems' architectures were simple; programs were crafted to run directly on the operating environment of the "host" system, which was either a mainframe or departmental computer. The way these computers were used is likened by many to the way the cloud is used, because all of the power of the computer was on the host and not the remote device, which was nothing more than a dumb terminal. But this sort of characterization of the cloud couldn't be more wrong. The free flow of connectivity, which is so critical to the cloud, was nonexistent in these computers. You had one connection to one application on one computer. To compare this to the cloud would be akin to comparing two cans and a string to a telephone network.

Users of these host-based systems quickly realized that applications had to be best-of-breed in order to be competitive. In other words, the marketing application had to suit the marketers, the engineering application had to suit the engineers, the accounting application had to suit the accountants, and so forth. From well-intentioned individuals, who were acquiring the best tools to do their specialized jobs, horribly diverse, fragmented enterprise environments developed. This fueled a steep rise in the number of "silos," or "smokestacks," of highly compartmentalized, segregated organizations. As the number of these silos and their customization increased, they only grew taller and less likely to work together.

While all of this was happening, PCs were revolutionizing the way software was bought and used by creating localized solutions for individuals. The result was even more diversity and disconnectedness.

In an attempt to unify this increasingly fragmented landscape, *desktop* technology innovation created the first stop-gap measure: the graphical user interface, or GUI, arriving with the Macintosh, X-Windows, and MS Windows. But these environments were, in retrospect, a patch. Their development was an appropriate response to the state of affairs at the time, and it was a step in the right direction. But it was not unification. Does having twenty windows open on your desktop allow you to work more effectively with the information? It clearly does not. As long as that information is fragmented at its core, a windows-based graphical user interface simply reflects, and in some cases magnifies, that fragmentation by pouring more and more information onto larger and larger screens.

The advent of the Internet and the widespread deployment of Internet standards such as HTML provided a common interface metaphor (the ubiquitous web browser) and the basis for integration through technologies such as web services, which allow websites to effectively borrow a function from another website. The web created the conditions for the arrival of a truly function-centered desktop to replace the application-centered desktop with which we had been struggling, and that many of us continue to struggle with.

It is not outrageous to predict that within a decade, at most, all talk of applications will fade away. Word processing, spreadsheets, and databases will all become part of a single integrated business environment in the cloud. I know that's a difficult thing to accept, especially given the proliferation of apps on mobile devices. But this proliferation is exactly the reason that applications are so untenable. It's as though, in a frenzy to isolate the millions of different things we can do with all of the computing devices we have, we've created a virtual archipelago of destinations, none of which are connected to one another. The effect is an attention deficit disorder on a scale that requires a whole new category of pharmaceuticals.

The question is not *how many apps does it take to get my work done, entertain me, and help me live a fulfilled life,* but rather *how few?* Simplifying these functions is the role that the cloud will play in navigating and delivering personalized information, tools, and content, and delivering them to the right device. Regardless of the device, which, if any, of the current metaphors for consuming this information is best?

That may be an easier question to answer through a process of elimination. The first thing to eliminate is the use of metaphors such as desktop windows interfaces. Window interfaces are the last technologies from the age of information scarcity—they were never designed to accommodate the age of information abundance. Information scarcity requires a portal that allows you to segment information into neatly defined buckets: a word processing document, a spreadsheet, a presentation. The same applies to enterprise-class applications, or what are known as ERPs or CRMs. These, too, are applications that provide highly structured environments where predictable transactions can be dealt with in predictable ways.

Companies such as Microsoft, SAP, and Oracle have, to their credit, already started moving to the cloud, but each will face significant challenges as it attempts to replace extremely lucrative revenue from packaged software with cloud-based services. Take, for example, Microsoft and its

When You Are Involved in the Most Complex Situations How Many Windows Do You Have Open On Your Desktop?

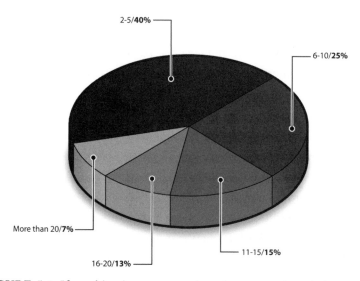

FIGURE 5-1 If anything is common to just about every knowledge worker's environment, it is the tremendous variety of applications, sources of data, and enterprise systems they rely upon to do their jobs.

Amazingly, the majority of knowledge workers have at least six separate windows open on their desktop at any one time, and 35 percent are navigating eleven or more windows.

What does all of this mean for knowledge work? Simply that it requires a tremendous degree of navigation and coordination, which can create the potential for risk, errors, and inconsistency.

Office suite of products, which are competing with Google's free Google docs suite in the cloud. Google already has both a short- and a long-term model for monetizing free software. Microsoft is only starting to phase over. But even with a clear business model in place for cloud-based applications, traditional vendors face incredible hurdles within their organizations when it comes to refocusing their marketing, sales force, and even existing customers on the merits of the cloud. Don't for a minute discount the significance of these challenges in overcoming the inertia of existing business model momentum. The incumbent syndrome, which I talk about at length in my book *The Innovation Zone,* is the single greatest limitation in catching up to, much less overtaking, a new competitor with no such legacy or bias toward what has historically worked.

The tablet is the next platform to consider as a possible portal to the cloud. In many ways, I see the tablet as a bridge between the PC and the ultimate evolution of the smartphone. *Tablets are the first toll toward a post-PC, mobile cloud–enabled world.* They offer an untethered and nearly always-on way to work and play. But tablets are hardly as convenient and inconspicuous as smartphones. They are also far less attached to us, in terms of being on our person, than smartphones are. Lastly, they are preferred to smartphones simply because of their form. For a demographic accustomed to having ample screen real estate in order to arrange many windows and one that is also handicapped by less-than-perfect eyesight, a tablet is easier to contend with.

Yet, all of these metaphors, from windows to tablets and smartphones are limitations of current technology. With flexible screens that can roll up or fold up for portability, projection capability for keyboards and images, and even direct projection into the eye, we are moving toward a smartphone that overcomes the technological obstacles that limit its function. The only question I have is how long we will need tablets to provide the bridge as we move toward more highly evolved smartphones. Interestingly, each of the technology limitations I listed has already been addressed in prototype devices. So our time frame may be much shorter than we might expect. My educated guess is that we will see much of this fully resolved in the next five years and all of it in the next ten.

At that rate, the notion of a portal to the cloud will become synonymous with a smartphone.

The Mobile Cloud

At the heart of the trend toward device convergence and personalization is the evolution of the mobile cloud as a means of interacting in real time and merging all of an individual's needs in a single, personal point of access.

Ultimately, the mobile cloud renders a smartphone a highly personalized device that integrates the most relevant sources of information and the underlying connections that make this information valuable to us. The mobile cloud also learns about our work habits, behaviors, preferences, and roles in order to provide a constantly changing and personalized experience of the world. The result is a person (or a business) that is always sensitized to his environment, marketplace, customers, and partners. In short, a cloud-enabled smartphone is a device that *knows* you, perhaps better than you know yourself!

The mobile cloud is intended to address two fundamental challenges we face when dealing with the complexity and speed of interactions in the cloud:

- Overabundance of information
- Lack of real-time responsiveness

Big Data and the Overabundance of Information

The development of the information industry can be read as a continuing story of new opportunities for adaptation created by unknown needs that arise from the advance of technology. For example, until the advent of the iPad, did you know that you needed a touch-based device with thousands of apps? But now you can't live without it. Why? Two words sum up the reason: keeping up.

Keeping up with the flood of opportunities to access and manipulate information has brought about a fundamental shift in the value proposition for information.

In all past eras, the overriding negative factor in working with information had been its *scarcity*—there was never enough available, and decisions had to be made with the certainty that some key facts were missing, perhaps the pivotal facts in the decision. Leaders and managers got used to working in this imperfect information environment, and there was never a question about whether the decision makers had the capacity to process whatever information was at hand. The classic business school grad was taught to dissect case studies, crank the numbers, analyze the options, and pick the one best suited to solving the problem. This is the way I was taught and it was the way I, in turn, taught my graduate students many years ago. But that method of teaching does nothing to prepare today's leaders for a world in which this situation has been turned on its head. The problem now is the human capacity to process the quantities of information available.

Examples here abound. I worked with one of the largest U.S. nonprofits, and the higher I looked within the organization's ranks, the greater the amount of time people spent just searching for information. The range was from about 10 percent of their time for administrative staff, all the way up to 40 to 50 percent for senior staff. The weighted average across the entire organization was 18.7 percent, or about one day per week. (Yes, there are organizations that only work five-day weeks!)

The costs for this sort of endless searching are staggering. One of the world's leading aerospace companies, which I had worked with, calculated the cost to the organization on an annual basis as being about $145 million per year, and management agreed that this number "sounded" reasonable! Although you might wonder if reasonable is simply a relative metric.

In today's information environment we are experiencing a radical transformation of the relationship between people and the information they have to work with. The incredible influx of readily accessible, yet completely disconnected, sources and streams of information inside and outside of the organization has made it clear that the means for navigating, organizing, and linking information with decision making is woefully inadequate. This is often termed the "Big Data" problem, since it is increasingly challenging us to find new ways to deal with the sheer magnitude of data available to every organization.

The problem in almost all of these cases is that we are attempting to evaluate large quantities of information with a high degree of recall but a low degree of precision. Recall is a function of casting a very large net that comes back with everything that *may be* relevant to your situation. Precision is getting only those items that are *most relevant* to your situation. As the time you have to react decreases (see the discussion of the uncertainty principle in chapter 3), relevance becomes far more important than recall.

However, if you think about the way we have built information systems to date, nearly every aspect of them, from the way information is organized and reported to the size of the monitors we use to view it, has been straining under the increasing amount of information available. It's in part why monitor size and resolution have been steadily increasing. But the reality is that we will never have enough screen real estate to solve the problem of overabundance. The answer is not creating more room for more data but rather connecting relevant pieces of data to each other so that we can minimize the amount of information we need to deal with.

Think about this for a minute using a simple analogy.

If I am trying to book the cheapest possible flight, hotel, and car package for a complicated trip, I have two basic options. I can surf the web for hours, going to all of the popular travel sites such as Travelocity, Orbitz, Priceline, and Hotels.com and entering my query each time. I'll have a dozen windows that I am comparing, none of which are in the same format.

Alternatively, I can go to Kayak.com (a cloud-based portal), enter my request once, and have Kayak surf the cloud for me to find the best deals among all the travel sites, airlines, hotels, and car rental companies. I can optimize my request for whatever is important to me, cost, duration of flight, connections, class of hotel, and so on, and get one unified view. This sort of unification of otherwise disconnected data is the essential differentiator among solutions that leverage the cloud and also simplify the interaction in such a way that the user enters and views only the essential information.

By using a simplified process, I limit both the data I need to enter as well as the data I need to evaluate. Add to this the ability to keep my preferences and past history of travel in the cloud, and I significantly reduce the complexity of my communications.

The result is an entirely new way to interact with the cloud that is far less cluttered and infinitely easier to use.

Living in Real Time

As the cloud expands to include more people and devices (recall that we projected nearly seventy billion connected people and machines by 2020), it will create an unimaginable urgency to perform work in the shortest possible interval of time. Trying to accommodate this in the way that we work today would be downright insanity. The volume of connections that we all have will make that simply untenable.

Most of us understand, through our own experience, that applications-based desktops create islands of automation. In spite of the value they have brought to the workplace, they have had the effect of separating and segregating functions that are intuitively part of the same process.

At this stage, we can only speculate about what the resulting landscape of the information industry will resemble once the mobile cloud has become a standard part of our lives. What we know for sure is that we will no longer refer to "desktops," since the range of functionality available from information appliances in many different forms will have long since left the image of a desktop behind.

Each organization will have moved its business model fully into the cloud, and the last remaining pieces of legacy software from the era of applications will be phasing out. Knowledge workers will have left behind their complaints that the isolation of applications and the contradiction between computer use and productivity made the workplace more frustrating than effective.

The mobile cloud will be regarded as a utility; we will use it to do our work without giving its existence a second thought. Just as we rely on the presence of a dial tone every time we pick up a telephone, we will expect that our personalized work environment will be always available, wherever and whenever we are.

Intelligent agents embedded in the cloud, working with a learned set of rules and user preferences, will decide whether or not to send a piece of work to a particular person. If the appropriate individual is not available to act upon a process step that is subject to a time constraint, these intelligent agents will route the work to another qualified individual of the community. In addition, these intelligent agents will pull information from the cloud necessary to complete the task without manual intervention.

Ultimately the mobile cloud will form the platform for a level of flexibility and spontaneity in how we work and live that is very difficult for us to imagine today as we try to coordinate our lives across multiple devices, applications, and sources of information. The result will be an ability not only to quickly adapt to the kind of uncertainty I've been describing but also to innovate at a pace and on a scale that will make today's innovators appear to have been standing still. Here too, as we will see in the next chapter, the cloud will alter the way in which we look at the basics of innovation, the risk it entails and the value it can deliver to the broadest possible global audience.

6

Innovation in
the Cloud

Great innovations should not be forced on slender majorities.
—*Thomas Jefferson*

Innovation always takes us by surprise. When the first, brick-sized Motorola cell phones were introduced in 1983, even the most ambitious projections were for fifty million phones in use in the year 2008. By 2010, however, more than five billion cell numbers were provisioned and in use around the globe. Fifty million to five billion is not a rounding error. How could we consistently be so wrong about the future? Because what we try to predict is the trajectory of technology rather than the trajectory of behavior. I'm reminded of that each time that I wait in line for the next greatest gizmo, wondering how silly it is to be so dependent on technology that just twelve months ago I was able to completely live without.

The fact is that every time we encounter massive change, such as that brought on by tablets, smartphones, cell phones, laptops, PCs—take your pick—it's nearly impossible to appreciate the true nature of the change or the way in which it will alter our behaviors. It's the reason humanity has such a miserable track record of predicting the true impact of innovation and change on the future. Thomas Watson, Sr., former president of IBM, is reported to have said that the worldwide market for computers would never exceed five. Apocryphal or not, this statement always sticks in my mind as a great metaphor for the way even the most visionary among us is stymied by the unpredictability of the future!

Whether it's the computer, the printing press, the automobile, the cell phone, or the iPad, we are amazed by our own ability to find applications for new ideas and adapt to change. It is ultimately the most encouraging and optimistic aspect of human nature.

New Behaviors = New Business Models

Innovation is a topic that occupies so much of our thinking that it would be impossible to talk about the cloud without also looking at how it affects innovation. However, as with the rest of the ways in which the cloud will alter our lives, trying to measure the effect of the cloud on innovation using our current notion of innovation does little to help us understand how the two will work together. The cloud changes innovation in some fundamental ways that we can only describe by creating a framework for innovation that allows us to look beyond the current ways in which we innovate.

Part of the reason it is so difficult to project the path of innovation is that big change rarely comes in the form of a single technology. Massive change is accompanied by a context of uncertainty, with so many forces interacting in chaotic ways that they defy any reasonable person's ability to project how the chaos will evolve. Just ask the Wall Street fund managers who had no models developed to run scenarios for the recession of 2008–09. But no matter how many scenarios you model, there are always many more that you simply cannot anticipate. The unknown is called the unknown for a reason.

Behavior is the unknowable variable in every innovation, and it is the variable that most determines the opportunity a new business model has to evolve and take advantage of the new behavior.

It's the Behavior, Stupid

We are at the tail end of an era that has focused almost entirely on the innovation of products and services, and we are at the beginning of a new era that focuses on the innovation of what I like to call "behavioral business models." These models go beyond asking how we can make what we make better and cheaper, or asking how we can do what we do faster. They are about asking why we do what we do to begin with. And the question of *why* is almost always tied to the question of how markets behave.

When Apple created iTunes it didn't just create a faster, cheaper, better digital format for music, it altered the very nature of the relationship between music and people. eBay did not just create a platform for auctions, it changed the way we look at the experience of shopping and how community plays a role in the experience. When GM created OnStar it didn't just make getting from point A to point B faster, it changed the relationship between auto manufacturer and buyer, and fundamentally altered the reason we buy a car.

Google did not invent Internet search—there were nearly fifty software vendors delivering Internet-based search, some for as long as twenty-five years before Google!—but Google changed the way we interact with the Internet and how our behaviors are tracked and analyzed, allowing advertisers to find and pay for buyers in a way that was inconceivable before.

All of these are examples of innovations in behavior that led to entirely new business models. Yet we continue to be obsessed with technology innovation. To paraphrase James Carville's now-popular political pun, "It's not the technology, it's the behavior, stupid."

The greatest shift in the way we view innovation will be that the innovation surrounding behavior will need to be as continuous a process as the innovation of products has been over the last hundred years. It's here that the greatest payback and value of innovation in the cloud has yet to be fully understood and exploited.

Unfortunately, far too many of us are stuck in an old model of innovation—just as surely as we are stuck in line waiting to take part in the new one.

Innovative organizations are those that can depart quickly from their planned trajectory and jump onto a new opportunity; they're organizations that recognize and take an active role in introducing new behaviors that were unknown. It is ultimately the speed with which companies do this and the willingness to experiment in new and unanticipated areas that determines the extent to which their innovation is "open."

This changes the idea of open innovation to mean more than going outside the company to find new ideas from experts; it means developing a collaborative innovation model that intimately binds the market to the process of innovation, in lockstep. That does not suggest that companies are held hostage by their customers, who only know to ask for incremental innovation in what they have already experienced. Instead, it means that companies need to push the envelope of innovation based on observations of what a market's behaviors are and then work closely with the market to identify how innovations can add value in unexpected ways.

The cloud is the ultimate *open* system for this sort of innovation, one that is influenced by factors that are both unknown and unknowable. In other words, no amount of time, information, focus groups, or traditional market research will increase the certainty with which we can innovate. The most important thing to do in the cloud is to realize that innovation must involve openness and disruption. Then we have to minimize the risk and uncertainty so that we increase the opportunity for finding novel approaches to solving problems and expand the ability to quickly scale, so we can address these problems once a resonant nerve is struck.

This is precisely the type of innovation that companies like Apple,

Google, Facebook, and Netflix have enabled by constantly challenging their customers to adapt to new offerings. For Facebook, this creates a fairly consistent market tension. Whenever Facebook delivers a new feature, such as its Timeline capability, discussed in chapter 4, there is an almost immediate market backlash, which is followed by a lull in the market's pushback and an eventual acceptance and integration of the new capability. This dance is repeated on a regular basis. While it does create some degree of tension, the result is a steady disruptive force that provides both Facebook and its users with more than just a path to sustained innovation; it also provides a periodic jump to a new type of behavior that would otherwise be seen by most companies as incredibly risky.

The benefit for Facebook is that it has a built-in cloud that allows any innovation to be immediately presented to its customers. The same holds true for Netflix. But this does not mean that the process is always going to gain ultimate acceptance from the market. In the case of Netflix, a critical new enhancement in 2011 separated the Netflix DVD business from its video-streaming business. Interestingly, the DVD-by-mail business was the original mainstay innovation that drove Blockbuster and most neighborhood DVD rental stores out of business and propelled Netflix to a dominant position in movie rentals. That was, in its time, a radical innovation with its own degree of risk, However, when Netflix made the decision to focus on its streaming business and charge separately for physical DVDs by creating a new brand called Qwikster, its customers mounted a revolt. The irony here points to the ongoing dilemma every innovative company has to contend with: focus on the legacy that makes money or move into the future? Markets rarely go willingly when a large incumbent player tries to do this.

When Netflix was a disruptive outlier it could get away with these sorts of tactics, but as a large company with a loyal following of more than twenty-five million subscribers, the pushback on innovation was enormous, amounting to a near revolt. The outcry was so bad that the company's founder and CEO, Reed Hastings, posted the following apology on the company blog:

> I messed up. I owe everyone an explanation.
>
> It is clear from the feedback over the past two months that many members felt we lacked respect and humility in the way we announced the separation of DVD and streaming, and the price changes. That was certainly not our intent, and I offer my sincere apology. I'll try to explain how this happened.
>
> For the past five years, my greatest fear at Netflix has been that we wouldn't make the leap from success in DVDs to success in streaming. Most companies that are great at something—like AOL dialup or Borders bookstores—do not become great at new things people want (streaming for us) because they are afraid to hurt their initial business. Eventually these companies realize their error of not focusing enough on the new thing, and then the company fights desperately and hopelessly to recover. Companies rarely die from moving too fast, and they frequently die from moving too slowly.
>
> When Netflix is evolving rapidly, however, I need to be extra-communicative. This is the key thing I got wrong.
>
> In hindsight, I slid into arrogance based upon past success. We have done very well for a long time by steadily improving our service, without doing much CEO communication. Inside Netflix I say, "Actions speak louder than words," and we should just keep improving our service.

The blog post went on to rationalize the decision. It was humbling for Netflix, but the company continued on its path of separating the services into Qwikster for DVDs and Netflix for streaming video. A few months later, however, after continued uproar from subscribers, Netflix relented, at least in part, and Hastings came back with another blog post, this one far more to the point:

It is clear that for many of our members two websites would make things more difficult, so we are going to keep Netflix as one place to go for streaming and DVDs.

This means no change: one website, one account, one password...in other words, no Qwikster.

Netflix did not, however, change its policy of charging separately for the two services. While the solution was a compromise, it was clearly driven by the marketplace and Netflix appropriately relented while continuing to force the innovation necessary to keep the company vital.

This sort of dialogue between the marketplace and its providers has never been as pronounced and apparently dysfunctional as it is in the cloud, where voices are amplified to an unprecedented magnitude. But that increase in the decibel level of market pushback can be a death knell for innovation. The cloud is not inherently for or against innovation, any more than the Internet is. Both are simply new platforms for conversations that have the power to drive both positive and negative momentum. And it is this point that companies need to pay especially close attention to.

Innovation is always a tense conversation between affected parties. That will not change and it should not change. It is the basic mechanism by which we align ideas with the value they can produce.

Not every new idea or invention has value. In other words, the risk of innovation does not go away. It has to be factored into the business and dealt with in real time, as Netflix learned with its introduction of Qwikster.

The other side of open innovation is that we need to be careful not to dismiss or underestimate the willingness of people, whether our customers or outsiders, to participate in an open model of innovation for reasons that often have nothing to do with direct monetary rewards. When Wikipedia first appeared on the Internet, skepticism was rampant. Few believed that people who had credible and thoughtful information on a topic would be willing to share what they knew for nothing more than the satisfaction and small dose of celebrity that being a self-professed authority might convey.

Yet Wikipedia has grown into a go-to resource for nearly every topic under the sun, with more than three million entries. What's even more striking about Wikipedia is the way it works in real time. Content problems—including profanity, bias, poor documentation of facts, plagiarism, and inconsistencies—are, on average, corrected within thirty minutes! No amount of editorial support could accomplish the feat without the vast collaborative behind Wikipedia.

Maynard Webb, chairman of LiveOps and past president of technologies at eBay as well as eBay's COO from 2001 to 2006, recounts how important it is to create community in order to benefit from this phenomenon of contribution. According to Webb, "We had people at eBay and at LiveOps do things for each other that were unimaginable. They competed with each other, and yet you had a PowerSeller willing to help another PowerSeller all day long. So much of it was the validation they got from each other. Community is huge."

What is especially interesting about this notion of community as it applies to innovation is that when it is leveraged correctly, as we will see in the next few examples, it acts as a critical counterbalance to the loss of flexibility that organizations experience as they grow. As shown in figure 6.1 the innovation lifecycle starts with an idea, and often a new organization, that has near infinite flexibility. As the idea grows it creates increasing value, but also increasing scale in terms of people, resources, partners and all of the structure needed to support the growing value. At some point the flexibility to alter the trajectory of the idea starts to suffer significantly. At this point value may also start to dwindle since the innovation cannot keep pace with new demands of the market and competitive threats. The power of open innovation that is driven by disruptive ideas, which form outside of the organization, can now play a critical role in sustaining flexibility and creating new value.

What if the same community spirit could be applied to more sophisti-

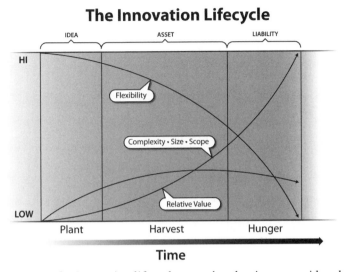

FIGURE 6-1 The innovation lifecycle starts by planting a new idea that has near infinite flexibility. As the idea grows it becomes a core asset for an organization and is harvested for its increasing value. Yet this also generates scale, complexity, and scope. These start to limit flexibility until the idea can no longer keep up with and adapt to the market and competition. The result is an ultimate decrease in value as the idea becomes a liability to new innovation. The counterbalance to this phenomenon is an open innovation process, which allows the entry of disruptive new ideas from the outside.

cated and higher-value cloud-based repositories? Some companies, such as design firm IDEO, which designed the original mouse for Apple, are already creating communities with the goal of spurring innovation.

The OpenIDEO Cloud

If the cloud is, in part, an engine for connecting, driving, and developing new ideas, OpenIDEO hints at how we can both tackle complexity and harness the creativity and resources of people along a full range of disciplines, experience, and ages.

Started as a technology platform for the global design consultancy

IDEO, OpenIDEO has become a global innovation community that generates hundreds of ideas for solving global social problems. In its first year, the OpenIDEO community—which numbered eighteen thousand registered users—fielded eight challenges sponsored by people and organizations as disparate as Unilever, the nonprofit Water and Sanitation for the Urban Poor, and chef and food advocate Jamie Oliver. Each challenge frames a critical question such as these:

- How might we increase the number of registered bone marrow donors to save more lives?
- How can we improve sanitation and better manage human waste in low-income urban communities?
- How can we raise kids' awareness of the benefits of fresh food so they can make better choices?

A simple brief lays out the hurdles that contributors should strive to clear when submitting ideas, and from there the structured innovation process takes off. In each phase—Inspiration, Concepting, Evaluation, Winning Concepts, Realisation—contributions range from a simple comment encouraging someone else's idea to actual products, like sketches, coding, and prototypes.

Contributions earn participants points toward OpenIDEO's measure of influence—the Design Quotient, or "DQ" for short. (Segmented according to the innovation phases, the DQ recognizes that innovation is more than invention and, at its best, draws on diverse talents; different people bring different strengths throughout the innovation process.)

As ideas progress from Inspiration through Realisation, they're shaped by ongoing collaboration, as contributors link and build upon each other's ideas. Similarly, it's the community—by promoting ideas through Applause and critiquing concepts through Evaluation surveys—that evaluates and short-lists the top concepts. In the Realisation phase—itself a community-generated improvement—OpenIDEO relays updates and stories about how the original challenge and its winning concepts progress. As it moved into its second year, OpenIDEO turned its attention to impact, exploring how this community and platform can ensure its ideas turn into action.

Of course, this raises the question: What's in it for participants and what's in it for IDEO? People contribute their ideas knowing that—by the terms of use—if their idea happens to be among the top concepts, they've granted the Challenge Host nonexclusive license for its use. Unlike at other challenge or competition platforms, such as NineSigma, InnoCentive, and Kaggle, or e-work sites like Elance, there are no cash prizes, no contracts for work, no promised recognition outside the community.

For IDEO, sure, hosting such a platform reinforces its brand as a proponent of human-centered design across all industries and sectors, including the global public good. But beyond goodwill, there's no obvious contribution to the bottom line. OpenIDEO is innovation in the cloud: people building value—or perhaps, more accurately, sparking potential value—not based on formalized organization structures or profit motive, but rather on their own ambition, energy, intellect, and desire to make a difference.

It's very easy to attribute this sort of altruistic behavior to people who have too much time on their hands, perhaps as a result of the current high unemployment. But don't be so quick to think in terms that are bound by the past. Look instead at how children play today as an indicator of how they will work tomorrow. The blatant disregard that most youngsters have for intellectual property is striking. When I use the term *youngsters*, I'm not just referring to preteens and teens. I teach a graduate class on innovation in which patent law is one of the most consistently debated topics. I've heard students in their twenties and even thirties propose the complete abandonment of patent law in many areas where the technology is moving so quickly that patents act as a vehicle by which to stifle or even prevent innovation. They argue that companies are using patents defensively to prevent others from putting in place ideas that might be seen as competitive to the current market offerings.

Large companies are notorious for acquiring other companies primarily for their patent portfolios, in order to remove their competition. For example, in 2011 Google acquired Motorola Mobility for $12.5 billion. A spin-off of Motorola, the company held seventeen thousand current and seventy-five hundred pending patents for smartphone technology. That values each patent at somewhere between $500,000 and $750,000, depending on how many of the pending patents are granted. Google may be the last company you would expect to stifle innovation. CEO and cofounder Larry Page blogged after the acquisition was announced that:

> The combination of Google and Motorola will not only supercharge Android, but will also enhance competition and offer consumers accelerating innovation, greater choice, and wonderful user experiences. I am confident that these great experiences will create huge value for shareholders.

Yet, you have to wonder if Google plans to actually develop these patents into usable technology or if it will, like any other large company that has to protect itself against competition, sit on the patents as a way to stall innovation that might have been possible if another acquirer had purchased and developed the patents. However you look at it, patents have become one of the most heated battlegrounds in the current marketplace since they can be used to form barriers to innovation.

While I don't expect these sorts of patent wars to go away anytime soon, it can change over time as a new generation of leaders emerges from a childhood during which the notion of protecting ideas has necessarily taken a back seat to the experience of sharing and collaborating on ideas. Again, as with privacy, protecting intellectual property through a closed process only has value if that protection exceeds the value of open and unprotected collaboration.

OpenIDEO in Action: The Local Food Challenge

In the case of OpenIDEO, a valuable collaboration was evident when the community teamed up with the Queensland Government in Australia and Queensland's IDEAS Festival 2011 to tackle the challenge, "How might we better connect food production and consumption?" The challenge drew more than 513 inspirations—comments, pictures, and resources to help spark ideas—and 600 concepts. From there, the OpenIDEO facilitators organized the concepts into themes, like Celebrating Producers and Transport and Traceability, and the community refined the ideas into twenty final concepts, ten of which the OpenIDEO team and challenge hosts named as winning concepts. The most active concepts garnered thousands of views. The ten winning ideas ranged from fresh food trucks serving low-income neighborhoods to a smartphone application, Eatcyclopedia, that would deliver information on a food's nutrition, source, processing history, and meal ideas (Eatcyclopedia's submission came complete with mockups that showed how the application would work).

Early in the Realisation phase, OpenIDEO reported four actions inspired by the local food challenge, from a very personal story—one man's transformation from a causal observer to an active participant in his own local farmer's market—to two distinct applications and guides in support of local food.

The challenge hosts used the twenty short-listed concepts as fodder at a workshop for policy makers and experts from across the government, the food industry, the education sector, and the community. With their knowledge of the local context, workshop participants were able to combine and build upon the original concepts to design four feasible prototypes, which were slated for assessment and implementation. Drawing links back to the original ideas, they proposed creating an "urban food hub" on unused land, publishing an online guide to the region's best growers and producers, and designing a social business supplying schools with healthy local food.

NineSigma

Another approach to cloud-based open innovation is illustrated by the work of idea intermediaries who act as brokers between problem solvers and companies seeking solutions. This kind of approach, called *open innovation*, leverages the power of a global pool of potential experts and radically changes the economics of innovation. Open innovation, or OI, in its simplest form is the process by which an organization engages people other than its employees, what we can generally refer to as the innovation community, in solving problems. For example, a provider of detergents may be interested in developing a new formulation that can work effectively in parts of the world where water and electricity are both in short supply or are not reliably delivered to homes. You would typically expect this company to turn to its internal research and development for ideas on solving the problem. Increasingly, however, as the need to come up with new ideas with greater speed and volume increases, companies are expanding their quest for new ideas to include anyone outside of the company who has an interest in solving a problem.

A variety of intermediaries have come to market to help facilitate OI. Known as idea markets, these companies are generally a meeting place for seekers of solutions and providers of ideas. Providers (also known as solvers) are compensated at an agreed-upon and published amount if their idea is accepted by the seeker.

One of the more interesting intermediaries in this space is NineSigma. Founded in 2000 by Mehran Mehregany, a professor at Case Western Reserve University who had worked at DARPA (Defense Advanced Research Projects Agency) in the 1990s, NineSigma predates the first use of the term *open innovation* by three years. At the time Mehregany worked there, DARPA had a recurring need to identify the best and brightest minds who had already worked in a particular domain. DARPA used the Internet as a means of identifying these individuals, using a combination of searches, which looked at the implied skills and capabilities of individuals based on what they had posted on the Internet. That process was the inspiration that caused Mehregany to consider applying the same approach to industry. The difference between NineSigma and other idea markets lies in the subtle notion of reaching out to identify capability in the cloud rather than simply waiting for talent to show up.

Andy Zynga, CEO at NineSigma, sees that the drive toward open innovation as not only strong among large enterprises, where it has its origins, but also in small and midsize companies. For example, 63 percent of those companies with revenues of $250 million to $1 billion are adopting open innovation strategies. New social networking tools such as crowdsourcing are making it easier for these companies to get in the game.

According to Zynga, "It used to be that 70 percent or so of all innovation spend was done by companies that had 25,000+ employees. That's flipped around. Today 70 percent of the spend is from smaller corporates." It is imperative for large companies to look for good ideas in these smaller companies around the world. That was the sweet spot Mehregany built his company around; look for innovators around the world for large clients who may not have the ability to search for themselves.

There were two basic obstacles at the outset. The first was that the NineSigma approach needed to be evangelized. Much of that changed when Henry Chesbrough wrote his book *Open Innovation* in 2003, making the concept of open innovation a mainstream topic. A few years later, a *Harvard Business Review* article by Larry Huston and Nabil Sakkab talked about the notion of connect and develop at Procter & Gamble, and how NineSigma helped them to build their innovation practice.

The second obstacle was that it wasn't clear which products in the marketplace were developed using open innovation. The problem was that NineSigma's clients often couldn't even tell themselves if a particular innovation ended up in the market or not. That's because when you're creating an innovation around a product, such as packaging, a component, or an ingredient, it usually ends up as a part of an overall innovation, and is not tracked separately

To help, NineSigma started by generating a sense of the company's needs using a cloud-sourcing platform. If a consumer packaged goods company wants to generate some fresh ideas from consumers, NineSigma will use a search engine that focuses on blogs and Internet background chatter to identify the lead users who others have said have significant influence in a particular area.

But to create a targeted and useful search for expertise you have to really understand what a company's needs are, and that's usually not an easy task. To give an example, Procter & Gamble was looking to produce a wrinkle-free shirt. NineSigma described this as a surface tension problem involving organic material. As a result of their search, they found a professor in Indiana who was working with integrated circuit chips and had a polymer that already addressed the problem of surface tension in organic materials.

To undertake this sort of massive search process NineSigma finds experts using a database of more than two million people, as well as a list of several million experts that they have access to through an affiliate network.

Since many of NineSigma's clients are large corporations with more than one billion dollars in revenue and substantial R&D organizations, you have to wonder why these companies need to surf the cloud to find talent and solutions when they are already heavily invested in employing and funding the world's brightest minds in their respective disciplines. But the flaw in that sort of reasoning is that internal and external innovation are mutually exclusive. They are not. Both can easily feed off of each other creating a powerful innovation synergy.

For example, NineSigma recently worked on a number of projects for a large industrial conglomerate, which has thirty-five thousand or so engineers and scientists on its staff, yet more than half of the proposals they received for new innovations came from people and places that they had never heard of before. That's always an enlightening moment for management at a company like Siemens. But it's not atypical. You can be the best in your field, go to all the conferences in your industry, and convince yourself that there isn't anyone else out there better at what you do. But in reality there almost always is.

Beyond Open

While OpenIDEO and NineSigma both provide a glimpse into the power of innovation in the cloud, they only tell part of the story. One of the most significant changes that innovation will undergo as the cloud becomes more of a factor is the degree to which we will be able to go beyond the past and current models of innovation. Discrete tasks that were formerly worked on by experts and a few highly trained individuals will be transformed into a process of continuous adaptation, much of which will be done without human intervention. That's not to say that innovation should be thought of as a process that can exist in the absence of conscious human thought, insight, and vision. Innovation is and always will be subject to the commitment of inspiring leaders and visionaries who are able to see beyond the moment and lead us into the future, despite our tenacity in clinging to the past.

However, *there are aspects of innovation that can be made much more systemic and that can be integrated more readily into the fabric of an organization or society.* To understand how this can be done, we need to provide a new structure for the way we talk about and define innovation. We have to recognize it as more than the process of inventing new products or services.

I explored the idea behind this new definition of innovation in my last book, *The Innovation Zone,* where I outlined a framework I call Innovation

2.0. Innovation 2.0 was intended to illustrate how all innovation has value, from incremental to radical, component to systemic. That framework works well inside or outside of the cloud. But what it does not fully address is the way in which innovation is spurred by the connections that we have talked about in this book.

Connections drive innovation by creating opportunities to couple existing inventions and ideas, but also to use the cloud's understanding of these connections, their trends, and their applications to infer derivative innovations that the market and providers may never have considered otherwise. I call this process derivative innovation, and it has four distinct levels.

Derivative Innovation

When we think of innovation, what most often comes to mind are breakthroughs that seem to take the market by storm. Historically, at least, this is the way we think of innovation, whether it is Ford's Model T or Apple's iPod. Yet this is not the reality of how innovation evolves. Innovation is a process that plays out at a relatively consistent pace. The breakthroughs are not so much one-time events or moments of immense achievement as they are transitions from one stage of innovation to another. When we look back these stages are clearly delineated by specific products, services, or events that act as mile markers. But these mile markers are nearly impossible to predict looking forward. However, we can better understand what stage we are moving into by looking back and recognizing the stages we have already gone through. By doing this, we can anticipate the pace of innovation and better understand the sorts of things we should be investing in as innovators and consumers of innovation. What is most interesting about these four derivative stages of innovation is that the cloud provides a unique catalyst for each one, but it also provides a uniquely qualified mechanism for the final two derivatives of innovation.

Because innovation builds off of existing inventions, we will refer to the four stages as *innovation derivatives*. I'm using the term *derivative* because in each successive stage of innovation we are bringing together and building on a foundation of more and more existing innovations.

To keep things simple, I'll use the abbreviations 1D, 2D, 3D, and 4D to talk about each derivative (first, second, third, and fourth) stage of innovation.

Derivative	Music	Cable	Telecom
First Derivative	MP3 Players	TV	Landlines
Second Derivative	iPod	Color	Wireless
Third Derivative	iTunes	Cable	Cell Phone
Fourth Derivative	Genius Mix	TiVo	Smartphone/Apps

Derivative	Electricity	PC	Software
First Derivative	Local Generators	Desktop Terminal Computing	Automation
Second Derivative	Regional Generators	Desktop Local	Applications
Third Derivative	Utility Providers	Networked PCs LAN	Suites
Fourth Derivative	Grid	Mobile PC/Laptop	Web

Derivative	Characteristics	Impact of the Cloud
First Derivative	Device-based, simple, new technology, long adoption cycle, friendly to existing business models and consumer expectations	Shortens adoption cycle, provides low-risk, low-cost platform for introducing device

Continued

Derivative	Characteristics	Impact of the Cloud
Second Derivative	Device-based, combines multiple first derivatives, introduces new business model, perceived as threatening to incumbents, has little or no precedent in the market, standards begin to emerge	Creates higher levels of collaboration among developers and the market, identifies influencers, provides real-time market feedback
Third Derivative	Information-based, slight or no departure from 2nd derivative device (almost unnoticed change in device by marketplace), exploits new business model fully, creates copy-cat innovators, creates competitive threat to old business models and devices, standards are selected by the market, competition among players of 3D peaks	Shortens time to develop new business models and new standards, increases diversity of offerings and competitive choices, allows smaller players to sustain a market position
Fourth Derivative	Experience-based, functionally a radical departure from all previous devices, adds significant complexity, changes user experience in a dramatic way, establishes new device and business model, creates a new industry or industry segment, competition begins to thin as leaders emerge from 3D	Creates an inherently experience-based capability, tracks behaviors, allows high levels of complexity to exist in the cloud without need for complexity in the device

First Derivative Innovation

First derivative innovation focuses primarily on the introduction of a new device. But the term *device* isn't limited to physical objects. A spreadsheet, word processor, methodology, or even a form of media can be a device. A device is simply something that can be easily described and understood as a new way of solving a problem.

For example, when spreadsheets were first introduced by Dan Bricklin and Bob Frankston, who invented VisiCalc in 1979, they were rudimentary software programs with little functionality beyond basic math. Typically, 1D innovation has a fairly long adoption cycle because there is little if any precedent for the device. This is why 1D innovation needs to be as simple as possible in order for adoption to occur. It's also why 1D innovators need to have patience and a longer-term game plan to avoid being blindsided by 2D innovators. In fact, *1D innovation is very dangerous and rarely the most fruitful place to be.* In large part this is because all the mistakes to be made will occur in the first stage of innovation, and the market may remember you more (if at all) for what you did wrong rather than what ultimately came out of the 1D stage. During this stage, the business models used by 1D innovators tend to be very similar, if not identical, to the model that preceded the innovation. Recent examples of 1D innovation are the early MP3 players introduced by Sony.

Most players at this stage of innovation are likely to fail as they rush into a market that shows early promise but requires more staying power than they had anticipated. This was true of the rash of early dot-com companies that flooded the market in the late 1990s. While a few of these companies, such as Amazon and Google, had the ability to ride out the storm, the vast majority are now long-forgotten experiments.

Because 1D innovation is so risky, few companies want to invest heavily at this stage. The preferred approach is to wait for someone else to make the mistakes and educate the marketplace before stepping in. But what if we could substantially reduce or eliminate the risk inherent in 1D innovation? That's exactly what the cloud does by creating a platform on which new devices can be quickly developed, prototyped, tested, and introduced to a market.

One critical area where 1D innovation can be especially difficult is the marketing of a new device. Because the market has no precedent for the device, marketing is very difficult. As a result, marketers often resort to putting the new device into an old category that the market already understands.

First derivative innovation does not require the cloud, but the cloud does allow a new device to be far more easily introduced and also allows the innovator to get fast feedback from the market, which will enable shorter iterations of incremental changes to the device.

Second Derivative Innovation

Second derivative innovation is where radical innovation usually attaches itself to the company that is most likely to take the innovation to critical mass. This was the case with Amazon and Google, but also with the iPod, which was a relatively late 2D entrant into the crowded MP3 marketplace, where devices such as Creative's Nomad and Diamond's Rio had built a near monopoly in the MP3 portable media player marketplace.

During this stage of innovation, multiple innovations, which the market has started to accept, are combined to create devices that are not only recognizable to customers but more importantly considered by incumbents to be a competitive threat to their market position. The result is acceleration in partnering among component companies, which drives more options and variations of the product or service. It is this acceleration that is most likely to be facilitated by cloud-based supply chains such as E2open, which we will talk about in chapter 7.

To understand second derivative innovation, let's look at the innovation of electricity during the late nineteenth and early twentieth centuries. The first derivative of electric power was driven by localized power generation, making electricity most cost effective when provided in-house by the factories that used it. But this created countless standards for the dynamos, motors, wiring, voltages, amperages, and machinery. As electric power became pervasive, the costs incurred in trying to resolve these problems started to approach and eventually exceeded the savings of internal economies of scale. In fact, many factories attempted to regionalize electric power and began to sell it to local shopkeepers and municipalities in an attempt to shore up an eroding financial proposition. These same municipalities eventually started to generate their own power and sell it back to local businesses and consumers. These were the first electric utilities.

Although we often compress the history that follows, from the first large-scale power plants in 1891 at Telluride, Colorado, and then in 1895 at Niagara Falls, it took decades for electrical grids to take shape across the globe. In fact, the European power grid would likely have been in a state of disarray for the better part of the twentieth century were it not for the decimation of regional and factory-based power plants during World War II, which made reconstruction of interconnected and centralized power much less expensive than rebuilding the hodgepodge of proprietary power plants and power sources in place before the war.

Third Derivative Innovation

However, the more interesting story is not about electricity but about what happened to the factories that used it. As power utilities came on line during the 1900s, factories, for the first time in history, did not have to worry about generating and managing power. They could instead focus on the things that really mattered—what they produced. It is at this point that electricity entered the third derivative stage of innovation, and the competitive landscape shifted drastically. During this stage, the innovation was not so much in the electric utilities that formed but in the industries they served, which were now free to focus on their core business.

It is no coincidence that manufacturing experienced a surge of innovation in the early part of the twentieth century as this transition was occurring. With the increasing ability to focus on their core processes and products, factories developed a far more sophisticated approach to manufacturing and innovation. The impact was felt across all industries, from moving assembly lines in automobile manufacturing to farming and agriculture.

What is most striking about this shift to external power generation, however, is that it happened over such a prolonged period of time and was barely noticed in terms of its value as an innovation. In 1905 there were fifty thousand individual power plants in the United States. Today there are approximately twenty-three hundred! The investment in infrastructure to replace this first wave of proprietary 1D innovation was so great as to be daunting, if not outright impossible, to justify for most organizations. It's the same reason that postal systems, railroads, highways, and telecommunications networks have all required massive investment or intervention on the part of government in order to mitigate the pain of replacing outdated infrastructure and offer some protection for new investments.

The point here is that innovation often remains suspended in the third derivative stage for some time as standards are developed that form the basis for long-term investments in innovation.

A more contemporary example is the MP3 standard, which has formed the basis for nearly all music delivered in digital form. Once these sorts of standards are put in place it becomes very difficult to dislodge them. As a result, innovation happens within the confines of the standard. In the case of the music industry, the third derivative innovation was the unanticipated breakthrough that digital music would have on the business of music. The notion of paying 99 cents for an individual song was originally derided by the entire music industry. The concern was not so much the value being assigned to a song but the fact that all songs had the same value and that listeners could exert more power over their playlists than studios could exert over the collection of songs on an album. The standards at stake here were the inherent belief in the relative value of music based on the popularity of the artist as well as the concept of an album, which had been a staple of the music business since its inception in recorded form. Both these concerns were founded in the reality of the past rather than the behavior of the future. Ultimately, the music industry, both studios and artists, benefited as much as consumers.

It is precisely this aspect of third derivative innovation that makes it so difficult to walk away from. Building a new business model is no simple task and nobody wants to leave it behind once it is established and accepted by the market.

That does not mean that innovation stops at the third derivative, only that it is restricted by the business models and standards that form during this stage. This is where the cloud can have a significant impact on innovation in the final and fourth derivative stage.

Fourth Derivative Innovation

Eventually, the standards that form in third derivative innovation become too great a limitation for the floodwater of innovation that is building up behind them. Like a levee holding back a hurricane surge, the model begins to crack, weaken, and eventually gets overrun.

This is when fourth derivative innovation begins to take shape. In 4D innovation, the greatest value of innovation is in how it is transformed to adapt to the user experience. This innovation differentiates offerings that have by now become commonplace and are nearing commodity status due to their standardization. The basic device, product, or service does not change radically but the way in which the user experiences it does.

In the case of digital music, a good example of 4D innovation is the introduction of Apple iTunes Genius mixes, which developed playlists for iPod users based on the user's music preferences and purchasing history. The device, standard, and content did not change but the way in which it was experienced by consumers did. This sort of customization of the user's experience is key to driving the type of innovation that occurs in the cloud, where endless combinations of content can be constructed in real time to suit the needs of the moment. What's critical about the cloud at this stage is that it allows the market to influence innovation directly through the expression of its interests.

It's interesting to note that, while so much of marketing has been reduced to focus groups and market research, breakthrough innovations typically make little sense to a market researcher or a focus group. The reason is simply that people only know what they have experienced. The late management guru Peter Drucker was a strong disbeliever in this sort of "ask the market" approach to innovation, as was Apple's late cofounder Steve Jobs. Both believed that while markets could express dissatisfaction with a product, they could not envision solutions that stepped sufficiently outside of the existing product.

However, this does not mean that a market cannot demonstrate its need for innovation in its collective behavior. The problem to date has been noticing that behavior and responding to it in a way that moves the market toward a new approach. Finding such fresh approaches has always been considered the hallmark of great innovators who can anticipate a market's movement while also shaping it.

This is impossible to do without the cloud, which is why 4D innovation only happens when an individual or a company is able not only to gather a critical amount of information about a market's anticipated requirements but to look beyond these based on deep analytics that can project a new need. None of this displaces the need for astute and visionary leadership. However, in the cloud the collective experiences of users can be used to determine the most likely new innovations and to provide a basis for a much faster cycle of innovation.

Letting the Outside In

Ultimately, achieving the state of fourth derivative innovation is less about drawing hard lines around internal versus external innovation and more about creating processes that have inherent permeability with both the market and outside ideas. But as we discussed at the outset of this chapter, this is all about intense collaboration. To call it purely market-driven is a mistake that allows a market to hold you hostage to a single stream of innovation. If Sony cofounder Akio Morita had allowed customers to design the first Walkman or Steve Jobs had allowed the market to dictate the way they bought music, neither the Walkman nor iTunes would have come into existence.

"Open" also implies that there is an element of uncertainty, randomness, and risk that we are willing to design into the innovation process. For example, when pilots hone their skills by training in flight simulators, they don't just fly in predictable situations but face randomized weather conditions and mechanical malfunctions. They will not necessarily encounter the same conditions when they are in the air, but their ability to deal with and improvise around the unknown gets better if they are exposed to higher degrees of uncertainty. The same applies to innovation. If we stick to a single stream of ideas and never create churn to disrupt that flow, we will not be as adept at spotting and leveraging new trends, opportunities, and options when they emerge.

A lot of people have difficulty with this aspect of open innovation, especially when it is opened up to the cloud, where the participants in an innovation effort may not have any of the skills and capabilities traditionally considered important for the task at hand. After having seen organizations consistently struggle with this:

I am drawn to the conclusion that we take far too much credit for being able to see into the future, and we rely on that "foresight" rather than marshaling our resources as needed when we actually encounter the future!

It's as though we develop such conviction in our ability to predict what's to come that we refuse to take a detour into reality when we run directly into it.

This ability to innovate based on an open model in the cloud goes beyond crowdsourcing, as it was popularly termed by Jeff Howe in a June 2006 *Wired* magazine article, to what we will call *cloudsourcing*. Cloudsourcing expands the idea of the crowd to include all of the world's talent. The point is not to simply incentivize individuals to submit ideas but to incentivize them to build upon one another's ideas. The two are worlds apart in terms of how difficult they are to implement and how much value they deliver. By the way, cloudsourcing is not just about individuals; it is just as important to acknowledge the role of groups and other enterprises in a crowdsourcing model.

Unintentional Innovation

We are not always innovating with intent in mind. In many cases, we stumble upon something that is completely ancillary to our original mission. In an open innovation model, you need to provide incentives. But how do you then foster the discovery of accidental knowledge that may not have been part of the problem you were trying to find a solution for? One of the biggest challenges of open innovation is in somehow capturing and connecting this accidental knowledge to intentional efforts. If a pharmaceutical scientist researching hypertension medications in one part of the company discovers a compound that grows an extra tail on mice while trying to cure their hypertension, will it be seen as an annoying side effect or a new opportunity? Well, it probably depends on how the researcher is incentivized. If it's based on the number of compounds discovered to reduce hypertension, you can rest assured that the side effect will be no more than a speed bump on the road to success.

These sorts of accidental discoveries will only increase as the store of knowledge we accumulate increases. And, in the spirit of open systems, this is knowledge available to an ever-increasing number of individuals and with a shorter and shorter shelf life.

As we will see in the following chapter, commerce in this new context of accelerated knowledge creation, discovery, and innovation will require a new way to look at risk, investment, and many of the traditional frameworks we have used to build organizations.

7
Commerce in the Cloud

Every act of creation is first an act of destruction.

—*Pablo Picasso*

The potential upside value of a cloud-based business is much higher than that of a traditional business, which needs to invest heavily in infrastructure, people, marketing, and distribution before shipping out a single product. The reason is that a cloud-based business can ramp up all of its resources in real time as demand increases. This means that you are investing only if the business succeeds. What is also interesting about this economic model is that since the cloud encourages greater experimentation it also results in a larger number of failures than a traditional business where risk discourages experimenting with outlier ideas. The importance of this subtle shift in how cloud-based businesses invest in innovation is critical to the evolution of commerce in the cloud for one reason, the burden of innovation starts to shift from large corporations to smaller ones. And this shift could not come at a more crucial time according to one of the twentieth century's most interesting economists, Joseph Schumpeter.

Creative Destruction

In 1942, economist Joseph Schumpeter sounded a wake-up call for capitalism with a prediction so disturbing that it makes Nostradamus seem tame. Schumpeter's book *Capitalism, Socialism, and Democracy* foretold of the demise of the Western world's central institution for innovation, prosperity, and growth: capitalism. Schumpeter believed that capitalism would ultimately result in a system of corporations and elitists that had lost sight of the core values of capitalism, namely the importance of the entrepreneur. At the same time, Schumpeter foresaw a tremendous increase in the number of educated people, but thought there would not be enough meaningful work for all of them. *To simplify Schumpeter's often tedious writing: he expected high unemployment, crushingly large corporations, and elite academics to bring about the death of capitalism.*

Today's contemporary reality is far too close to Schumpeter's vision for comfort. We have become enchanted with large corporations that are termed "too big to fail," we have staggeringly high unemployment rates that refuse to retreat, many of our most prestigious academic institutions teach values that border on socialism, and we have lost sight of the importance of small business as the fundamental driver of employment, innovation, and economic growth.

Consider that there are more than twenty-six million small businesses in the United States alone, and they employ half of all U.S. workers. In fact, during the first decade of the twenty-first century small business created 70 percent of all new jobs in the United States. These same businesses create thirteen times more patents per employee than do large businesses.

Despite this overwhelming engine of innovation, when the United States put in place a $787 billion stimulus package to aid in the recession of 2008, only $730 million was earmarked for small business. That's less than 1 percent for a segment that produces 50 percent of all jobs.

This discrepancy speaks directly to Schumpeter's concern about the erosion of entrepreneurship that capitalism would create. Schumpeter's projections are uncanny in their accuracy. But Schumpeter noted that, while the trends were clear, he did not wish for capitalism to take this path. Like a doctor telling his patient that too much drinking and smoking would lead to an early demise, he was pointing out a fatal behavior that only his patient could correct.

Schumpeter gave a name to this disease, which has since stuck as a moniker for the process of dismantling a system through an ongoing process of disruptive change. He called it *creative destruction.* To be fair, Schumpeter was not being at all flattering in his use of the phrase. However, many of us today use the term to describe a positive force for change. I prefer the positive nature of creative energy to change something for the better, and that is the way we will use it in our discussion.

Schumpeter's view was a gloomy one:

> ...in capitalist reality, as distinguished from its textbook picture, it is not (price) competition which counts but the competition from the new commodity, the new technology, the new source of supply, the new type of organization (the largest scale unit of control for instance)—competition which commands a decisive cost or quality advantage and which strikes not at the margins of the profits and the outputs of the existing firms but at their foundations and their very lives....It is hardly necessary to point out that competition of the kind we now have in mind acts not only when in being but also when it is merely an ever-present threat. It disciplines before it attacks.
>
> Joseph Schumpeter, *Capitalism, Socialism, and Democracy*

However, what Schumpeter could not have foreseen was the advent of the cloud and the profound impact it would have on capitalism and the global free market. In a somewhat perverse twist of fate, Schumpeter's creative destruction is embodied in the cloud in a way that has the potential to put capitalism back on track.

The first step in creating any new economic, political, or social system is arguably the most radical and tumultuous—deconstruction of the existing system.

Something needs to so disturb the balance of power and credibility of the existing system that movement to a new system seems painless by contrast, and inevitable, even though the precise nature of that new system may be far from clear.

Taking It to the Street

The greatest force for Schumpeter's creative destruction in today's markets is the dissatisfaction with the approach taken by large corporations and Wall Street, which profit from the lack of an efficient path to innovation and the intense concentration of wealth. The way in which many of these institutions have been run and the greed that they have embodied has resulted in a counter-elitism movement that threatens to be as profound as any force of the free market.

In 2011, this phenomenon led people to take to the streets on Wall Street and at trading exchanges around the United States to protest rampant corporate greed and the disparity in wealth being created by large banks and financial institutions. Enabled by mobile technology, these on-demand crowds, or what are popularly termed "flash mobs," had formed before. But this time they were not a casual exercise in free expression but a coordinated protest against a specific set of injustices.

If Schumpeter were living, he may have interpreted these gatherings as support for his theory were it not for the fact that the protesters included a far broader cross section of society than just academic elitists, and their targets, large corporates, were the very institutions that Schumpeter was concerned would undermine capitalism.

Cloud Capitalism

Although the continued mania for mergers and
an illusion about the importance of the role that
as cornerstones of our economy, it masks the eve
entrepreneurship, access to capital, and small bu
95 percent of all enterprises globally are small- a
ness employing nearly 70 percent of the world's
has been a shift to a much more granular econom
ing in this equation, however, is a mechanism b
can be supported by the same economies of scal
enjoy.

P•TAC® is a registered trademar
of Ad Craft of Arkansas, Inc.
(501) 372-5231 adcraft@sbcglobal.ne

The cloud is that missing link in the evolution of capitalism and free
markets, and offers a counterbalance to Schumpeter's grim diagnosis for
capitalism. I'd even go so far as to propose that the cloud is an absolute
necessity for continued economic prosperity. As markets, enterprises,
and distribution channels rapidly disintegrate into increasingly smaller
pieces that can be reconstituted rapidly, the cloud becomes a requisite
mechanism for coordinating this quantum increase in the complexity
and variety of the economy.

A trivial example is the scenario faced by each of us in using our
smartphones. With a seemingly limitless variety of apps, which track
everything from our calories to our spending, it has become a full-time
job to sift through, organize, and try to integrate apps with each other.

I realize that this sort of discussion opens the door to a classic chicken-
and-egg debate. Is the cloud leading to complexity or is complexity leading to the cloud? This may appear to be a meaningless and pedantic
debate, but I believe it sheds light on the underlying factors that extend
beyond the adolescent cloud as we know it today and allows us to look at
how the cloud will reshape all forms of commercial and social institutions by helping us manage this dramatic rise in complexity.

If we look to biology as an analogy, it is clear that all life tends toward greater complexity and diversity as it evolves and develops higher levels of intelligence. In the case of intelligent life, evolution has resulted in ever more complex organisms and collections of organisms. Keeping pace with this complexity has required sophisticated nervous systems and social orders. For intelligent life, this often translates into embedded intelligence, or a set of instincts that govern community interactions. For example, think of how hierarchies are typical structures in some intelligent species, while swarms govern the behaviors of others. The cloud represents the evolution of intelligence in the systems that support an economy and allow it to evolve to greater levels of complex and ultimately intelligent behavior.

It's clear, however, that not all organizations are evolving in the cloud at the same rate. For those slower to disintegrate into easily reassembled parts, the cloud eventually tears down the walls placed between the parts of an organization, its people, its suppliers, its customers, and potentially all the relationships in its vital value chain.

But consider that the walls placed between people, partners, and processes have been constructed at great sacrifice over years of business development to compartmentalize and protect competitive positions relative to the buying preferences of carefully identified customers. Are the individual participants in the economy's value chains—today's successful large businesses, what Schumpeter called corporates—likely to stand by while wholesale decimation takes place before their very eyes?

In fact, in the development of business over the past century, such transformative changes have taken place over and over again. The only difference this time is the speed with which the impact will be felt.

Take as one example the monopolies created at the end of the nineteenth and the beginning of the twentieth century by the activities of the "robber barons" in iron, railroad, real estate, and natural resources industries. These players of monopoly capitalism built enormous, integrated value chains to insure the operating standards, scale, and, not incidentally, profitability desirable to minimize competitive risks. These relationships were built on the principle of locking in partners as part of an impenetrable value chain as well as locking out competition by preventing suppliers from partnering with competitors and thereby creating enormous barriers to entry.

Ultimately, these kinds of barriers to competition are being torn down further by the cloud. Although interventions such as governmental bailouts of companies and countries that are too big to fail may hasten their demise by artificially buffering them against the forces of a free market, the underlying dynamic has consistently shown that a free market will erode uncompetitive structures as new forces seize on technology change as a way to create a scale of syndicates rather than the scale of individual corporations. In fact I'd go further to propose that structures-of-scale, whether economic or political, that are based on the centralization of authority, are doomed to fail as has been proven throughout history.

> Whether it's the Roman Empire, British Imperialism, the Soviet Union, or even the more recent European Union, the downfall of these structures-of-scale is centralization, a flawed process which leads to an inability to innovate locally.

In very practical terms what this means is that surviving the seemingly unstoppable progression to organizations of ever increasing scale requires us to change our current business models to integrate and embrace the cloud as a means of more evenly distributing authority and innovation. In some ways this promotes a much more complex strucure for organizations. However, although cloud-based organizations can still be dauntingly complex in their interactions, connections, velocity, and volume, they can still be governed by very simple rules. DNA contains the blueprint for all life yet it consists of merely four base amino acids that can only be paired in certain ways, yet the systems that result are anything but simple.

The Value Chain in the Cloud

It is impossible to go much further in our discussion without first describing in more detail what we mean by the term *value chain* and outlining a bit of its history. The concept of the value chain has become an immutable law of business and, more specifically, competition. Yet until now it has remained a topic that focuses on how companies can manually build and sustain intricate networks of internal processes and coalitions of business partners. In the cloud, the notion of a value chain takes on an entirely new dimension, as the intelligence we have just discussed becomes the foundation for these networks and intelligently starts to create these partnerships.

Originally introduced by Michael Porter, the term *value chain* represents the collective partnerships, resources, and processes that bring a product or service to market. In Porter's view, the entity at the center of competition is not necessarily the traditional organization defined in terms of physical resources such as buildings, factories, and employees, but rather the collection of all the activities that combine to create value. Although Porter introduced this framework long before the advent of the cloud, or the Internet for that matter, the value chain is an especially relevant way to think about the cloud, because the cloud is nothing more than a vast collector and coordinator of resources and processes.

In Porter's classic view, value is added during the production process that takes raw materials and transforms them into a finished product, when the product is distributed, and when the product is sold to the customer. Each of these activities may exist within the boundaries of one corporation or among any number of separately functioning entities. The ability to create value is indifferent to the composition of the value chain, as long as the price customers are willing to pay for a product or service exceeds the costs of production.

The cost of creating value is affected by the degree to which the specific activities in the value chain are coordinated and integrated. A poorly structured value chain may result in delays during the transfer of information from one task to another, causing the time to market for a product to expand beyond a window of opportunity. For example, a delay could mean a significant loss of opportunity for a pharmaceutical company bringing a new drug to market. Delays and the resulting loss in value underscore the principal element of effective value-chain management—managing both the interdependent value-creating activities and the linkages that connect them.

In addition to internal linkages, there are external linkages to other organizations, from value chain participants such as vendors and suppliers to downstream constituents such as customers and distributors. Linkages occur when the performance and execution of one activity affects other activities.

Value is created not only in the processes that generate the information, but also in the ability to deliver it to the right individuals at the right time. Indeed, delayed or misdirected information is often the greatest source of inefficiency within a value chain, and these processes should be the first to be evaluated when an organization is looking for opportunities to optimize a value chain.

Porter's premise was simple: maximizing the efficiency of a value chain brings costs down and differentiation up, creating the two basic forces of competitive advantage. At the peak of the industrial economy, the best way to achieve this was by assembling all the various functions across the value chain into a Byzantine patchwork of value-creating activities under one roof. The true father of this model is Henry Ford, with his vision of the factory village where iron ore would enter one end and a complete automobile would come out the other. It is this model of vertical integration that defined the old economy, where everything fit on one balance sheet, from the sheep that produced the wool for filling car seats to the steel foundries that created sheet metal to the stamping machines that formed metal into car parts.

Now, let's apply the basics of a value chain to the cloud. If the premise is that the linkages that connect a value chain are its most valuable elements, how does the cloud impact the creation of linkages? Since the cloud will become the fundamental means of managing connections, it's safe to assume that the process of creating value chains will itself become far more efficient, expedient, and economical. As the cloud begins to make these connections faster and lowers their cost, the aspect of differentiation becomes a short-lived phenomenon and one that is more contingent on the ultimate value it delivers to the market than on the impediments it creates to new entrants. The basis of competition now starts to shift as well.

During the twentieth century, the notion of "economy of scale" dominated our thinking on competitive advantage. The degree of competitiveness was measured in terms of how vertically integrated an organization could be and the degree of top-down control it could exert over individual value-creating activities. In simple terms, economy of scale is the ability to derive greater value from one large entity than a collection of smaller ones. It is this notion that drove the design of value chains, and, in many cases, organizations themselves. Consider GM, the standard-bearer of vertical integration for many decades. Pick up a copy of *Forbes* or *Fortune* from the 1950s or 1960s and it will likely be filled with gushing praise for GM and its management. The economy of scale for GM was so great, how could it ever lose?

GM was the most admired company in America, if not the world, for decades. During the golden years, in the middle of the twentieth century, GM could do no wrong in the eyes of the business press and management pundits. It's ironic, then, that GM became the poster child for the type of corporation that could only be sustained through a government bailout. What went wrong? The answer lies not in size but in speed.

An Economy of Speed

At the outbreak of World War II, the U.S. government mobilized the country's manufacturing sector into a war machine by turning to the auto industry for the production of war materials. At that time, a B-24 plant in California, the heart of aircraft production, was producing one bomber per day operating under optimum conditions. Henry Ford's Willow Run plant in Ypsilanti, Michigan, used auto industry production-line techniques that allowed Ford to produce one B-24 Liberator bomber per hour! Clearly, the notion of an economy of speed was important long before the advent of the cloud.

In fact, the U.S. auto industry was an early adopter of other pre-cloud technologies that emphasized speed, such as EDI (electronic data interchange), which enables more efficient communication among trading partners, and JIT (just in time inventory), which ties suppliers intimately to the production and manufacturing process. However, this early dabbling did little to change the giant, vertically integrated structures of U.S. auto manufacturers. Instead, they—along with other large corporations—used these systems to build even steeper barriers to entry and larger economies of scale. Walmart is notorious for building an entire ecosystem around suppliers that were held hostage to its systems and processes. Their message was the classic sort of arrogance that Schumpeter feared: "If you don't like playing by our rules then take your game elsewhere." As a result, while speed did increase, when measured as a relative time to market, many small businesses could only compete if they became part of these monolithic empires. The dirty little secret, however, was that the primary reason these small companies were held hostage had less to do with the efficiency of the processes or systems of large organizations, but rather their proprietary nature. If you were a supplier or partner in these enormous value chains you had to invest in and build linkages to systems that only worked with that value chain. While industry standards such as EDI (Electronic Data Interchange) alleviated some of that burden there were always nuances to each value chain that departed from, or added to, established standards. This effectively hardwired many smaller partners and suppliers into value. An easy way to think of this is to use the analogy of consumer lock-in which occurs when you chose a broadband provider for your home cable, internet, and phone service. Each provider requires that you use their cable box, set-top devices, and of course a yearly agreement to invest in their service with a penalty for early termination.

Another example is that of the value chains that have existed in publishing. Until only recently it used to be that the only way to publish a book was to go through a publisher, who, in turn, had access to book wholesalers and distributors. You could self publish but the chances of getting your book distributed widely was as likely as a musician trying to sell their songs without a record label. Consider how drastically both of those scenarios have changed in the past decade with the advent of e-books and iTunes. Today, anyone can write an e-book, post it to Amazon's site, and instantly be part of the largest book distribution network available. The same applies to independent artists who want to distribute their music through iTunes.

Even in the behemoth automotive industry value chains have changed dramatically during the past two decades. Japanese auto manufacturers were among the first to adopt models that relied much more on disintegrated value chains. While the high-level process flows of building cars in Japan varied little from those in the United States, there were significant differences in the structure of their value chains that sounded an early warning for the advent of a cloud-based model. Rather than seeking to assemble all components of the value chain under one roof or on a single balance sheet, Japanese manufacturers organized value chains into what they called a "keiretsu," or coalitions of suppliers, manufacturers, and distributors. By breaking the activities into parallel yet independent operations, Japanese manufacturers operated more efficiently than their U.S. counterparts, benefiting from advantageous capital structures that became possible because they were free from the burden of financing the entire value chain. The real source of competitive advantage, however, is derived from the greater speed of responsiveness to shifts in market demand that this model enables.

Most of the credit for Japan's early success in the U.S. auto market is given to the combined U.S. recession and energy crisis, which resulted in a rapid shift of market demand toward cheaper, fuel-efficient cars during the late 1970s and early 1980s. If cost and energy efficiency were the only factors, however, it would have not been Japanese automakers but Volkswagen, with its more established distribution channel and greater brand recognition, that emerged victorious in this economic environment. But the reality is that this notion of a sea change in buyer behavior is greatly overstated. What actually happened was a series of subtle demographic shifts that over time allowed Japan to reshape itself according to the desires of the U.S. market, rather than to try to mold the market into its own image. Think speed over scale, as well as fluidity over momentum.

In every case where Japan overtook U.S.-based automotive players, American manufacturers held the advantage of greater scale and in most cases had the basic technology in place to rival that of their Japanese competitors. The real secret of Japan's success was its ability to get products to market faster by reconstituting value chains at a rate that was equal to the changing demands of the marketplace. By leveraging its superior responsiveness early in the cycle of new product introduction, Japan has been able to set the agenda in its favor and force competitors to respond to it.

Although the automotive industry is an extreme example of value chain integration, it illustrates dramatically the importance of creating connections that allow for a quick reassembly of the many parts that go into complex products and services. It also forms a very visible model that sets consumer expectations for how fast a company should be able to respond to changes in a marketplace, such as energy prices and family demographics.

This change in expectation applies to virtually every industry. We have simply come to believe that any company that is not able to continuously meet our changing needs is unworthy of our business.

Order Out of Chaos: A New Model for Scale

If we bring together Schumpeter's economic model of creative destruction and Porter's concept of the value chain and look at how the cloud impacts each, we end up with an entirely new way to look at both the prospects of capitalism and the process of competition. This new view redefines traditional notions of achieving scale in terms of the liabilities it entails as well as the benefits it can offer.

By leveraging the power of the cloud to create a platform on which businesses can build the connections needed to form value chains— value chains that do not require hardwired preexisting relationships— this new model creates a means of real-time collaboration that disrupts an incumbent's ability to close a market to new innovations from outside the status quo.

A prime example of this is the emergence of a new class of cloud-based companies, including CBANC, E2open, and GXS, that are acting as intermediaries in the creation of complex value chains. E2open, for example, has introduced the notion of a "supply chain control tower" that acts in much the same way that an FAA control tower at an airport does in managing air traffic into and out of airports. E2open works with companies to make information, such as inventory, ship time, and availability, visible to business partners in the cloud.

These control towers serve several critical functions. First, they monitor all the business rules and resources needed to perform a process, such as manufacturing a product, and ensure that all of the required steps and components are in place to meet a market need before that need arises. The control tower provides the ability to anticipate changing demands and market behaviors based on knowledge gathered from all of the suppliers and buyers of a particular product or service. For example, if demand for a product is projected to increase, the control tower can add a qualified supplier to the value chain in order to fulfill this increased demand in real time.

Second, the control towers provide a means of creating trust among business partners that may not have already been put in place through agreements for how individual partners will share information with each other. This can even be applied to basic sharing of best practices.

For example, CBANC has created a control tower for the sharing and exchange of banking industry practices and procedures among banks that have never worked together or may not have even known to ask each other for assistance.

CBANC is a particularly interesting example of how cloud-based intermediaries can help small- and medium-sized businesses scale without having to invest in extensive research and development. In the case of CBANC, that takes the form of sharing best practices, policies and procedures, vendor buying experiences, and key surprises in exams specific to banking.

Myers Dupuy, president of CBANC, realized the value this cloud-based collaboration would have for community banks when he worked with a client who had a legal agreement that was in high demand at other banks. CBANC was founded by Hank Seale, a visionary founder of several start-ups in the banking industry. Hank wanted to find a new business collaboration model for banking that would help community banks gain an edge in the fiercely competitive banking industry. While Dupuy was thinking about ways to address the needs of community banks, one particular experience became an epiphany.

I worked with a banker in California; let's call her Sally, who was a cash management officer. She had built the perfect cash management agreement. Sally's bank had invested about $10,000 to $15,000 of staff time, lawyer time, and board approval time for this one document. It just so happened that in every bank install I did after hers, I would get the same question, "Do you know of another bank with a really good cash management agreement?"

I would call Sally and say, "Hey, would you mind sending that cash management agreement one more time to another banker?" She probably sent it out ten times on my behalf and had given it out twenty times to people she knew.

At one point, she finally said, "I can't do this anymore. We've given this document away about thirty times which means about $300,000 of generosity my bank has given out to possible competitors without any way to get any value back." This was an organic moment that happened while we were trying to figure out how we were going to build my CEO's long-term vision for a collaboration model that could help small banks group together and be as strong as the biggest banks. That's when the light bulb went off.

We realized, "This isn't about discussion forums. Banks don't need discussion forums to chat and keep up socially. They needed a way to value and barter their work, and to block their competitors specifically. They needed to get some form of value back in return for the time they spent creating their work. What could that be? It couldn't be based on real dollars because that would create legal and regulatory implications." That's when it dawned on us that we should build a virtual currency that would only work inside our network. The bankers would set their own price and exchange their intellectual property in a virtual free market.

It was truly one of those "aha" moments. We started to put in place the framework for an exchange mechanism in the cloud that would act as a formal clearinghouse for banks to share information, documents, agreements, best practices, and virtually anything of value which they wished to share.

Here's a typical example of how the system currently works without CBANC as the trusted intermediary. A banker spends $500 on a piece of work from a service provider or partner institution and they have no distribution rights for that work. Let's just assume that their heart's in the right place and they never intend to do anything wrong with it. However at some point they leave their job and a new person comes in. They see the piece of content on their network, have no idea it came from a third party and send it off to a friend who innocently asks for help. Unknowingly, they've just violated intellectual property laws and put themselves and their friend at risk.

What we've done is replace that risk by requiring our users to acknowledge that they own full intellectual property distribution rights when they upload a piece of content.

We've also indemnified the seller from a lawsuit if a bank buys their content and decides later it hurt their bank. That way everyone sleeps at night and the regulators are comfortable that the exchange is a controlled transaction rather than an unregulated gift of content that could belong to someone else.

The demand for the virtual currency is now so high, because the content that backs it is so in demand, we can now drive behaviors with our users that you would not think possible. If you asked 100 banks, "Would you ever go online and post anecdotal experiences about your last regulatory exam so everyone can see it?" The answer would universally be "no." Yet the incentive to get a thousand CBANC points, which they can trade for other documents which they do not have, is causing our members to share substantive, anonymous anecdotal reports about the key issues and surprises from their last exams. In addition, they are helping their peers prepare for upcoming exams, and they feel good about that. Those thousand points that they got could save them hundreds of hours. That's a sound investment of time—take ten minutes to write a quick report and save potentially hundreds of hours!

Another great example of the power of the virtual currency is users' willingness to write reviews of their vendors. Rapidly changing technology, regulatory, and economic factors mean that bankers have to rely more and more on outsourcing mission critical business functions to third-party vendors. It is not uncommon for one bank to do business with 300-plus vendors. If you take a small community bank, they do not have the staff resources to conduct proper due diligence on all of these vendors, especially when the services necessary to stay in business (think: emergence of mobile phones and mobile banking) changes every six months.

What they need is a safe, organized place where they can read candid reviews by their peers of vendor performance. That did not exist prior to CBANC in the banking space, but the virtual currency our users want drives them to write vendor review after vendor review, and now banking professionals have access to candid, unbiased stories of vendor performance that they can read and evaluate before they ever pick up the phone and call the vendor.

Ultimately, when we look at all of the data we are collecting about how our members behave and what type of information they exchange, there are numerous ways in which to monetize the value of this information that both benefits our members and the growth of CBANC's business, especially as we extend this model across other industries.

The CBANC approach opens up the door to an entirely new notion of virtual currency as a mechanism for exchanging value through the cloud. This may be one of the most intriguing and ultimately most powerful advantages to using the cloud. Imagine for a moment that the points that are used in the CBANC model become universally accepted across a critical mass of cloud applications, from specialized areas such as banking to consumer clouds. What might this look like? Why would virtual currency have benefit over real currency?

First, consider that much of what your children are doing today in online gaming already involves this sort of virtual currency. Enormous black markets have been created by the equivalent of digital sweat shops where young gamers toil away gathering virtual currency on games such as *RuneScape*, in virtual worlds like *Second Life*, and in dozens of other online contexts. These kids are being conditioned to use virtual currency and to trust in it, although in its current state it is far from trustworthy.

However, the issue of trust is one that can be addressed as well as any other aspect of the cloud's integrity.

An early example is Bitcoin, a virtual currency that has been widely used and exchanged for real currencies, goods, and services. The idea behind Bitcoin is really no different than any other virtual currency. However Bitcoin goes to great lengths to preserve both the anonymity of its users as well as to secure its virtual currency. In an AlterNet article about Bitcoin Scott Thill describes the mechanism for doing this in detail.

> "A public peer-to-peer transaction ledger, called a block chain, is stored on every computer running bitcoin and records every transaction ever made. The ledger weighs hundreds of megabytes in size, and is validated every 10 minutes by a computer working to secure the network, called a bitcoin miner, which wraps blocks of broadcasted message transactions in cryptographic hash functions. Transactions are entirely public, while those who transact are nearly private. The result? An emergent digital economy for the iGeneration.[2]"

While Thill's description may sound almost as cryptic as the Bitcoin transactions themselves, it does illustrate the lengths to which Bitcoin has gone to secure its currency. What is clear is that virtual currencies will form an increasingly larger part of the transactions that take place in the cloud and make the use of online exchanges, such as CBANC, even easier to use.

While these sorts of intermediaries existed before the cloud, they did not offer the tremendous savings, scale, and speed that CBANC or E2open can provide. For example, think about the way travel agents were once the norm when you needed to book air travel and hotels. Today, few of us would think of going through a travel agent, with all the online options available. The reason is only partly due to the convenience of booking arrangements from home. The greater value is in being able to save money while also having a larger number of options, as well as greater flexibility and control. Online intermediaries such as Priceline. com and Kayak.com are able to provide individuals with the same sort of economies of scale that were once afforded to only the largest travel agencies. The same is true of cloud-based intermediaries such as Groupon, which offers individuals the buying power of a large organization by negotiating lower prices with sellers based on the proposition that they will be able to get to a larger community of buyers.

However, the benefits are not limited to cost reduction. The other aspect of this new model is that it disrupts traditional locked-in value chains and creates a greater degree of competition by opening up the value chain to companies outside of the incumbents. Where travel agencies had once relied on partnerships with selected air carriers, cruise lines, and hotels to negotiate the best deals in anticipation of buyers, online intermediaries turn the tables and instead rely on their ability to attract a larger volume of buyers, identify actual demand, and increase options in real time. These new business intermediaries justify their value through the scale that they can build on behalf of their members. This would never have been possible outside of the cloud.

At this point, I'll guess that you're wondering why a large company would need to leverage an intermediary's economy of scale? As we'll see in the case of intermediaries such as E2open, the size of the business may change the benefit of working with an intermediary but it is critical for businesses of every size. While a large business may not need the economies of scale I've described, it will still need the agility that a cloud-based intermediary can offer.

But why limit the conversation to large companies? The primary initial recipients of the value these intermediaries provide are small- and medium-sized businesses, which could never have leveraged scale. In the case of CBANC, the initial beneficiaries are community banks. These companies can now buy scale on demand, as and when needed. For larger companies, the appeal is that many noncore areas where these companies may have expended valuable resources can now be addressed through cloud intermediaries.

This new means of achieving scale without having to build it internally hinges on three fundamentals.

1. Removing barriers to the entry of small business and the growth of entrepreneurship reinvigorates a free market.
2. Free markets must move at speeds that are unattainable by organizations that attempt to lock in suppliers and partners.
3. Perhaps most importantly, only by meeting the expectations of consumers for nearly real-time changes in products or services can companies hope to win the confidence of the marketplace.

This new model of the market cannot be supported by the same methods we have used to build organizations to date. It relies on an ability to create a set of standardized means by which we can collaborate, share, and transact across even the most complex value chains.

A basic tenet of the cloud is that size does not determine speed. Speed is determined by factors such as influence, time to community, higher levels of experimentation, lower risk of experimentation, and the ability to reconstitute a product or service in real time. Unlike the behemoth integrated value chains that dominated most of the twentieth century, the value chains formed in the cloud do not abide by rigid, controlled supply chains. Instead, the cloud consists of constantly shifting relationships among community members. Because of this, size alone does not define community ownership—that is, it is no longer justifiable for the largest player to own the largest supply chain. The communities are instead owned by their members.

What this means is that the faster you can create a community of suppliers, partners, and distributors to respond to a demand, the more likely you are to succeed—as a community and as a part of it.

Sounds simple, right? Sure, until you get mired in the myriad tasks

involved in forming a supply chain, from identifying partners to negotiating terms and contracts to justifying the costs of building each new
network. This is why large businesses still dominate in the face of enormous market inefficiency. Have you ever asked yourself, "How in the
world does (fill in the blank) stay in business given how badly they seem
to operate?" In short, traditional value chains have created insurmount-
able barriers to innovation and evolution. (If you want to learn this lesson
the hard way, try to compete against an industry behemoth.)

Here is where the rules change in the cloud—in a big way. The cloud
represents a new mechanism for establishing markets at this higher level
of complexity through the use of cloud-based platforms. Such platforms
act as catalysts for a new marketplace, which is much more complex and
far more sophisticated than anything our traditional business institutions
are prepared for. These trading platforms, or what have also been called
exchanges, are likely to be the greatest value proposition for new business
and the central metaphor for the way all business is conducted over the
next hundred years. Most importantly, they will erode the bedrock of traditional value chains and open the door to a new era of entrepreneurship.

Why are these exchanges so important? Consider that in complex markets, such as automobile manufacturing, there are a multitude of mechanisms for forming and managing value chains that are as complex and as
well entrenched as the tributary system of the Nile. A seemingly endless
cascade of tens of thousands of suppliers contributes to the production of
an automobile. And the path from innovation to the construction of any
new model requires an enormous amount of time and effort to establish a
new value chain of partners, suppliers, and distributors.

This also assumes that all of the buyers and sellers in any marketplace
are known to each other. That is clearly not the case, since much of every
business's effort involves promoting, marketing, and selling its services or
products to organizations that need its goods but are not familiar with them.

Now, suppose it were possible to remove much, if not all, of the
tedium, market and pricing inefficiency, and process latency involved in

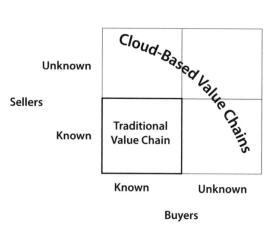

FIGURE 7-1 Traditional value chains are built to respond to a known set of market needs with a known set of value chain partners. Cloud-based value chains provide a much higher level of interchange among partners, greater spontaneity in addressing new needs on the part of the market, and increased innovation by bringing buyers and sellers together to form new value chains and new buying communities.

identifying, qualifying, and engaging with partners? What if we were to remove the transactions from the process and instantly coordinate the community of providers and suppliers (current and potential) based on the demand side rather than the supply side of the industry? The result would be an extraordinary increase in the velocity of innovation and market efficiency, not to mention a flood of new enterprise.

The E2open Story

One of the best examples of this sort of cloud-based trading platform is E2open. E2open was founded by a group of high-tech companies—including LG Electronics, Acer, Toshiba, Nortel, IBM, Hitachi, Seagate, and Solectron—which saw the need for an exchange among all of the companies in an industry that were sharing suppliers and common parts.

The principle is simple: create an established ecosystem of interchange-able organizations that can build value chains in real time based on the nuances of the market. However, the infrastructure required is incred-ibly difficult to create and put into practice. When the approach was first attempted in the late 1990s there were nearly 1,000 such exchanges built. Nearly every one crumbled under the enormous weight of investment and time required to put the pieces of the exchange in place.

In many ways, these exchanges create an operating system for a busi-ness that introduces trust, financial and legal terms, and visibility into the processes, demand, and inventory of members. The difference is that an exchange like E2open has to do that for thousands of members. The investment is daunting but the payoff is huge, especially for large com-plex projects that involve hundreds or even thousands of suppliers.

For example, in the case of the Boeing 787 Dreamliner, which used E2open, in partnership with Exostar, the supply chain had to be agile enough not only to accommodate thousands of suppliers but also to allow suppliers to be instantly rearranged based on Boeing's needs and fluctua-tions in their production schedules.

With suppliers across the globe, any number of problems—from natural disasters to raw materials shortages to basic reconfigurations of a product—can result in an immediate need to change the way a supply chain is configured. For example, the computer company Dell's battery supplier, LG, had a massive fire in the second-largest battery chemicals plant in South Korea, which cut off Dell's access to batteries for its lap-tops. Without the ability to quickly shift its supply chain to other provid-ers, Dell would have been forced to shut down production and shipment of computers. You can imagine the sort of chaos that results from inci-dents of this kind. Today's supply chains are so tightly reliant upon these fragile global networks that even small disruptions can cause big headaches.

At the same time, demand chains—the buyers of products and services—are incredibly volatile as well. For cell phone manufacturers, the introduction of a new device may peak in a matter of months, requiring repeated and frequent supply chain reconfiguration. The cost of doing this can quickly erode margins and stifle innovation.

E2open offers an alternative that effectively minimizes risk by providing visibility and exception-based management between brand owners and suppliers, no matter what the underlying disruptions may be. This takes the notion of a cloud-based utility to an entirely new level of sophistication. The service is so reliable that IBM has increased its pull replenishment levels to 85 percent through E2open's global trading network; in addition, the company services large players such as Vodafone, IBM, and Motorola Solutions.

The underlying network is a critical part of how the cloud enables this level of service. There are 29,000 companies established in the E2open network; when supplier A suddenly comes up short, a company can instantly switch to supplier B or C. Not only can a company get connected to the supplier, it can have real-time visibility into the supplier's inventory, shoot a message out to an alternate supplier saying, "I need another 100,000 components, what can you give me?" and instantly get the commitment. This is not just getting someone on the phone, it's an electronic commitment that is virtually as fast as a person could read an e-mail.

In addition, every supplier and customer in the E2open network is always looking at the same dashboard with the same information about supply and demand levels, allowing companies to respond to variances in a way they couldn't before. This is what E2open calls "a single version of the truth." That concept has profound implication in practice, because it takes the guesswork and potential error inherent in supply chain negotiations out of the equation, increasing reliability and confidence in making changes.

Trying to build this scale of redundancy and reliability into a proprietary supply chain is inconceivable in the absence of the cloud, in the same way that it would be virtually impossible to expect that every company could self-insure against natural disasters and risk. The investment in money and technology to implement an exchange would be prohibitively high for any small company and most large companies as well. In fact, it takes, on average, four months for most companies to on-board a single supplier. With E2open, a customer has full access to the entire network of suppliers in less than half that time.

But there is another benefit to doing this in the cloud that goes well beyond the near-term reliability we've described. The next generation of supply chain that is taking shape in the cloud is one that focuses on being truly demand-driven, so that the forecasting is based on demand signals, or what are typically called *polls*, rather than on past performance and demand.

The idea behind polling is to understand the real-time behavior of a market in such a way as to predict some of its future behavior. This means being able to sense every order, as it happens, allowing you to anticipate demand and then manage a much more efficient supply chain.

This may not sound radical. Since Dell pioneered this model of a demand-driven supply chain, in the 1990s, it has become a competitive necessity. But these models reflect the buying behaviors of one company's products. What if you had the ability to monitor all of the buying behaviors for an entire category across an industry? What kinds of behaviors might emerge and how could you leverage those to not only respond to but even predict buying trends?

E2open calls this *collaborative execution,* which is the ability to take real-time data, through analytics, anonymize and aggregate it and make real-time decisions about a supply chain. For example, the data can inform decisions about how to change allocations, how to deal with shortages, or how to manage demand spikes; one can even go further and ask, "Am I best in class in what I do by comparing myself to the performance of my peers?"

This is the idea behind creating what I call a *business operating system* that allows organizations to manage not only their own resources but the resources across an entire value chain. Without this capability, you can't reform a supply chain quickly enough to respond to changes in the market. Similarly, the market doesn't have a single voice to tell you what it wants or why its demand for a particular product or service might change, so the risk of experimentation is very high.

For example, if a market suddenly starts to demand a product in a certain color or a product with a specific set of features, you would typically not know it until well after the demand has occurred. *Acting upon this kind of information about the past is like driving while looking in your review mirror.* It's not that you can't do it if you're on a straight and wide road, but every time you hit a twist or turn and drive off of the road, you will end up slowing down and making errors in judgment. As a result, you eventually exhaust the desire to innovate.

I recall having a discussion with John Croker, a retired air force general who was responsible for teaching military doctrine to military leaders. He gave an example of the importance of counterbalancing the instinctive response to avoid risk and uncertainty that involves driving a Humvee: You are driving a Humvee in a war zone along a winding, high-risk roadway on which you know other soldiers have been ambushed. Your instinct is to drive as fast as you can to avoid being the target of an attack. However, if a sandstorm suddenly cuts your visibility, your instinct to speed is tempered a bit by the prospect of running off of the road. So you slow down. If the sandstorm cuts your visibility even further, you slow down even more. If you follow that logic to its inevitable conclusion, you will at some point stop altogether, making you a prime target for attack. The officer's point was that soldiers in today's uncertain and unconventional theater of war must fight the instinct to slow down by trusting the intelligence they receive through assistive technologies, which can guide them through scenarios where visibility is lacking. This is no different from the way organizations must respond in counterintuitive ways by relying on real-time data about markets rather than on hunches and historical analytics.

Exchanges such as E2open provide the ability to create supply chains across many partners that can align instantly to the needs of a market, while still being able to innovate. In a conversation I had in 1999 with the late Peter Drucker, he described precisely this sort of framework for the organizations of the future. I had asked Peter what he felt was the most profound shift in the structure of the organization during the twentieth century. His response was that it was the shift from vertically integrated companies built around the notion of ownership and standardization of product to companies that were aligned around partnership strategy and products that were customized to be sold as services. In this model of *the organization,* survival without the ability to use the cloud-based intermediaries as the cornerstone for alignment and customization becomes nearly impossible.

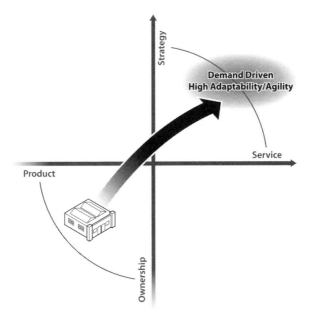

FIGURE 7-2 Perhaps the greatest shift in business during the last 100 years is that of the movement from businesses aligned around product and ownership to those which are aligned around service and strategy. The former was a much simpler organization to manage as compared to the complexity, numerous partnerships, and fast adaptation required of organizations aligned around strategy and service.

Less Is Greater Than More

While the cloud is big business for major providers of cloud-based technology, such as Amazon, Google, HP, and Microsoft, the biggest beneficiaries of the cloud will be the small businesses that employ nearly 90 percent of the world's working population and produce 65 percent of global GDP. These businesses are incredibly productive and efficient when compared with larger businesses. For example consider that small business in the United States:

- Represents 99.7 percent of all employer firms
- Employs just over half of all private sector employees
- Pays 44 percent of total U.S. private payroll
- Has generated 64 percent of net new jobs over the past fifteen years
- Creates more than half of the nonfarm private gross domestic product (GDP)
- Hires 40 percent of high-tech workers (such as scientists, engineers, and computer programmers)
- Makes up over 95 percent of all identified exporters
- Produced thirteen times more patents per employee than large patenting firms; these patents are twice as likely as large firms' patents to be among the 1 percent most cited

Yet the first challenges any small business faces are funding, staffing, and scale. Each of these can be a monumental challenge not only to the business but also to the potential for innovation that small businesses provide to the overall economy. If you look at the numbers above, it's not hard to understand why small business is such a critical part of sustainable economic growth. Diminishing the role that these engines of the economy can have is like throwing the plankton out of an ecosystem; it may take some time but eventually every organism, including the ones at the top of the food chain, will suffer.

If these businesses can flourish and grow, on the other hand, the positive impact on the economy is considerable. In fact, while the Small Business Administration claims that 64 percent of net new jobs during the period from 1995 to 2010 came from small business, nearly all net new jobs during the first decade of the twenty-first century came from small business. This is due to several intersecting dynamics.

First, when large businesses are hit hard by an economic dip, one of the first areas of response is cost cutting through job reduction and decreased spending on innovation. Both of these accelerate the growth of small business, which end up being started and staffed by many of those shed from large corporations. Not surprisingly, many of these individuals will also leave with innovative ideas that their former employer was reluctant to invest in because of the added cost and risk. When large companies get scared, the innovation antibodies come out in droves. But in the absence of competition from powerful corporate players, these newly planted small businesses flourish like ferns after a forest fire, when the jungle canopy no longer blocks their sunlight.

Second, recessions are especially good times to introduce a new idea, not only because the attention of larger players is diverted to operations and cost cutting, but also because the marketplace is ready for some light to illuminate their path out of the darkness. Some of the most iconic innovations had their start in the worst economies. The iPod, which gave birth to a decade-long series of innovations in computing, was introduced in 2001, a time that was as dark economically and nationally as any the United States had experienced since the Great Depression and the Second World War.

Third, everything is less expensive in a bad economy. The life cycle of most small businesses is five to ten years, and the time when you need to squeeze the most out of every dollar is at the outset.

It all seems somewhat counterintuitive, but after having been through many of these cycles myself and having worked on my own small businesses and those of others:

It is absolutely crystal clear to me that large-scale economic difficulties create the most fertile soil for planting new ideas.

But what these periods have lacked until now is an effective funding vehicle for small business. Traditional lenders, such as banks, venture capitalists, and even angel investors, tend to get much more conservative during a downturn, falling into the classic joke of only wanting to lend umbrellas when it's not raining. The cloud has started to change that.

New players such as Kickstarter, of New York, have taken the idea of crowdsourcing into the cloud by developing a way to successfully match investors and donors with recipients who use the money to fund creative projects; call it *cloudfunding*.

More than 700,000 individuals have contributed over $75 million to fund Kickstarter projects, roughly a hundred of which are introduced daily. The setup is pretty simple: recipients set their own financial goals, one or more Kickstarter investors takes an interest in the project and makes a pledge; if the goal is reached within the set timeline, the money changes hands and the creator moves forward with her plan. Donors receive products or experiences defined by the project's creator, depending on the level of the pledge.

It sounds amazingly simple, though hardly novel—basically like an online dating service for start-ups and investors. To a degree it is, but what's novel about Kickstarter is that it fills a void where "traditional" early funding sources often leave off, and requires far less red tape than microlenders such as the Grameen Foundation, which specializes in small loans to people in impoverished and developing countries. Kickstarter also serves as a critical testing ground for new ideas, quickly validating their ability to attract attention and deliver value.

In a way, Kickstarter offers a pathway for ideas that would otherwise likely die a quick death on a cocktail napkin or a slow death as their inventors tried to promote the idea among friends and family. Among the projects recently seeking funding on Kickstarter was the open-source electronic bulletin board Teagueduino, of Seattle, which had attracted $3,387 in pledges with thirty-five days left to collect the other 85 percent of the money its creator was looking for. During the same period, an intellectual, salon-style social gathering known as Tertulia had netted $12,370 (123 percent of what was expected, with nine days left for other patrons to donate); the writer of *Speakeasy Dollhouse*, an immersive, biographical murder tale, had attracted $3,980 with twenty-nine days left on the calendar to attract the remaining 60 percent of the targeted amount.

Kickstarter's biggest matchmaking successes include 2009's *Designing Obama*, a book that explored the visual art and design of Barack Obama's presidential campaign. The project raised $85,000, but was eclipsed in 2010 by several projects, including the open-source social networking project Diaspora (which topped $200,000); the film *Blue Like Jazz* ($350,000); and TikTok multi-touch watch kits (just shy of $1 million).[3]

The interactive, collaborative niche that Kickstarter established in the cloud sets the organization apart from other funding sources. "Real" people whose dreams would be hampered by a lack of funding can do "what they love, something fun, or at least something of note,"[4] and then use Web 2.0 tools like blogs and online videos to keep the world apprised of their progress. This is a far cry from the venture capital world, where funders require seats on their beneficiaries' boards of directors in order to keep tabs on how their money is being used.

The Kickstarter cloud allows for other types of personal interaction between funders and beneficiaries. On his blog, Phil Simon, author of *The New Small: How a New Breed of Small Businesses Is Harnessing the Power of Emerging Technologies,* opens up about exactly how the funding for his 240-page, self-published book will be used. The maker of the online game

The Demolished Ones went so far as to give contributors of $75 or more the chance to give input for the game.

Without the cloud, none of these collaborations and interactions would have been possible. One-way communication and information delivery simply doesn't allow for such relationships, especially not in the real-time format that's enabled on the web.

Most Kickstarter projects raise $5,000 or less,[5] but that doesn't mean that the model is limited to no-name companies. When NASA decided to develop its own massive multiplayer online game (MMO) in 2011, for example, it turned to Kickstarter to raise money for the beta version of the project. *Astronaut: Moon, Mars, and Beyond* is NASA's attempt at creating an educational game that's exciting and targeted at today's tech-savvy kids and teens. Able to run on computers, tablets, and "select consoles," the project hit its $5,000 Kickstarter goal and was in development for a late 2011 release.[6]

As with any innovation, there are downsides to using Kickstarter. In his online article "The Pros and Cons of Using Kickstarter to Fundraise,"[7] software engineer Philip Neustrom discusses his experience using the site to raise some of the funding for LocalWiki software. He singled out the 5 percent cut of funds that Kickstarter takes and the additional 2-3 percent taken by Amazon as Kickstarter's credit card processor. That may not sound like much but given the low margin nature of many of the businesses that Kickstarter funds, 7-8 percent can be significant. In addition the Kickstarter model uses an all or nothing mechanism which requires that anyone who pledges to a project through Kickstarter is only charged if the total amount of funding sought by the business is reached. The reasoning is that anything less will compromise the chances for success. The downside is that you will get all of your requested funding or none of it.

Fitting into the Kickstarter mold does come with some unorthodox requirements, such as producing a video detailing why you want the money. It's also not just a roll of the dice. If you want to convince investors, you must write about—and provide updates on—the desired funding and you have to widely publicize your project on your own.

Challenges aside, Neustrom and many other participants give Kick-starter largely positive reviews. The company isn't alone in the "cloud-funding" space. Others, such as San Francisco-based IndieGoGo, use a similar format to fund for-profit, creative, and charitable campaigns for a smaller cut of 4 percent.

Nearly 150 years ago Adam Smith described the force of an invisible hand that shapes free markets. Cloudfunding is a form of that invisible hand, hovering over ideas and capital and bringing the two together; in the absence of cloudfunding, it would be either horribly inefficient or simply impossible to pair such ideas with those who will finance them.

Cloud Currency

If there is a single concept that best defines the evolution of commerce in the cloud it is that of liquidity. Liquidity, simply stated, is the ability to translate resources into value. The faster the translation occurs, the more liquid a given resource. For example, cash is far more liquid than a piece of real estate, because the former can immediately be transformed into another item of value whereas the latter must undergo a series of intermediate translations before it can be exchanged for another item of value.

This transformation of value as it takes on varying forms is central to the concept of liquidity. To make the discussion more concrete, consider the analogy of a liquid taking the form of its container. No matter what shape the container is, a liquid will easily adapt to its container's most intricate details—in the same way that cash can be immediately translated into any other item of value. But the immediacy of this value translation is contingent upon two other factors, market breadth and discount.

The point is that the degree of liquidity requires a context in order to be measured meaningfully. In other words, if only one buyer and one seller exist, liquidity has no degrees. Increase the number of buyers, and the resource being used (currency) is discounted as buyers bid up the price, spending more of the resource for the same amount of a particular good. Increase the number of sellers, and the market broadens, decreasing the price of the goods. This is the basic law of supply and demand that we have all grown up with and which Alfred Marshall popularized when he published his *Principles of Economics* in 1890.

However, the law of supply and demand is not as pure and efficient as we make it out to be in today's markets, since it relies on some fundamental inefficiencies and imbalances. Some of the best examples are markets such as diamonds and oil, which are controlled by cartels of suppliers. My apology to those readers who hold fast to the belief that most of the diamonds sold to consumers for jewelry are in fact worth a fraction of the value De Beers exacts for them through artificial supply controls. This does not mean that there is no inherent value in these commodities, simply that the value is often manipulated by artificial price controls of inefficient markets. When a significant dearth of buyers and/or sellers exists, a market is considered to be thin or narrow. Thin markets may result in high discounts or price gouging, require regulation, or simply die off. At the other extreme of this phenomenon are commodity markets, which consist of readily available goods with ample supplies of buyers. Commodity markets tend to be relatively efficient because they are fairly broad.

This leads us to an interesting phenomenon. Efficiency seems to provide greater leverage for the buyer while inefficiency tends to favor the seller. This is the essence of the fear that the cloud engenders in most traditional businesses. Namely, if markets get more efficient then prices will plummet and margins will disappear. Again, we can point to the diamond trade, which nearly collapsed when word got out after the dissolution of the Soviet Union that Russia was sitting on a stockpile of raw diamonds. Putting these diamonds into circulation would have the same effect on diamond prices that releasing the world's petrochemical reserves would have on the price of gasoline.

So what of that? If it is true, and markets are in fact a zero-sum game, then won't cloud-based trading networks such as E2open drive suppliers out of business, possibly leading to a thin market as suppliers dwindle? In the case of artificially controlled markets, where cloud-based trading networks can offer alternative channels for procurement, the effect is no less than that of taking away a protected monopoly. Yet, as has been the case with the breakup of some of history's most notorious monopolies, from Standard Oil to AT&T, the resulting component companies have been far more successful despite the turmoil of breaking up.

The reason is that the value of their products and services has been greater when presented to the market in smaller pieces that are more easily recombined with other pieces of the economy, a constant theme that we have been repeating in the context of how the cloud creates greater value.

Therein lies the power and beauty of liquidity, which adds a new dimension to the cloud. To better understand this idea, let's look at traditional markets as consisting of two axes, as show in figure 7-3. The horizontal axis represents the market, or demand chain, and the vertical axis represents the suppliers, or the supply chain. To gain some insight, let's add to each axis the labels of known and unknown; each reflects the degree to which we know the needs of a market or the possible partners in a supply chain.

Each axis is labeled from 0 to 1, with the value 1 at the center of the X/Y coordinate system. If the demand chain axis is equal to 0, there is no variability in the product and the marketplace has well-defined needs that apply to all buyers. However, if the demand chain axis is equal to 1, there is high variability of the product and *each* buyer's needs must be addressed individually. The same applies to the supply chain axis. If it is equal to 0, then the supply chain is well established and does not change easily. To understand the 0:0 quadrant in the lower left think of Henry Ford's early efforts at defining the automobile industry—the supplier wanted to control and own every aspect of the raw materials and production and the market did not expect to have any choice in options such as color, interior, or configuration. On the other hand, a 1:1 on both the supply chain and demand chain axis indicates that the supplier is often changing the supply chain to offer a large number of options, which the buyer expects to be able to chose

From Mass Production to Mass Innovation

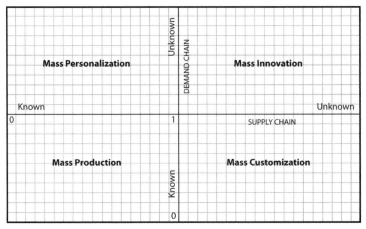

FIGURE 7-3 If we fully understand each buyer's needs and behaviors, and are able to partner with all of the suppliers needed to deliver a particular product or service, we would expect that we have built a perfect business model, or what is often referred to as *one-to-one* or *mass customization*. But in this figure that would only place our business at the center of the four quadrants. This is actually only the foundation for cloud-based business models.

from based on their preferences. This is the way we buy automobiles today. Based on our preferences we can chose options when we buy a car that requires the supplier to pick and chose different partners in their existing supply chain to provide these options.

Given that scenario, you might assume that a rating of 1:1 would be the ultimate state of any marketplace. You would be right in terms of the way suppliers and buyers have interacted up until now, in the absence of the cloud. But in reaching that conclusion, you have completely ignored the impact of the cloud on both suppliers and buyers.

An amazing phenomenon takes place when you move to the upper-right quadrant of figure 7-3, the domain of the cloud. As cloud-based trading networks begin to take shape, they accelerate the velocity of transactions within a market by making it possible for buyers to request variations on products that don't reflect the past capability of the supply chain. For example, iTunes has not just changed the music industry but has grown the industry by introducing new business model innovation where buyers drive the demand for music by creating their own playlists. The supply chain then offers suggestions for products that the buyer may not have considered, such as iTunes Genius mixes. This type of innovation instantly recognizes the changing behaviors of the market and reconfigures the supply chain accordingly.

This mass innovation occurs in the cloud as trading networks take on the function of matching supply chain to demand chain by tracking the competencies of the supply chain at a low level of granularity (using our iTunes example, this would be the ability to buy individual songs and to combine them into customized playlists) while also tracking the preferences and behaviors of the demand chain across discrete buyers and communities.

The result is the formation of new products and services to instantly meet the combined requirements of multiple buyers. This is what we called *fourth derivative innovation* in chapter 6. Staying with our iTunes example, you as a consumer benefit from the preferences and buying patterns of others who have purchased similar music. In practical terms, the cloud now knows intimately the abilities of a large breadth of the supply chain and can map these to the constantly shifting requirements of the market, thus increasing the velocity of innovation, creating constant novelty in products and services (thus maintaining margins), and continuously reforming the supply chain to meet the demand chain.

Now, going one step further, you can envision the liquidity that results from recombination as a third dimension that leaps out from the two-dimensional graph we are using to illustrate supply and demand chain. The effect is to create a third multiplier (demand/supply/liquidity) in the market in novel ways.

This novelty cannot be predicted in the traditional ways that supply chains have reacted to markets. Focus groups, surveys, and classic market analysis no longer work. As the late Steve Jobs once quipped, "You can't just ask customers what they want and then try to give that to them. By the time you get it built, they'll want something new."

Only by building supply chains that keep pace with the unpredictability of the demand chain can enterprises succeed in the cloud.

However, capturing the trust needed to make this model of recombinant commerce part of a sustainable economic model may seem nearly impossible. After all, if it were possible, why hasn't the supply chain done it yet? Therein lies the answer. The demand chain has not had the clout to make it happen, except in a few commodity markets, because of the supplier leverage in our lower left quadrant.

Now the tables are turning. Demand chains are driving markets, making for strange bedfellows among suppliers—and creating bonds of trust where none would have imagined. To be blunt about it, suppliers have to find ways to build these bonds to survive.

Consider how the cloud accelerates the ability to address latent opportunity by providing far greater liquidity in the formation of supply chains. The central promise of the cloud is to make typical the sort of innovation that has previously been atypical.

The challenge is that since childhood we are taught not to repeat the mistakes of the past. History is a vast series of lessons learned and we ignore them at our peril, or so we are told. But what if we challenge that belief? Might it be that, as with so many generalizations, such as Schumpeter's creative destruction, we have lost the essence of truth by using too broad a brush to outline the parable? I know I'm treading on sacred turf here, but I doubt that I am alone.

If a basic characteristic of the cloud is its increased velocity and turbulence, then the past may be an anchor preventing an organization from moving forward to new success and stalling the liquidity of a market. The key to surviving under these conditions is a competency in continuously rebuilding the value chain to drive liquidity through both the demand and supply chains.

Organizations that succeed in the cloud have reached the stage

How the Cloud Increases
Market Liquidity for Mass Innovation

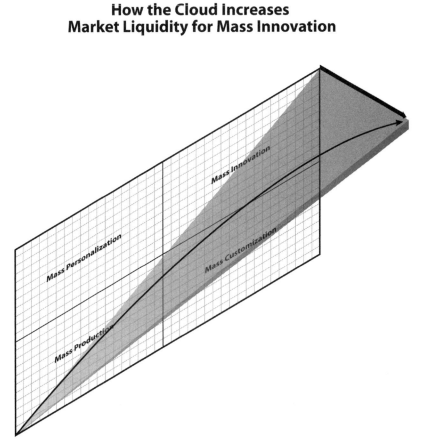

FIGURE 7-4 Cloud-based opportunity results from the ability to create liquidity in a market by going beyond the one-to-one model of business shown in figure 7-3 and identifying market behaviors and supply chain partnerships that are not obvious to either the market or suppliers.

where their knowledge of the past plays less of a role in guiding their future than does their understanding of current circumstances and an innate ability to create liquidity by processing and responding to these circumstances. Knowledge of the past is only valuable inasmuch as it provides a perspective on the future. The cloud, on the other hand, equips an organization to respond to as-yet-unknown forces for change.

Trust in the Cloud

When the topic of trust comes up it is most often in the context of the relationships between people. Trust, after all, is a basic human emotion that relies heavily on how we assess another person (that is, we evaluate whether someone has a trustworthy character or demeanor). However, trust is also a cornerstone of commerce. When talk of trust turns to online relationships, what we often fail to recognize is that trust is structural not just intellectual. In other words, trust can be legislated, documented, proceduralized, and incorporated into the bedrock of commerce in tangible ways.

Consider, for example, the last time you bought a house or a car that required a mortgage or a loan. It's not likely that you had a personal relationship with the banker, the real estate broker, the underwriters, the escrow agents, the appraisers, or even the seller. Yet you all established trust among each other by adhering to contractually binding rules for the transaction. These were not rules that anyone came up with just for your particular transaction. They are rules that take concrete form in the many documents, laws, contracts, procedures, and regulations already in place for the transaction.

Without these structural aspects of trust in place, far fewer homes would be bought and sold. Structural trust is, in fact, a method of facilitating commerce by decreasing the level of uncertainty inherent in dealing with otherwise unknown parties.

But what often slows down complex transactions that rely on this sort of trust is the one-off modifications that need to be made to the many pieces of the transaction. This is especially true when any new party enters the community of trade. In a perverse way, the very mechanism that creates more liquidity is the culprit in stifling greater liquidity. In the cloud this presents a significant impediment because potential partners are mostly unknown.

So, what if it were possible to incorporate not only the structural elements of trust into the cloud, but to go even further and allow for their instant modification to meet the needs of new participants? Effectively, this would provide trust by validating the identity, competency, and past performance of the participants.

In his best seller *The Quest for Cosmic Justice,* Thomas Sowell introduces a principle that provides a great context for the softer side of the cloud. Sowell believes that the complexity of modern life has led us to pursue a misguided ideology of righting everything that is wrong with our world by imposing a set of cosmic values.

According to Sowell, under social values, all things are fair and equal, and change is based on merit—in effect, this is the premise for a free market, where competition should bring the best products and services to the market. According to Sowell's cosmic values, all things are *not* fair and equal; therefore, we undertake human intervention as a necessary means to make the world fairer. Sowell's insight is that, although the intent behind intervention is understandable, its consequences are often disastrous.

The application of Sowell's argument to social issues, such as equality and justice, is easy to appreciate. But it also applies to the economics of the cloud.

In many ways, intervention has become the essential value proposition of economic policy, whether we're talking about the new economy or the old economy. Whether it is the Federal Reserve Bank of the United States adjusting lending rates, central banks bailing out failing corporations or buttressing failing economies, or global tariffs promoting or discouraging international trade, intervention has become a tool by which we attempt to manage the inherent uncertainty of complex economic systems. But what if we could build organizations in the cloud that were able to adjust themselves to market conditions in a way that did not require ongoing intervention? What might that economy look like? To answer that we need to look at how the cloud changes many of the fundamentals of how we work so that organizations become adaptive in real-time to this dramatic increase in complexity.

8

Work in
the Cloud

Globalization has changed us into a company that searches
the world, not just to sell or to source, but to find intellectual
capital—the world's best talents and greatest ideas.

—*Jack Welch*

Today, the complex movement of raw materials, goods, machinery, ideas, and people is a commonplace task that we take completely for granted. While the cloud may be helping us to become masters of the supply chain, we are only starting to understand how to master the knowledge chain, the collection of activities involved in packaging, transporting, and coordinating knowledge work, which increasingly takes place in the cloud.

Facilitating the knowledge chain is a daunting task, as knowledge work represents the bulk of the work performed in every industry. If you doubt that, just look at the amount of time and effort you personally devote each day to tracking down the right information, tools, and people to get work done. We have all become conductors of an immense orchestra whose players and instruments are scattered about the globe. Add to this complexity the looming promise of living entirely in the cloud, and it becomes clear that knowledge workers just don't have the right tools to get the job done.

While the cloud will eliminate many of the economic barriers and increase the convenience and reliability of computing for businesses, it will also radically change the way knowledge workers do their work. In other words, if you think it's hard to manage the knowledge chain today, just wait! We are on the cusp of a revolution much more dramatic in its impact on knowledge work than mass production was on manufacturing.

Moving Knowledge Work to the Cloud

As we've already seen, the cloud is much more than a utility that simply shifts the burden of computing power and data storage from users to a third party. Unlike electric utilities, which only move power, in the cloud we are also moving work and all of the tools needed to perform it. It is this subtle but profound change that creates the greatest opportunity for the enterprise of the future since it is no longer limited by talent tied to geography.

However, the movement of work to the cloud requires us to package up a great deal of scattered and disconnected information, links, applications, rules, regulations, skills, roles, and even the workers necessary to perform the work—and this is not a trivial matter. Think of the problem in this way: tools for knowledge work to date have focused on either *the content*, that is the documents and files, or *the process*, that is, the sequence, timing, and flow of content. Tools for knowledge work in the future have to focus primarily on *the work*, that is, the tools, methods, connections, and judgment needed to *act* on the information.

In the same way that the supply chain is about aligning around partnering strategy, the future of work is less about the assembly line than it is about orchestrating and managing the unexpected. To address this, a new category of cloud-based technology is evolving that deals specifically with the way we package and transport work in the cloud. It's called *case management,* and the basic idea behind it is that work is naturally organized as a case. The fundamental difference between the case concept and today's work environment is that a "case" becomes the defining metaphor for work rather than a file folder, the dominant image used in desktop computing as a metaphor for content.

Much like a folder on a desktop, a case allows you to store similar documents and files in one location. However, a case also enables you to store or link to all of the connections, rules, regulations, people, and applications needed to do the work in the cloud as a single object. Once created, a case can move from person to person or machine to machine, with everything it needs to be worked on. There is no need to find the right applications on your local computer, download software, or even locate the right people; all of this is connected to the case.

This would be like having a car that comes fully equipped with connections to the right mechanics, parts, maintenance schedule, driver behavior, and even the performance and maintenance history of similar vehicles. Furthermore, imagine that this car could find its way to the repair shop and tell the mechanic what was wrong with it, not unlike the basic idea behind services such as OnStar, which make the car an intelligent self-servicing machine.

Another analogy for case management is transportation. To consider the impact of the cloud on knowledge work, we can compare it to the impact that the steamship and railroads had on economies of the early twentieth century. Railroads and steamships transported workers, materials, and in many cases the fuel, such as coal and oil, needed to grow the global economy and to radically redistribute its population. Case management does much the same for knowledge work; it is the mechanism that can *connect and contain* all of the components that go into today's knowledge work and provide a way to collaborate while the work travels across the globe.

To better understand exactly what case management is, consider a mortgage process, an example of a classic complex knowledge chain. As with most knowledge chains, a mortgage process involves a complex set of collaborations among a wide group of people who form a loosely connected network of players, including bankers, mortgage brokers, underwriters, investors, credit reporting agencies, inspectors, appraisers, lawyers, real estate brokers, government agencies, administrators, loan officers, processors, assistants, escrow officers, notaries, closers, funders, account executives, and, of course, the buyer.

The amount of information that flows through this process is daunting, but so is the intricate set of activities and regulations involved and the complex connections each has to the people who perform the work. If you were to try to map the process, you might well end up with a neat and tidy flow chart, but in practice that chart would be close to useless, as all of the exceptions, nuances of each situation, and unexpected delays set in. Today, all of this knowledge work is coordinated in multiple paper and computer systems such as files, folders, faxes, local and remote storage, and directories, which are managed through a combination of automated and manual processes. Items get lost, and have to be resubmitted and reverified. With all of the technology we have to throw at the process, we wonder why it still takes most banks three to four weeks for a *simple* mortgage to be written, a time frame that hasn't changed much in over three decades!

However, some banks are seeing enormous competitive advantage in speeding this process and reducing errors by using case management to gather, package, and orchestrate these myriad components of the knowledge chain into a "case" that progresses through the process with all of the necessary items and links needed to write the mortgage. This means that all of the knowledge workers in the process have access to all of the information, links, people, and resources they need to get their work done. This is where virtually every solution to knowledge work that we have put in place to date falls short.

Unlike industrial-era work, knowledge work does not have one process flow, one manager of work, or one way to do the work.

In knowledge work, every worker has the potential to be a conductor and to redirect work as needed based on judgment and experience.

While a high level of complexity has always been part of the need that information systems were intended to address, the reality has fallen far short. For example, if you look more closely at our mortgage process you will find that many of the steps involved use different tools, software applications, networks, content, formats, and methods. Often the work is redirected, sent back, rerouted. Much of the time to process the mortgage ends up being taken not in the tasks but in manually getting work out of one system and into another. (Just think of how often you have to fill out the same information in multiple forms.) And just because much of this information is stored electronically does not mean it all works easily together. By some estimates, 90 percent of the time and effort in a mortgage process is the coordination of this nontask activity. That 90 percent is the white space in the knowledge chain that has simply not been addressed until the advent of case management.

If the problem were limited to the current state of affairs, we could probably just continue to deal with these issues. But complexity is not going away. In fact, things are going to get much, much worse, to the point where the complexity I just described will destroy many processes. Here are a few reasons:

- The increasing prevalence of risk and uncertainty
- Continued pressure to cut costs
- Increased transparency and governance
- Quantum increases in the size of the global educated workforce

The Increasing Prevalence of Risk and Uncertainty

The global interconnectedness of markets is creating unprecedented levels of uncertainty and risk. Incidents that could once be contained to a small geographical area or population now seem to ripple across the globe at light speed. From the near financial meltdown of world economies in 2009 to the effect of the 2011 Japanese tsunami, we have seen markets react instantly and synchronously. This effect is what I termed the *uncertainty principle* in chapter 3. Moving in the smaller windows of opportunity that uncertainty demands means we need faster coordination within our entire value chain of partners and customers, as well as far better levels of agility and resiliency. The hardwired and often-haphazard nature of many processes does not allow for either. Case management promises to deliver on both by coordinating and delivering work to where it needs to be with all of its relevant resources and connections intact and ready for action.

Continued Pressure to Cut Costs

While the recession of 2008 to 2010 may have been cyclical, the associated wave of cost cutting is not an episodic phenomenon. While we may well have triggered renewed attention on the topic through the difficult economic cycle of the last decade, the pressure to run efficient and lean operations will continue to increase as global pressure and competition also increase. Cost cutting is like an arms race in which there is always a better weapon system over the next horizon.

This relentless global cycle of cost cutting will not end soon—even as we proceed through the innovation and investment portion of the economic cycle. This means that organizations will put every aspect of their processes under intense scrutiny in order to optimize resources and create new efficiencies. If you consider that our mortgage example is just one of countless instances in which up to 90 percent of the process time is spent on nontask and nonvalue-adding activities, it is clear that eliminating as much of this waste as possible must be an area of intense focus. Case management addresses this directly by creating work product that is always ready to be acted on, requiring little time to search for the right information, tools, and methods to get the job done.

Increased Transparency and Governance

The mandate to create transparency also plays a critical role in forcing organizations to better define and then shed their noncore activities. In a recent study we conducted, we were amazed to find that the vast majority of organizations do not partner with or outsource to outside organizations and contractors due primarily to the fact that they do not believe they understand their own processes well enough to describe them! Even more perverse is that some of these organizations see this lack of "describability" as a competitive advantage, sort of like a secret sauce, though it's a secret even to themselves!

Transparency provides a means of sharing processes with partners, contractors, and customers in order to involve each when and where appropriate so that work can be expedited. Implicit in transparency is a solid understanding of your processes.

Managing work as a *case* is an ideal way to increase transparency while also maintaining the right level of security and privacy. For example, in the United Kingdom, tax authorities have created cases for every taxpayer. These are available to the taxpayers, employers, financial institutions, and the tax authorities. The cases stay with a taxpayer for life and provide a simple and error-free collection of all of the documents, rules, filings, individuals, and links to relevant data (for example, sections of the tax code effective when the filing was made). In this way, the burden of record keeping is greatly reduced, precision is increased, access to information is simplified, regulations are always linked correctly, time frames are recorded, methods of calculating tax are documented, supporting documentation is archived, and the people or roles involved are all connected to the case.

Quantum Increases in the Size of the Global Educated Workforce

One of the most important benefits of case management is its ability to provide a reliable platform for collaborative work. While this is important in any situation that involves multiple people and tasks, it is especially important when your workforce spans time zones and cultures. When those working on a process are not in the same place or the same time zone, the work product must be able to stand on its own and provide the next person in line with the necessary components to get the work done. In many ways, the work has to become its own administrator, with the intelligence to deal with changes as it flows through the process.

Fueling this mass migration of knowledge work will be a concerted effort to educate more of the world's population. The number of universities in developing countries around the globe is increasing at an astounding rate. For example, India today has nearly three hundred universities and more than ten thousand colleges, a tenfold increase since the 1950s. Consider that in India alone there are over five hundred million people under the age of twenty-five—what the Indian press has dubbed its generation of Zippies. While only a few of those people are today competing in the global marketplace, the pool of talent is enormous and the competition is fierce. Infosys, one of India's largest outsourcers, hires nine thousand employees yearly from more than one million applicants.

Across the globe, the trend to educate more of a country's citizens is reflected in a growing pool of talented and capable workers. This will create a massive increase in the number and quality of knowledge workers who will need tools to better share and collaborate on work across a broad global spectrum. For this knowledge-based workforce, case management will be as critical to success as plowshares were in the agricultural age.

Surviving and Thriving in Complexity

When you consider the impact that the cloud will have on knowledge work, it is difficult to conceive of knowledge workers maintaining their sanity much less getting work done correctly and effectively unless they are provided with tools to manage the growing complexity of information. Without a case to provide the superglue and an intelligent system to handle the complexity and coordination of knowledge work, business will simply be unable to keep up. In a free market, this is not an option. Competing companies will need to look toward case management to allow them to continue accelerating and growing their businesses while also equipping their workers with the tools they need to be able to continuously innovate.

Imagine that all of these underlying forces are like the fault lines on which many of the world's largest cities have been built. We cannot ignore their potential consequences, but it is not an option to move the city. Instead, we have to build cities and economies that can withstand earthquakes and survive the future. In that same light, we need to build businesses that can apply case management so that they can grow and thrive in spite of their complexity and the complexity of their markets.

A Lesson in Moving Work

Henry Ford understood the power of moving work nearly one hundred years ago. Ford did not create new technology or even radically change existing technologies. Rather, his genius lay in a simple change in the movement of work.

In contrast to what most of us are taught in grade school, Ford's innovation was not mass production or the principle of interchangeable parts. Both had been in use for at least a hundred years before the invention of the Tin Lizzie. In fact, Ford did not even create the assembly line. Ransom Eli Olds and the Cadillac Motor Company were already using complex interchangeable parts and assembly lines in their manufacturing processes.

Ford's innovation was so simple that it is overlooked in most history books. His assembly lines moved—work was transported to the worker, not the other way around. While assembly lines had until that time involved workers moving to and from parts bins and the object being built, Ford was inspired by watching the moving overhead conveyers in a meat packing plant where stationary butchers each performed higly specific cuts at each station. Using the same basic concept he revolutionized the automotive assembly line. The cornerstone principle of the twenty-first-century organization will be that the work, and all of the tools needed to do the work, can be moved to workers—wherever they are.

This is not a revolutionary concept when applied on a small scale, but when considered in the context of today's information-based global economy, it directly challenges what is perhaps the most salient feature of modern capitalism and the cornerstone of industrialism: the centralized enterprise, in which workers come to the work.

Work 2.0

There's an old riddle that goes something like this: I leave home, take three left turns, and return home. So where do I work?[1]

Here's a more current version.

Jason Ander got up for work today. He put on a pot of coffee and curled up on the couch with his laptop. He logged on and began where he left off yesterday, at the kitchen table, solving the problem of using algae as an alternate energy source. However, Jason isn't employed, at least not in any contemporary sense of the word. Yes, he gets paid for his work, but only when his ideas are accepted. The rest of the time Jason pays his own way. No fringe benefits, no paid vacation, no employer-paid health insurance. And that's just the way Jason likes it, because that also means less uncertainty, less company politics, less structured work time, no commuting, and lots of success that is entirely his own.

His work exists everywhere and nowhere in particular. He finds assignments by taking on challenges from intermediaries such as InnoCentive and NineSigma, which cast a global net for solutions to problems that traditional R&D departments can't solve. Or Jason finds projects on Elance, oDesk, and Live/Work, marketplaces for talent that operate like eBay; on these sites, companies and individuals find talent, in some cases without having to pay for it up front. Good ratings and a good fee? You're hired!

Jason never leaves home, avoids office politics, and never gets laid off. So where does he work? Jason works in the cloud. More and more people around the globe are working in the cloud and many more will. In fact, the greatest shift that will happen over the course of the twenty-first century will be in the movement of jobs to the cloud. In the same way that the nineteenth and twentieth centuries were typified by the transportation and movement of people and goods, this century will be all about the movement of work and ideas.

However, the shift to the cloud is not just about technology and globalization. It's also about uncertainty. The more connected the world becomes the more uncertain the results of our interactions will be and the less likely companies will be to keep as many people on the payroll. Every business wants to operate at its most effective yet lowest level of full-time staffing. Our traditional structures for organizations, employment, and problem solving are unable to keep up with this new rate of complexity and connectivity. We need something radically different, and that is exactly what Jason is becoming a part of—a cloud of resources that is always available and always ready to solve problems.

Cloud-based employment will also be accelerated by the tremendous influx of educated workers, who are being turned out by an ever-increasing number of institutions for higher learning around the globe. In the United

States alone, colleges graduate about 1.75 million students annually.[2] The result is an ultimate *human cloud* that connects talent and problem solvers under one virtual global rooftop.

There are a number of firms in this space, such as LiveOps, Guru, oDesk, and Freelancer, which play the role of a cloud-based matchmaker and account for a billion-dollar industry which is doubling each year. However, the matchmaking goes well beyond the popular view of simply outsourcing work to contractors. While this can be done with relative ease, even without the cloud, there are ways to do this in the cloud that go well beyond a simple outsourcing model.

For example, earlier we mentioned Amazon's Mechanical Turk, which has created a way to easily post simple tasks, such as copyediting or data input, to an online bidding system that matches the task with a pool of global talent. In much the same way that you would post an item on eBay and wait for people to bid on your item, you put up an item of work and wait for workers to bid for the job; Mechanical Turk acts as an online marketplace for work.

It's important to understand a bit about how Mechanical Turk works, a method alluded to by its name. In the late 1700s an amazingly complex chess-playing machine, called The Turk, was built by a Hungarian inventor, Wolfgang von Kempelen. The Turk was constructed to resemble an elaborate tabletop chess cabinet with an intricate mechanism of exposed gears and levers and complete with the torso of a mechanical, turban-topped manikin that would play against an opponent. For a period of nearly one hundred years, The Turk toured Europe and America, playing against thousands of opponents, including Benjamin Franklin and Napoleon. While it was presented as a fully automated chess-playing machine, The Turk was nothing more than an elaborate hoax. Inside was a human using magnets and levers to move The Turk and defeat its opponents.

The illusion of The Turk speaks to our desire to automate even the most complex tasks, a desire that certainly continues to this day, as demonstrated by IBM's Deep Blue computer-based chess machine, which won against Garry Kasparov in a match in 1997. But it's also reflected in the seventy-year legacy of modern computing and IBM's latest effort in the quest for machine intelligence that can outwit humans—its supercomputer Watson, which won in a televised broadcast of *Jeopardy* in 2011.

Despite these successes, we can all agree that there are clearly still many tasks that can only be accomplished by a human. Playing off this fact, and the online availability of a global talent pool through the Internet, Amazon introduced its Mechanical Turk in 2005 as part of its web services offering. A web service is an early precursor to cloud-based applications. These are small applications with very specific purposes that can be easily delivered over the Internet and integrated with other applications. Often called *widgets,* examples of these include credit card authentication, address verification, stock market quotes, and other features that can be easily plugged into a website without having to be rebuilt each time.

However, unlike its other web services, which were fully automated pieces of software, Mechanical Turk used humans as the engine that processed information required to complete a task. These tasks were called Human Intelligence Tasks, or HITs. Amazon originally built hundreds of these HITs for its own use, for example to search the Internet for duplicate web pages. Over time the list of HITs grew to include all sorts of rudimentary tasks such as transcription of podcasts, posting to blogs, even generating friends on Facebook or page hits for a YouTube video.

The problem with Mechanical Turk and other approaches of this sort is that they are rarely, if ever, used for larger projects that require a high degree of quality control and consistency. The reason is that these marketplaces are not actively managed; the workers are not vetted for capability, other than a simple peer review. What you end up with is an economically attractive way to farm out small tasks but no way to engage a qualified team of workers for a critical project. If you want a few hundred names entered into a spreadsheet or some basic research done to identify the contacts at several companies, Mechanical Turk is ideal. But what if you wanted to have tens of thousands of biological images scanned by qualified workers who could identify the unique cellular structure of a specific virus in each of those images? Achieving an adequate and reliable level of quality will likely require a very specific set of skills and a rigid benchmark.

This is where cloudsourcing comes into play. In the cloudsourcing model, workers can be mobilized through platforms such as Crowd-Flower. CrowdFlower has a pool of 1.5 million workers around the globe that it can deploy as part of a systemic problem-solving network to attack large-scale projects that demand a degree of integrity that has otherwise only been available through formal employment or managed outsourcing relationships. *The power of these cloudsourcing platforms is that they can parse the work into small chunks that can then be broadcast to a vast network of prequalified workers.* This means that complicated projects may require only a few hours of work rather than the months it may have taken to accomplish them through traditional approaches.

Look at our earlier example of the images that need to be scanned for a virus. CrowdFlower would break the project into myriad smaller pieces of work, each one of which might take a few minutes of a single individual's time. By creating the workflow for the project, monitoring quality levels, and filtering out unacceptable work, CrowdFlower can guarantee a certain level of quality for even the largest tasks. Interestingly, Crowd-Flower relies on Amazon's Mechanical Turk for about 10 percent of its workforce. This sort of partnering creates an intricately woven network of providers across otherwise unmanaged cloud-based human resources.

Can this approach be used on every piece of work? Of course not. Even CrowdFlower cofounder Lukas Biewald admits that this is a basic solution for tasks that can be easily broken down into component work. Yet when you consider how much of your work, or that of your enterprise, falls into this category of high-volume, low-brainpower work, which can still require an expensive and capable worker, it's easy to come up with hundreds of scenarios where this kind of sophisticated cloudsourcing model can significantly increase the speed of the task and free your resources for work that is more meaningful to your business. According to Biewald, CrowdFlower takes advantage of the human "cognitive surplus" that is able to get online and work in small increments of time to collectively solve large problems.

But cloudsourcing does not stop with basic tasks such as data entry. As the pool of global talent available not only increases but also becomes far better educated and less expensive due to all the factors we've already discussed, the notion of going to the cloud for more complex work becomes just as feasible. A number of companies are now delivering these sorts of highly skilled workers through the cloud.

One of them, Elance, stands as a popular option for both employers and contractors. The company's core mission is twofold: to use the cloud to help employers whittle down their choices and stay within their budgets and to connect providers with paying projects that they wouldn't know about otherwise.

Launched in 1999 in Mountainview, California, Elance is the brainchild of a Merrill Lynch bond trader, Beerud Sheth, and Srinivas Anumolu, a New York Life portfolio manager. The pair were working on Wall Street when they decided to take their knowledge of electronic trading marketplaces into the human cloud, to allow employers and independent contractors to interact in an eBay-like fashion, with little or no outside involvement.

Sheth and Anumolu were inspired by an article written by Massachusetts Institute of Technology professors Thomas W. Malone and Robert J. Laubacher, "The Dawn of the E-Lance Economy," which looked at how employment is turning from a company-centered model to what they call a "Business of One," where work ends up being employee-centered.

The two launched their venture with $1.2 million in angel funding, a pittance compared with the sort of funding most start-ups require. Without a strong brand to attract customers—either the talent or the hiring companies—they initially populated the site with friends, family, and online message board participants, all of whom were encouraged to sign up as providers.[3]

Why would someone sign up as a provider, other than doing it as a favor to Sheth and Anumolu? Part of Elance's initial value proposition was that the risk of signing up was nonexistent. You shared a bit of your experience and area of focus, perhaps posted a portfolio of your work, and then just waited to see if an opportunity arose for you to bid on. The experience was not unlike what is happening on many cloud-based sites for photography, where amateur, aspiring, and even professional photographers post their photos in the hope that someone will decide to pay to use them. Sites such as 123RF.com have had extraordinary success using this strategy.

The Elance site grew from there, as both the supply of talent and hiring companies became aware of its existence. Today, the Elance human cloud is a leading gathering place for companies in need of outsourced talent and for freelancers, contractors, and part- and full-time employees who already have a job, but are searching for additional work. More than 500,000 computer programmers, sales and marketing experts, language translators, and application developers peruse Elance's human cloud regularly to seek out new gigs; they then place bids and connect with potential clients. From the first communication (typically the bid itself) straight through to the final payment, the entire process takes place in Elance's human cloud.

From its humble beginning, Elance has grown to more than 50,000 gigs posted in its cloud every month and over $400 million paid for projects since its inception.

With all of that money funneling through its cloud, you may think that Elance has cornered the market. However, this is just a drop in an enormous pool of talented workers who are available globally, in no small part due to a void that has been created by high rates of unemployment and underemployment. Pairing laid-off workers with companies that wouldn't necessarily shell out the money for a full-time computer programmer or marketing specialist, but that *are* willing to pay a few bucks to have their individual projects handled by experienced pros, makes perfect sense during an economic downturn.

In 2010—with the nation and the global economy in one of the worst job crises in history—Elance reported a 40 percent year-over-year increase in freelance earnings through its site.[4] In an interesting economic twist of fate, the funds that used to cover employee benefits are being rerouted through Elance's cloud, directly to independent contractors. In some ways, that is a much more efficient model: the work is still there, but not efficiently addressed by traditional models of employment.

But don't confuse the initial circumstances that are propelling Elance with the longer-term trends that will make this sort of work the norm. The Elance approach has another twist that makes it a long-term play: it creates an unusually broad range of fees for any particular project.

If you post a job for the development of a website on Elance, you are likely to get bids that range from a few hundred dollars to several thousand. The difference will depend on the geography of the worker, his portfolio, organizational overhead, and myriad other factors.

Interestingly, you might initially consider low bidders to be weak in terms of skills or experience. In actuality, they may be very skilled but in greater need of the work and with little opportunity cost to weight the work against. In other words, they are very good but very hungry! This is where the efficiencies of a free market start to change somewhat dramatically. If you get a few bids at $200 dollars and a number of others at $2,000, all else being equal, why not take the risk of a $200 bidder? What is the worst that can happen? You're out $200 and can always come back and go for a higher bidder. While that may not apply to decisions that are time critical, there are many cases were a $200 hedge bet is a wise move that risks very little.

As a consultant, I've often used this practice in hiring Elance workers for projects such as report layouts, website development, or research when I can afford to wait a few extra days to see if the low bid works out. If it does not, the risk is a small one. But if it does work out, I now have a resource that I can leverage with enormous effectiveness.

Both sides of the Elance equation benefit from this peculiarity: freelancers post profiles and select jobs that fit their work styles, experience, and need (or expand their portfolios by taking on bigger, more complex projects); employers peruse the site for good candidates, invite them to bid, and then see who else they can attract, outside of the obvious candidates, through a more general bidding process.

In addition, the Elance cloud includes a variety of devices for managing the project such as milestones, payment, tracking, communication, and work submittal tools that users need to collaborate with one another. And if the project doesn't go as planned, there's always the eBay-like "feedback" section, where employers can post their two cents and give as many or as few stars as they want, based on performance and satisfaction.

Kevin Rose is one of Elance's highest-profile matchmaking successes. In 2003, Rose started social news website Digg after putting his project out for bid, hiring a developer, Owen Byrne, for $10 an hour, an incredible rate to begin with, and then working with that provider (and later hiring him full-time) to build out his concept. Within eighteen months, Rose's new company had generated $60 million in revenues. Digg has since morphed into one of the most visited sites online, and is yet another example of how the cloud is shaping our lives.

Smaller projects that don't hold quite as much clout abound in Elance's cloud. In the one-minute video "What My Elance Cloud Commute Looks Like," writer Ted Bendixson shows the world how he works from his laptop, travels the world, and manages to run a thriving copywriting, blogging, journalism, and amateur videography business, courtesy of Elance.[5]

Cloud workers like Bendixson enjoy the luxury of being able to pick and choose their projects, and maybe not work on any at all (for those long trips to Burma, for example) if they don't feel like it. Elance enables this type of lifestyle, while at the same time ensuring that companies get their pick of the litter when it comes to independent contractors.

Of course, as with any significant economic shift, there is a clear near-term downside to the human cloud. Namely, highly paid freelancers who had been able to command much higher rates are now scrambling to compete with lower-priced alternatives. In many ways this is not unlike the phenomenon that drove manufacturing offshore. But the reality is that, like it or not, we are bringing new skilled workers into the global workforce at a high rate, thanks to better education, connectivity, and low-cost computing access. In 1980, the global workforce consisted of about 960 million workers. By 2000, the global labor force had grown to 1.46 billion, and Delphi's estimates put the current size of the workforce at just over 2 billion, with no end to the growth spurt in sight.[6]

The clouds are closing in and there is no going around this weather front. We can only go through it, as tumultuous a journey as it will be. The good news is that efficiency in any free market or economic system eventually finds a point of equilibrium, which benefits everyone involved.

Although we currently live in the era when pink slips are the hottest accessory for high-paid, experienced professionals, the human cloud will outlive this and permanently shift the means by which we reshape the way careers and companies are built, but most importantly—especially in the case of the American economy—the investment we make in quality K–12 learning will be the key to developing this sort of workforce.

9

Learning in the Cloud

Education is all a matter of building bridges.

—*Ralph Ellison*

In 1998 I was introduced to the late Peter Drucker by a close mutual friend. Drucker was one of the twentieth century's great thinkers and is considered by many to be the father of modern-day management. I recall so vividly my first encounter with Drucker in person. We were in a booth at a small Italian restaurant in his hometown of Claremont, California. I had come prepared with numerous questions to ask and was more than a bit starstruck at the idea of sitting across the table from this brilliant mind.

But what I recall most was Drucker's firm response to one of my very first questions. I asked him if he thought that technology was the greatest force driving progress during his lifetime. He looked me squarely in the eye and said, "You technology people all want to believe that the greatest achievements are based on new technology." Well, that should have put me in my place, but I persisted. "Well, to what would you attribute the great achievements of the past hundred years?" His reply has stuck with me ever since because of its profound simplicity:

The greatest progress in the last century has been the result of access to higher education. The GI bill, for example, did more to prepare the U.S. economy for the second half of the twentieth century than any other single policy or technology.

Granted, we could argue about the way progress is being measured. But it is clear that when you look at the way that nations have developed their capacity to compete on a global scale, it is directly tied to their investment in and effectiveness at education. I'd claim that this is not just a function of higher education but also a very effective K–12 education. But we have a long way to go. Even basic literacy is still a struggle for much of the world. According to UNESCO, 20 percent of the world's population is still illiterate.[1] In an information-driven world, this is indeed a sad testimonial on how we use technology to facilitate the most basic need to educate.

Nowhere is education more critical than in developing countries, which desperately need to enable their populations to work in tomorrow's knowledge-based economy. Yet access to classroom education is virtually nonexistent in many parts of Africa and India. Much of this is due to the high cost of traditional education. But the economics are about to change drastically.

By the time this book is published, India will have brought to market a $35 Android-powered touch screen tablet (Android is Google's mobile operating system). The Aakash (Hindi for "sky") tablet is meant to bring the power of the cloud to the widest possible number of users.[2] Thirty-five dollars may be a couple of weeks' pay for the 75 percent of India's population that makes less than U.S. $2 a day, but the relative affordability it offers will change the economics of access to the cloud in ways that have been unthinkable.

At the same time, a U.K. nonprofit has developed an even cheaper mini computer called the Raspberry Pi. At U.S. $25, the credit card–sized computer needs to be plugged into a monitor and keyboard.

The Aakash and the Raspberry Pi are examples of what is perhaps the greatest innovation in education for the twenty-first century: affordability. These devices will provide a portal into the cloud that will alter the face of global education in ways that we can hardly begin to imagine today. They will solve a problem called "the last person," which columnist Thomas Friedman has written about, namely, getting computing to the last person in India[3], or for that matter, the world.

Affordable access to the cloud will impact this global push toward fostering the basic skills needed by knowledge workers, and the degree to which this type of education succeeds is intimately tied to how we will prosper as a global economy.

The Academic Factory

Historically, educational "power" in the classroom has been concentrated at the individual instructor's level, and collaboration between classrooms—let alone with other institutions or outside learning resources—was sporadic at best.

Since the time of Aristotle's Lyceum, nearly 2,300 years ago, students have trooped off to schools, universities, and all manner of brick, mortar, and ivy-clad buildings of learning. *The idea of the university looms large in the collective consciousness of an industrial culture.* This was a large part of the industrial ethos that led to the sort of work and worker that were captured perfectly in the 1936 film *Modern Times.* Who can forget the image of the hapless Charlie Chaplin tightening bolts on a large flywheel? Chaplin, along with his fellow workers, had been minted in lots by the educational factories to function as yet another cog in the machine.

In the mid-twentieth century, workers spent the first twenty years of their lives gaining enough education to work for the next forty. As technology entered the office and factory, individuals found themselves spending a greater amount of their working lives learning such things as how to use PCs, new software applications, business processes, and so forth, instead of actually contributing to core business objectives. Yet, the rate of change and innovation across all industries is increasing, while at the same time the volume of information grows. We have reached a state of gridlock, where most of us spend too much time jumping from subject to subject struggling to keep pace. The irony is that, as the need to relearn throughout our lives has increased dramatically, the tools to replace the classroom have not.

The Open Classroom

The way we educate our workforce is changing quickly, however. Institutions of higher learning, such as MIT, have already open sourced the entirety of their curriculum by making course content free and available to the public. K–12 schools in the United States are investing heavily in the concept of Innovation Zones, which are experimenting with personalized courses, virtual learning, and intense interschool collaboration geared to students' strengths and weaknesses. New institutions such as the University of Phoenix and Kaplan Learning have started to disrupt traditional classroom education by offering courses online. While these for-profit enterprises are often critiqued for not being as well equipped with traditional PhD- level academic professors they are also much more likely to be able to scale their business model and also leverage talented instructors who are much closer, from an industry perspective, to the materials being taught in a classroom.

According to Robert W. Wrubel, Chief Innovation Officer at Apollo Group, the parent company of the University of Phoenix:

"We're going to transform the entire notion of the nation state over the next two decades. In a knowledge-based economy transformation occurs when unskilled workers transition to semiskilled and ultimately to skilled workers; that drives and transforms lives and countries. Globally, the demand for that far exceeds the capacity and the ability to serve that need. Because of funding challenges across the globe we just can't build enough classrooms and hire and train enough teachers. It's a problem of pure scale that stems from the fact that we built a very expensive educational model that was groundbreaking in the 1800s and served a small percentage of the population that needed to be knowledge workers at that time. While the vast majority of the population worked in jobs that required little if any formal education. Now, however, we've got to make knowledge workers out of 80 percent of our working population and we simply can't afford to scale the current business model for education to meet that need."

Wrubel's point is not that traditional education is at the end of its lifecycle but rather that a blended model is needed, which, in his words, "redefines education as a journey that is not episodic—a separate time when you are part of an intensive learning experience, and then you pull out, and you go into the job and workforce—but instead a lifelong process." I've seen this myself both at Bentley University where I teach graduate courses and advise on the MBA program and also at Kaplan University, where I am an advisor to their online program. Students who come back into the classroom as part of this journey, after having worked for some period of time, are not only more motivated to learn but better able to use and to appreciate tools that allow them to control the pace and scheduling of the learning.

Amazingly, this same notion of learning in a way that integrates the classroom with the student's life, rather than the other way around, is also being applied to K–12 education. In New York City, local innovation zones have been experimenting with personalized online learning for students who have suffered from chronic tardiness or absenteeism. These students are often labeled as uninterested or unable to keep up. However, after putting in place an online classroom that the students can attend, educators found that many of these same students do extraordinarily well when tested. The fact is that we've bought into a factory-based model of education that is leaving far too many people behind; it's the equivalent of trying to drive a modern automobile on a cow path. No matter what the horsepower, you would end up stuck in the muck.

I don't mean to throw out all of traditional learning. Early parts of the learning process may be best accomplished in a traditional classroom in parts of the world where access to bricks and mortar classrooms is available and cost effective. There is nothing like an inspired and passionate teacher to motivate students. I've been party to both sides of that equation as student and professor, and I value that interaction immensely. But I've also seen the power and reach of virtual learning. I am not suggesting we chose one and forsake the other. What I am suggesting is that we do not make this a zero-sum proposition and instead look at the merits of both and use each where needed, while also using each to leverage the other.

There is another hidden advantage to the model used by institutions such as the University of Phoenix, which often goes unnoticed.

Because of the large volume of students and the online access they have in real time to the university, innovation of the learning models themselves can happen on a scale and with a velocity unheard of in traditional academic institutions.

This means that the University of Phoenix can use enormous collections of data about students' course experiences and turn them into insights about how people actually learn, which can then be used to personalize the way learning is delivered to students. That level of personalization is a facet of learning that will be enabled through the cloud on an unimaginable scale, making the classroom of tomorrow as tailored to each student as your experience would be today with a private tutor.

According to Wrubel, "The University of Phoenix is using the same principles that we see in emerging cloud-based platforms like Amazon, Google, Facebook, and even eBay, where you see the combination of marketplaces and data and insight driving better and better experiences, which in turn drive better and better outcomes at dramatically lower costs of delivery."

This personalization has another benefit. In a cloud-based educational model the learners' identity is a persistent identity that they carry with them through all of their jobs. Their resumes change to reflect all of their activities including book learning, certificate learning, video, and experiential learning. You become not only a real-time learner in the cloud but also a real-time talent who is able to move in lock-step with the market and the needs of current or potential employers.

All of this is just the beginning of how education in the cloud will alter traditional classrooms. Wrubel has another vision of how higher education will change that may be the most disruptive element of all as we move to the cloud. His vision ties in directly to much of what we have been saying about the way that the cloud is driven by influence, if you recall our discussion about how you can't plow a cloud in chapter 1.

To illustrate this Wrubel asks a simple question, "What makes up the great educational institutions today?" It's an interesting question, especially for those of us who paid dearly for a university education or who are doing so for our kids. Wrubel's answer is worth pondering.

"People would say, "Well, their incredible legacy and heritage, or their tremendous research, or the fact that they only let in the smartest people on the planet." So even if you emptied Stanford of all the faculty, by having a really tough admissions process, you'll get an education by just putting the kids in dorms together, but what makes these guys great are these huge celebrity faculty and researchers that live there, and when you really go, "Well, are they indentured servants?" "No, they're just agents. They're free agents just like LeBron James is."

So have they been given access to big markets the way sports stars in the NBA were in the '70s and the '80s? So what happened once we realized that the power wasn't really the franchise; the power was the star, and once the star was given sneaker deals, it changed not only the game and the audience, but also the stars, who could be bought, you just had to give them access to big platforms and audiences. Similarly, when movies get big distribution, the stars can command a far larger share of the profits.

I believe we're on the verge of great change. As we start building broader-scaled audiences for education, we change the economics of the stars who drive the brands and the value of the elite and semi-elite institutions. For example, Clayton Christensen is one of the top-ranked business professors at Harvard. Well, we said, "We're not going to buy Clayton, but what we will do is offer a pay-per-view for his best lecture. Then we'll apply production values to it that no one at Harvard could ever afford, because we can serve an audience of hundreds of thousands of students. Suddenly, if you start doing that on a dramatic scale, you shift the whole underlying premise and foundation of what makes up the brands of all the universities and you give access to talent that was all sheltered for the 200 future hedge fund managers—they go to Clayton Christensen and read about disruptive innovation."

Remember, however, that what is key in this transformation is that all of education is shifting, including traditional institutions of higher education. For example, at Stanford, three professors have opened up their classes, at no charge, to anyone who wants to access them online. One of these classes, An Introduction to Artificial Intelligence, had 160,000 registrants, 35,000 of whom stuck it out and continued the class. The class, which was taught by two professors, Peter Norvig and Sebastian Thrun, both of whom also work at Google, now ranks as the most widely attended online university class in the world.[4] While non-paying students do not get college credit for the class, they do get a certificate of completion signed by the professors. For many, that is more than enough to demonstrate their ability to themselves and potential employers.

Yet, for most, the dream of an open virtual university is still just that, a dream. Like the promise of flying cars, it is a vision of the future that always seems to be just a few decades away.

In large part, this is because of the fundamental social and cultural role that classrooms and campuses play. Few of us can imagine replacing the face-to-face interaction of our school experiences fully with any technology. There is magic to in-person communication, dialogue, and debate that is simply not translatable in virtual environments. Myriad cues and nuances that we do not completely understand, but which inform and influence us, take place in the classroom and are not easily replicated, if they can be replicated at all.

But what if I was to tell you that we are on the precipice of a radical change in the way learning will take place because of the capability that the cloud delivers? It would be hard to accept at first. After all, most of us have experienced some form of virtual learning and have, at best, put up with it. But what we are experiencing is traditional learning being delivered in what I call a *just-in-case* mode. What I mean by this is that much of what passes for virtual learning today consists of recorded video, slide decks with voiceovers, low-quality video connections that don't convey the nuance of human face-to-face communications, and curriculum-based classes. While some learning may be facilitated by these approaches, most is not. What we need today is *just-in-time learning.*

Just-in-time (JIT) learning revolutionizes both the way we deliver and the way we consume learning by providing it in context when, where, and how it's needed. Let's use a simple analogy to illustrate the point. If you are a clinician performing a medical procedure in a remote area and need to quickly consult a specialist, it is highly unlikely that you will turn to a prerecorded class about the procedure. You do not have the luxury of time. You need the information immediately and you need it in context; in other words, it has to be learning that can be applied to your current situation. This type of contextual real-time content requires that you be able to access a specialist who understands the critical nature of both your situation and your task.

The role of the cloud in this case is to perform three key tasks: understand your context, connect you with the right people and content, and provide a level of communication that is not only as good as what you would expect from a face-to-face encounter but raises the bar and provides an even better level of communication. Now, remember that I said just-in-time learning needs to be deliverable when, where, and how it is needed. The key to creating an even better experience than a face-to-face encounter lies specifically in the "when, where, and how." This means that the learning must be available on demand without regard to time or location and that the interaction with the learning system must provide real-time access to all of the necessary content, as well as a quality of visual communication that conveys the nuances of an in-person interaction.

Visualizing this level of real-time connectivity and video quality is difficult to do, since so much of what currently passes for JIT learning is typified by the YouTube experience, where content is recorded and video, even in HD quality, is less than adequate to replace an in-person interaction.

Taking the Classroom to the Cloud

Education is an area where the difference between the Internet and the cloud becomes especially pronounced. YouTube is an Internet-based metaphor for learning. If you watch any twelve-year-old try to find out how to do something on his own, his first stop is usually YouTube. While this is certainly a move in the right direction, from just-in-case to just-in-time learning, it only works if you have the luxury of time to find what you are looking for; you need to have the time and patience to weed out the irrelevant and the inadequate, and at no point does it offer the immediacy of real-time communication.

A cloud-based educational model differs from this Internet model by drawing on an understanding of the context of the problem and by using your digital locker, thereby connecting you with the resources currently available to handle the problem. It also delivers these resources, be it a person or data, in a form that is easily integrated with the needs and expectations of your experience. I know that's a mouthful, so let's go back to the example of our clinician in the field. Just to make it more interesting, let's say the clinician is somewhere in a remote part of Latin America with only electric power and Internet.

Three years ago Cisco took on this challenge of reaching remote areas in Latin America with real-time learning by establishing a Center of Innovation in Mexico, which developed a series of cloud-based solutions for health care and education. These initiatives integrate mobile connectivity, content, and high-definition video telepresence in self-contained vehicles that can take the clinic or classroom wherever it is needed. The mobile units connect to a cloud that has a specialized set of resources for each application.

Using one of these resources connected to a health-care cloud, the mobile clinic allows a doctor to instantly access specialists and the full range of a hospital's diagnostic capabilities, and to conduct remote medical procedures in real time while conferring with colleagues. What is especially amazing about Cisco's approach is that all of this is done in a way that not only rivals face-to-face interaction but actual ups the ante by allowing collaboration that is better than face-to-face without the need for physical proximity.

At this point you're likely saying, "But hold on, nothing can replace face-to-face interaction. Too much is communicated by physical presence that can never be communicated in telepresence." This is the same argument we've been hearing for years when it comes to virtual learning of any sort. You're right, if you're thinking of yesterday's video technologies, which not only lose much of the subtlety conveyed in real-time HD-quality video but also fail to deliver an integrated solution to learning that takes into account the context of the situation. Cisco is solving these problems in two ways.

First, the quality of the video that can be delivered in the cloud through a standard Internet connection is light years ahead of what we've become accustomed to on the web. In a cloud-based video solution the computing power needed to perform the necessary encoding and compression is intelligently determined and performed by hardware specifically designed for the demands of high-definition video. While there is a proliferation of video on the Internet, most of it is processed and broadcast by general-purpose hardware at a quality that simply does not convey nuance. Think about what makes face-to-face communication such a unique medium. When two people are talking to each other face to face, they are constantly scanning eye movement, subtle gestures, and expressions that are an integral part of human communication. Capturing these subtleties of communication requires a high-definition image that can be magnified to approximate the actual physical dimensions of the person's face. This may sound insignificant but it is critical to the quality of the communication and the degree of engagement between participants, and it is something that demands specialized hardware.

There are other advances also coming in the next few years that will further capture the nuance of face-to-face communication. For example, if you've ever been part of a video teleconference, you know that one of the most disconcerting things is likely the lack of eye contact. Because each person is looking at her screen, the immediacy that eye contact brings is lost. Don't believe this? Then pay attention to a broadcast of the nightly news. The gaze of the newscaster is trained directly on the camera, causing you to feel a direct connection to the person. But this is a one-way communication. When the communication is going in both directions or involves multiple parties, the lack of eye contact results in an instant detachment from the person on the other end of the conversation. By increasing the quality of the video and by also using embedded cameras that are able to see through the screen, in much the same way that a two-way mirror works, your gaze is directly at the remote person. In addition, the focal point of your eyes can be tracked so that the system knows who you are addressing in a multipoint collaboration, for example a video connection with four people.

The second thing that Cisco has done is to integrate the capability to bring in content from the cloud just-in-time from sources that are relevant to the discussion. In our clinical setting, these might be x-rays, ultrasounds, and medical records. Because all of this exists in and is connected to the cloud, the content is available in real time no matter what the location.

You might be thinking, "But this isn't education, it's collaboration." Precisely my point.

We have become so accustomed to thinking of education as something that is done in advance, as preparation for the real world, rather than something that must continue whenever it is needed.

This does not obviate the need for traditional preparatory education. In every discipline there is a basis of knowledge that is required to perform the essential tasks required of a professional in that field. We'll see how the cloud is also assisting in traditional just-in-case learning. But as every field increases in its complexity, it is also becoming more likely that no one person can be adequately prepared for all the situations he will encounter. The cloud provides the ultimate antidote to this complexity by creating an on-demand set of resources that can collaborate as and when needed.

It's especially interesting to note that Cisco began its efforts to develop this sort of cloud-based technology in Mexico, a developing country. When you stop to consider where education has been most limited by economic and geographical constraints, it is clear that developing countries have been at a distinct disadvantage. Studies by the International Institute for Applied Systems Analysis in Austria have shown that increasing the primary education of a country from 40 percent of the population, typical in many African and Latin American countries, to 100 percent and increasing secondary education from 0 percent to 50 percent can double GDP. In this regard, the cloud may be one of the great equalizing forces in bringing developing countries to a level global playing field, or at least much closer to it. In my estimation, the global economic impact of the cloud will make developing countries among the fastest-growing economies and labor pools during the twenty-first century.

Of course, tapping the potential of the talent in developing countries requires an ability to deliver education to a much larger audience than any number of brick-and-mortar classrooms could accommodate. To do this, new approaches are being developed to help in traditional primary and secondary educational settings.

Viral Learning:
The MOODLE Model of Education

The cloud that's transforming the way we do business is also finding its way into traditional education. One example is Moodle, one of many options that's making waves with its open-source course management system (CMS), or learning management system (LMS). Popular among educators worldwide, the system enables a dynamic cloud-based approach that teachers use to manage and promote learning.[5]

Amazingly, the site is completely free, making it especially attractive for the frugal public school sector and easily available to developing economies. That's exactly what Martin Dougiamas had in mind when he kicked off the Moodle project in 1999. A former webmaster at Curtin University in Australia, Dougiamas was "frustrated with the existing commercial software at the time" and felt that Moodle could do a better job. It would be another nine years before Moodle officially moved into the cloud, enabled by Amazon's technology in 2008.

Today, Moodle is used by more than 10,000 sites and has a large developer community that regularly contributes to and enhances its features.[6] The approach is not unlike that of Wikipedia, which relies entirely on contributions from individuals who are self-motivated to contribute content, research, and expertise.

Initially designed for the university environment, Moodle is applicable across a broad range of organizations worldwide, many of which use it to conduct courses fully online or to support face-to-face teaching and learning.[7] In fact, the words "Go home tonight and check Moodle for your homework assignments" echo daily in the hallways of K–12 and higher educational institutions around the world.

The technology that drives Moodle is straightforward. With a username and password, students, teachers, and administrators can access the system and use it for course and learning management, for distance learning, to participate in forums and wikis, to build collaborative learning communities around specific subject matter, and to complement face-to-face courses (a process known as "blended learning").[8] Key to the blended learning approach is the concept of using the mode of education that is best suited to the students, whatever their needs may be; that includes giving access to students who have no physical access to a classroom as well as augmenting existing classrooms.

Using Moodle, an English teacher can use the cloud-based system to upload reading assignments, post questions based on those lessons, collect and grade assignments, and point students to further information and research resources. The sheer number of users it has attracted since inception confirms the site's usefulness. As of September 2011, Moodle has logged some impressive numbers:[9]

Number of registered Moodle sites:	56,198
Countries:	214
Courses:	4,768,448
Users:	45,088,793
Teachers:	1,104,594
Enrollments:	19,249,750
Forum posts:	79,365,836
Resources:	42,463,907
Quiz questions:	80,033,351
Total registered uses:	1,091,075
New users each 24 hours:	790
Registered user access each 24 hours:	1,482

The idea of an educational cloud involves much more than just a virtual classroom. The educational cloud stands out in its ability to handle very large deployments with hundreds of users as well as the single classroom with one teacher and fifteen students. Its broad applicability makes Moodle a cornerstone example of how the cloud can extend the reach of education. Because it exists in the cloud and is serviced by an army of volunteers, the approach is self-sustaining and also self-evolving. As the needs of the marketplace change, Moodle morphs in near real time to deliver the most relevant content.

As part of Amazon's cloud, Moodle's applicability goes well beyond the K–12 space. Leading universities like University of California, Berkeley, for example, offer free webcasts and podcasts to the public via the Moodle platform.[10]

And at Maidu High School in Auburn, California, teachers use Moodle to give students the option of *not* going to school.[11] This is a prime example of the way the Innovation Zone model is creating personalized learning environments. In 2011, the school used the open-content system to offer online-only courses through a neighboring school's online learning program, which offers all of the classes that students need to graduate and move on to college.

With a little imagination, it's not hard to envision Moodle as a radical departure from the factory-based type of learning most of us have become accustomed to. Located in a central repository, learning materials offered online will provide the same level of education as classroom instruction, and will include book chapters that are scanned and uploaded, online lessons, videos, assignments, and chats with advisors— all at no charge, and with no need for local IT support.

Springville High School in Alabama is also using Moodle to create collaborative learning environments in the cloud.[12] There, teachers can extend their classrooms via a safe, online environment where students access assignments, quizzes, and other materials. To prepare for the new setup, eighth-grade students began enrolling, receiving content, and taking quizzes online before they ever met their ninth-grade English teachers.

The approach caught on quickly and faculty soon began adding classes to Moodle, which became a "one-stop shop" for students to access make-up work, handouts, presentations, and any work they needed to review from any computer, at home or at school. Today, Springville High School's Moodle program contains classes across all subject areas, and it continues to grow.

At Great Corby School in the United Kingdom, Moodle serves as an online environment for students, teachers, and parents.[13] In fact, the cloud-based system serves as a vital part of the school's community by allowing students to enhance their learning both in and out of school, facilitating the dissemination of information to parents, and helping administrators keep track of minutes, agenda, meeting dates, and photos of school events. According to Kirsty Williamson, a KS1 teacher at the school:

> Our Moodle is an environmentally friendly and cost-effective way to keep parents informed of school events and any information they need. And all of the content is password protected to ensure the safety of our children Overall, teachers value and enjoy using our Moodle as it promotes personalized learning and, in a small school with mixed-age classes, the ability to differentiate is key.[14]

What Moodle is doing is hardly unique. Similar organizations, such as the not-for-profit Khan Academy boast having delivered more than 95 million lessons using their open classroom with 2,700 recorded video lessons. Amazingly, every single piece of content on the khanacademy.org site is free to anyone, student or not. While Moodle and Khan Academy may be drops in the ocean of effort needed to truly create a global workforce of skilled knowledge workers, they do create a clear compass setting for where the cloud will take us. The notion of an open classroom is no longer limited by existing boundaries, be they social, economic, national, or political. Sure, it may be a frightening proposition for many schools that hold on to the value of a brick-and-mortar, often ivy-clad, building in which classrooms exist. These may likely continue to be the most prized locations for learning. But the history of civilization's advancement is not a history of better learning for a few elite members of society. That was done nearly as effectively 2,000 years ago in the great city of Ephesus as it is today in the hallowed halls of Harvard. It is instead a history of expanding access to education across ever-widening and diverse populations by removing the obstacles that stand in the way of both educator and student.

Educating Democracy

In the cloud, the sort of open education represented by Moodle is not just a surrogate for the classroom; it fundamentally alters the value proposition of a classroom. And while it does not completely replace a bricks and mortar classroom in all cases, it does make learning in the cloud even better than classroom learning in many ways.

David DeHaven who is the Dean of the School of Information Science at Kaplan University, which has a strong online presence, believes that online learning can be better than the classroom in many cases. "I think it's actually going to be better, and I'll tell you why. The reason is that we're going to be able to pull in very rich resources in real time, aggregate them, and because it's cloud-based, make these resources scalable and mobile. We're going to be able to deliver learning to any device while at the same time, providing collaboration and connectivity that allow rich interaction among the students. I don't think you're going to use that entirely in place of the classroom experience. But I do believe it will create a powerful alternative to the classroom that can stand on its own."

I know that the concept of a classroom entirely in the cloud is a stretch for many of us who have been taught in classrooms of brick and mortar, but cloud-based learning is quickly becoming second nature for the current generation, which spends, in many cases, more time learning outside of the classroom in social media, through online gaming, and via rich, pervasive media. If you have kids, look at the way they play. Games such as the virally popular *Minecraft*, where you build elaborate structures and cities in a globally cooperative setting on servers located throughout the cloud, are an incredible illustration of just how different this sort of learning can be.

Don't make the mistake of setting these games aside as simply a form of entertainment. If you could engage kids in a classroom to just one-tenth of the degree that they are engaged in online gaming, you would have likely achieved super-teacher status.

This link between engagement and learning is one that is pervasive with the current generation of gamers but which also confounds the prior generation.

My son Adam plays many games online that I see little educational value in at first glance. For instance, consider online war games. Their realism and the degree to which they make play out of a scenario that involves a battlefield is for me profoundly disturbing. Yet, this is a reflection of how modern warfare is being fought in military installations around the world where high tech soldiers are operating drones and using lethal force thousands of miles away from the battlefield. Do I like this? Absolutely not. Does it make war antiseptic in a way that I find troubling? Of course. Would I prefer, if Adam some day becomes a soldier that he fight a battle by joystick rather than in a trench? Do you doubt that any parent would?

This discussion of gaming may seem a departure from our educational theme. It is not. My point is simply that we are re-engineering education in ways and in experiences that we are just beginning to understand. A generation of kids is being raised to expect a level of realism from all education that does not just mimic the real world but is indistinguishable from it. If we do not bring that experience to the classroom we will lose the attention of this generation faster than you can change the channel on your TV.

The ultimate power of the cloud is to broaden the reach and gravity of education across as many minds as possible by enaging these minds wherever and whenever they are. However, there is something beyond even engagement that offers an even more compelling value proposition for education in the cloud, and it's one that most of us do not consider often enough. Education leads to empowerment: it broadens our appreciation for our potential both as individuals and as a society. The overriding trajectory of this empowerment is the creation of a society in which we collaborate much more freely and place a much higher value on the process of collaboration. This eventually leads to an appreciation of the role of democratization as a political institution in which the individual perceives a greater likelihood of prosperity. The protection of that prosperity then becomes a central theme for individuals and institutions. The result? *It's been said that in the history of the world, no two established democracies have ever gone to war with each other.* While this is a hotly debated statement, depending on how you define a democracy and a war, it does hint at how democratic self-interest translates into intereliance and the need to maintain stability wherever and however possible. Beyond degrees and accolades, this democratization may be one of the greatest benefits that universal education can confer.

The dramatic changes in education that we have outlined in this chapter will ultimately be the greatest force in changing the way we experience not only the cloud but life itself. They will set the expectation for what our play and our work should look like and also what our personal and professional interactions should feel like. To imagine that future at this point may require a fair amount of speculation and conjecture, but the hints are already there and unlike past changes of this magnitude, we will not have to wait for generations to pass in order to experience this change and the behaviors it will bring with it. So before we leave the cloud let's take a final journey into that future and try to paint a picture of life in the cloud.

Working, Living, and Playing in the Cloud of 2020

Here's to the crazy ones. The misfits. The rebels.
The troublemakers. The round pegs in the square holes.
The ones who see things differently. They're not fond of rules…
You can quote them, disagree with them, glorify or vilify them.
About the only thing you can't do is ignore them. Because
they change things. They push the human race forward.
While some may see them as the crazy ones, we see genius.
Because the people who are crazy enough to think they
can change the world, are the ones who do.

– Apple Inc.

What do you value most? Think about it for a minute.

We each have our own yardstick for success, and yet I would claim that whatever our individual ambitions, desires, and hopes, none of us can achieve them on our own.

At the start of this book I said that the cloud was all about the formation of a new type of community that would alter the rules of risk, innovation, scale, and success. While I've talked about all of the ways in which the cloud is changing, or will soon change, each of these, what

I've left out is the long view of the cloud—and by "long," I'm thinking in terms of many decades, perhaps a lifetime. Given that time frame:

What the cloud will change most is the way we build and leverage community for the betterment of humankind.

It's one thing to benchmark the cloud revolution based on how well it leverages the way we build community when contrasted with the way we build community using existing technologies such as phones, computers, and the Internet. It's another thing altogether to consider how the cloud may change the fundamental nature of human community itself.

So I'd like to take a short flight of fancy into the long view of the cloud to consider what the world might look like in fifty years, when we are brought face to face with unlimited amounts of information and computing power at the same time that ten billion people will be intimately connected one to another and nearly a trillion devices.

A few things will not change, so it's best to begin with those. We are humans and will remain driven by human desires, values, and conflicts. The desire to accumulate wealth and the basic appeal of ownership will not go away, nor will the appeal of leadership, achievement, or the passion for experimentation and exploration. While the forms they take a hundred years from now may seem vastly different to us, their underpinnings will be as familiar as the goal to reach the moon would have been to Columbus: both entail seeking out new worlds. It's just that the scale and complexity of the goals will increase by accelerating orders of magnitude and the tools we will need to both propel and sustain that growth will also need to change.

Nearly 150 years ago Karl Marx postulated that the economy is the fundamental force behind all human development. Eras change, wrote Marx in his manifesto *Das Kapital*, as the factors of production (technology, resources, and organization) change. As wrong as Marx was about the mechanics of his grand plan, in this regard his work was correct. Eras do indeed change as the tools we have to effect change evolve. However, what Marx did not understand, what he could not have understood, were the ultimate mechanics of the cloud.

Could any economist, politician, or revolutionary of any persuasion have predicted that community on a global scale would be something that came from within and was not imposed from without? Would any visionary have known that the disintegration of organizations, nations, and institutions would lead not to destructive disorder but rather to a constructive chaos that furthered the reach of democracy? We've seen the overnight dissolution of governments due to social networking. We've witnessed the rise of what were considered third world countries due to profound shifts in education and the availability of technology to drive education and commerce. The answers are clear, but only in retrospect.

Marshall McLuhan's global village descended upon us overnight. We were infected by its virus while we were still trying to figure out where to scratch. Global communications and instant connectivity have created opportunities and challenges few of us could have predicted. From the formation of terror cells and networks to the tremendous intereliance of the world's economies, the changes are as profound as those wrought by either World War, and have taken far less of a human toll. The radical changes we are seeing today are not only transitioning the factors of production from industrial to informational, more importantly they are transforming the very nature of how we build and leverage community, on a scale of unimaginable proportions.

In thirty years' time you will not only be able to build your own persona, but I would postulate that this persona will be indistinguishable from you, your fortune, your livelihood, and your membership in modern society. In fifty years' time that persona will perform work for you and collaborate with other personas around the world. Will you live a life of leisure, as has been promised across the entirety of industrial humankind's evolution? I doubt it. We are not driven to leisure as a species. We are driven to challenge ourselves. The question will become, What are these new challenges?

This sort of thinking is a shift that will turn the world on its head by delivering the means and the mechanism by which to deploy value to a spectrum of humanity broader than any political ideologist could have dreamt of.

We may well have the opportunity before us to move not only goods and services but indeed to move humanity itself forward a few steps in the process.

In more than five hundred years of technological achievement we have barely scratched the surface of humanity with technology. Despite the overwhelming proliferation of communications technology, the majority of the world lives in isolation. There may be one billion e-mail addresses and five billion enabled cellular devices but at least half of the world's population lives on less than U.S. $5 per day, below any reasonable standard of poverty.

We can rightfully say that the vast majority of humanity has better things to worry about than communications technology, things like shelter, food, and survival, as we'll see in our discussion about Maslow's Pyramid later in this section. But what of the ability of the cloud to change this? My premise is that we have the opportunity with the cloud to not only change business and commerce but indeed to move humanity itself forward in a quantum way in the process.

We have grown up in a world where the possession of material things has been the greatest measure of wealth and prosperity. We are fast transitioning into a world order where intangibles such as data, the understanding of behaviors through analytics, identity, influence, and the ability to form connections and communities are becoming a significant factor in creating wealth. As we've seen in this book this is true for Google as much as it is for GM.

The radical changes of our time are not only transitioning the factors of production from industrial to informational, but, more importantly, are opening up new possibilities in the legal configurations that provide structure to the ownership of those factors of production. Consider, for example, the discussion we had in chapter 4 about who owns your digital locker and to whom access to its contents can be granted.

If you have any doubt about the value of all this information in the cloud, consider that the most lethal war in this century will be the one that attacks the cloud, since it will be the means by which we orchestrate our supply chains, the delivery of food, fuel, medicine, and services to the world's population. It will be the repository for data about our economic, educational, medical, and military institutions.

Speculating on the long-term impact the cloud will have is clearly like gazing into a crystal ball. We are limited in our ability to appreciate the future impact of the cloud, just as early users of technologies such as the airplane, telephone, and radio were unable to see the far-reaching effects of such advances in their own time. Perhaps we are even more limited given the speed with which changes are occurring in the agility of our communications infrastructure.

It is not that we fail to understand the technology. Technology is fairly easy to predict. We understand the effect of Moore's law; what we do not understand are its effects on our behavior, and, through this, its implications for our social, economic, and political systems. We are trying to prepare ourselves for those things that we don't know we don't know.

We have before us a Gordian knot of monumental proportions. It is the very nature of revolution to so disrupt the order of things that the view of the future is obscured. However, we can speculate. First, it's clear that we will become completely dependent on the cloud as a means of orchestrating our lives, relying on it for everything from how we communicate and collaborate to how we experience entertainment and gaming. For many of us, that dependency is already here. *Even today, in a survey conducted by Cisco, one out of three people indicated that the Internet was more important to them than food, air, and water.*

Our dependence on the cloud will become a natural part of how we define the experience of humanity. And this will apply to nearly all of humanity, from people in the largest cities to those in the smallest, most remote villages. After clean water, food, and shelter, the cloud will be the next most indispensable resource that every human being on the planet will need to move beyond the foundation of Maslow's pyramid, which defines the progression of needs from basic physical needs at the base of the pyramid to self actualization at the top. What is especially interesting about my claim is that if you review the steps in Maslow's pyramid, which the cloud will precede and form a foundation for, almost all are enhanced significantly by the use of the cloud. For example friendship, family, achievement, problem solving, creativity, and spontaneity are all enabled and enhanced by the cloud. My contention is that at some point in the not too distant future they will not only be enhanced by but also be dependant on the cloud in the context of modern civilization—in the

Abraham Maslow's Hierarchy of Needs (called Maslow's Pyramid)

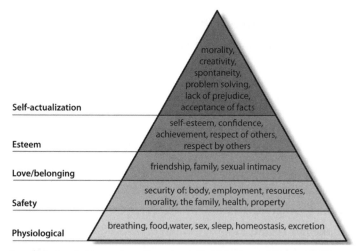

Abraham Maslow's hierarchy of needs, called Maslow's Pyramid, illustrates the progression of human needs through five levels from the most basic physical needs to that of self-actualization.

same way that today we could say it is essential to have basic telecommunications in order to satisfy many of these same needs.

We will first see this transformation of our need for the cloud take place in the ways we use cloud-based community to counterbalance the increasing complexity and uncertainty in our lives by developing networks of hyperconnected relationships that travel with us wherever we go. These mobile communities will act as a support system that allows us to leverage ever-decreasing windows of opportunity and the architected serendipity I talked about in chapter 5.

But this will soon morph into more than just an address book in the cloud or a tweet, text message, or post to Facebook friends. Within the next five years, our mobile communities will become the foundation for lifelong education, career security, and personal peace of mind. We will become as accustomed to the immediacy of interaction that these intricate communities provide as we are today to the interactions with coworkers and neighbors.

Value will be exchanged among members in these communities through not only traditional networking, for example helping you find your next gig, but increasingly through the exchange of virtual currencies. These virtual currencies, which we talked about in chapter 7, will play a significant role in balancing and hedging our individual portfolios against the volatility of national currencies.

For our children, the cloud will create a standard of collaboration and free exchange of ideas that will revamp the patent and trademark system.

Intellectual property will undergo a radical shift as the use of patents as defensive tools gives way to the notion of collaborative ownership of ideas and the hyperfluid exchange of ideas.

As difficult as that is to accept for those of us currently embroiled in patent wars, the generation growing up hyperconnected will see far greater value in the free and open exchange of ideas than can be provided by the closed and protectionist approach we have grown up with. They will encourage each other to work to leverage each other's ideas in ways that today we would think of as absurd. They will have to do this in order to move at a pace that allows them to keep up with the rate of change and the sheer magnitude of the problems they will face.

Don't be too quick to dismiss this new open collaboration. Some of the greatest achievements to date have come from open alliances among nations that would otherwise be adversaries. Think of the alliances that helped save the world from the brink of disaster in World War II, the collaboration that resulted in the International Space Station, and the ways in which the global community has dealt with near pandemics. These all portend a level of collaboration that will become commonplace as the cloud grows, and as communities develop that cross national borders and form bonds that are even stronger than the sovereign interests of their members.

The hyperconnected generation will also bring a new set of attitudes toward gamification of the workplace. Having grown up spending what, to their parents, appears to be an alarming amount of time in front of online games, they see gaming as a natural mechanism for socialization and problem solving. This expectation will carry over into the way they expect to work and the tools they want to use. This will undoubtedly create gaming interfaces for work that would likely be nauseating to today's workers.

The cloud will provide a platform for commerce that makes the role of small- and medium-sized business dramatically more significant in the global economy. Large corporations will not disappear. Their role in helping to scale new ideas will continue to have immense value. But their role as the controlling economic influence and the source of new ideas through traditional research and development will quickly give way to the speed and economic efficiency of small companies that can experiment with far less risk and quickly ramp up new ideas. Along with this will come a new era of what I like to call *everynuership*, in which everyone will have the chance to be an entrepreneur without the huge risk—mortgaging your home or gambling your career—that was once associated with starting your own enterprise.

As part of this trend we will also see developing countries in Asia, Latin America, and Africa thrust onto the economic center stage as they develop the capacity to educate, care for, and secure their nations through the cloud.

At the same time, this will cause the migration of populations away from cities in developed economies and will permanently alter the way we view cities as hubs of commerce. Hubs of commerce will no longer exist in the physical world as anything other than a center of gravity for lifestyle and entertainment.

The cloud will create a surprising resurgence in manufacturing through the introduction of micromanufacturing; the creation of most physical goods will happen at a regional level in neighborhoods and even in homes through on-demand 3D printers that will deliver products minutes after they are purchased. Companies such as Shapeways. com are already providing this capability to, in their own words, "harness 3D printing to help you make, buy and sell anything you want."[1] Ultimately we will use similar technology in the cloud as a means of building and buying objects that can be printed in the home as easily as we today download a PDF file.

The idea of legacy will take on new meaning as legacy clouds, which capture, store, and protect our digital footprints throughout our lives, provide access to us long after we are gone. These legacy clouds will create a new form of ownership over our personas and digital lockers that has as much, if not more, value to our heirs as any other part of an inheritance.

The cloud will alter the practice of medicine from a disconnected clinical experience to a fully mobile experience. Our bodies will be constantly monitored by our onboard smart devices, linked to the best resources for our current health care needs, and constantly fine-tuned to achieve a level of preventive medicine that has no analog in today's health care system. Our personas will have personal virtual advocates who speak for us when we can't. If we are injured, the cloud will know where we are, what happened to us, and what we need in order to be healed, from coordinating transportation to the closest facility with the ability to deal with our situation to personalized pharmaceuticals adeptly matched to the genome stored in our digital locker. We will go far beyond medical records to medical avatars that represent every aspect of our medical history, genetic profile, and personal preferences.

Pharmaceuticals will not only be personalized, based on our genome, but also tracked in real time, with each pill, capsule, or liquid embedded with its own connections to the cloud in order to determine patterns of use and conformance to prescribed directives.

The cloud will also secure us from crime by creating a prospective model of law enforcement. Our sensor-based world, interconnected through the cloud, will allow us to deal with the prevention of crime in the same way we use a real-time GPS to avoid traffic. Law enforcement is already using software to do this in Santa Clara. According to the *Journal of the American Statistical Association*, "On average [Santa Clara] predicted the location and time of 25 per cent of actual burglaries that occurred on any particular day in an area of Los Angeles in 2004 and 2005, using just the data on burglaries that had occurred before that day."[2]

Perhaps most disturbing, the cloud will become a standard theater of war, with cloud wars and cloud terrorism among the biggest threats to the peace and security of our world.

This reminds me of a particular episode of the 1960s science fiction TV show *Star Trek*, in which an alien civilization had "ethical" wars. In this form of war, virtual bombs were dropped on cities and causalities came not through physical destruction but rather by calculating who would have been killed and then ushering them, without protest, to euthanasia centers. The citizens of this alien world were willing participants in virtual warfare as a way to avoid the horror of physical war. The cloud-based warfare I am speaking of is not an antiseptic or clean war. Nations and organizations such as Al Qaeda will attack the cloud in ways that will cause massive physical destruction by hacking our security, economy, food supplies, and health care systems in ways that amplify human suffering by orders of magnitude over today's conventional warfare. This will not replace war or terrorism; instead it will amplify it like a match doused with gasoline.

Yet, even with all of the advantages and threats I've outlined, I've barely begun to describe how the cloud will alter our world. But I'll bet that you question and intuitively resist even the moderate degree of change I've described.

Why? Because change does not come easily to minds that are set on patterns of behavior; individually and institutionally, that are nearly impossible to break free of. Simply put, change is not easy. Consider that only 20 percent of patients who suffer a heart attack actually change their behavior over the long term to a lifestyle that will prevent a future heart attack. Why are we so resistant to change? It's not that we fear change, as much as that we're unable to let go of habits that have been reinforced through decades of experience, the patterns we talked about at the outset of this book.

But there are things that can accelerate change, and most of them are driven by crisis. I have no doubt that the same will be true of the cloud. A crisis of immense complexity that threatens nearly every institution—social, political, and economic—will drive us to the cloud as a refuge and a means of survival.

How immense will the crisis need to be?

Well, begin by asking yourself a simple question: How far has humanity advanced in the last one thousand years? Pick nearly any metric of productivity. For example, how many people can a single farmer feed, how much faster can we travel great distances, how much longer is our life expectancy? Amazingly, none of these answers offers an increase greater than a few orders of magnitude, at best. Interestingly the metrics that have advanced the most are those that allow us to create faster and large communities, such as, radio, the telephone, and transportation. For example, a thousand years ago, a person could have trotted on a horse at about 8 miles an hour, with most horses able to cover about 20 to 30 miles in a day; today, a 747 cruises at 565 mph and its range is 7,713 nautical miles. Yet even these advances will pale in comparison to what is to come in the cloud.

Whether it is Moore's law, which predicts the doubling of computer processing power every two years, or Metcalfe's law, which states that a network's value is equal to the square of its nodes, the inescapable conclusion is that our ability to create connections today is barely a glimpse of what lies ahead.

Despite all our progress, we are still only connecting a relatively small piece of humanity to the cloud. Of the seven billion people on the planet, only two billion have access to the Internet. Of these, I'd estimate that less than half, or about one billion, are using the cloud in some manner, from social networking with Facebook to participating in cloudsourcing or in online exchanges such as E2open. And yet we talk about the radical ways in which the cloud has already altered our lives. Whose lives? Certainly not the lives of the other 85 percent of the world.

At the same time, you could claim that within the community of today's cloud users an even smaller minority is using the cloud to form communities in which realizable economic value is being created rather than just casual experimentation and entertainment. When you tally up the cloudsourced workers, contributors to idea exchanges such as Nine-Sigma and InnoCentive, and cloud-based value chain participants, I'd estimate that the total represents 1 percent of the one billion, or ten million people worldwide, who make up the cloud's entire working population. That's not quite two-tenths of a single percent of world population.

Yet, this small group can make one hundred trillion possible connections, according to Metcalfe's law. The practical reality is that a very small number of these connections will *actually* be made, but at least we have a benchmark of sorts.

What might it mean if we were able to increase the number of participants in the cloud and the resulting economic value of this community over the next decade by changing this equation by even a slight margin? If we double the number of participants in the cloud, the possible connections increase four times, to 400 trillion.

Raise this same number of actual cloud participants to a full 1 percent of the world's population (at the present time), and 5,000 trillion connections are possible. That is more than four orders of magnitude higher and more than fifty times greater than the number of community connections that are available online in today's world. Yet we are still including just 1 percent of the world's population! Try to imagine how much might change if we can get into double digit percentages of participation.

You can see where this is going. The numbers are staggering, and I still haven't factored in the even faster increase and even larger number of machine-to-machine and person-to-machine connections. In this world, you can understand why I believe that the cloud will be to businesses and to our lives what the evolution of intelligent life was to the process of evolution.

What's more, and what we must be sure not to underestimate, is that the cloud will be built and owned not just by multinational corporations but by an intricate and unimaginably complex ecosystem stretching all the way down to the individual. And it is here that the cloud will ultimately have its most profound impact.

The greatest possession in the coming century will be the community and the connections we form within the cloud.

Throughout this book I've tried to make it clear that the cloud still represents the extremities of markets and the economy to which power has been slowly but surely shifting for centuries. We've talked about how every social, political, and economic system is being further decentralized into entities that are apparently uncontrolled by centralized authorities and instead ruled by their communities. So why not go the next step now, and envision what it might look like to move that power further into the hands of the people who make up those communities, to amplify their voices and ambitions well beyond today's constraints?

Why limit the idea of the cloud to large enterprise or global value chains? For that matter, why limit it to business, large or small, as we know it today? The cloud is already being used by individuals to build instant communities that serve their economic and personal interests, from the toppling of governments to the protests on Wall Street. That trend will only grow in its impact and implications.

Think of it. Whether you are creating a business or a political party, the greatest impediment has always been the time it takes to create community. When this changes, how might the world change? What will it look like, this brave, new, cloud-based world, this globally hyperconnected community?

Let's keep it simple and personal. Imagine a dimly lit lawyer's office with solemn faces staring blankly across a dark mahogany conference table. A son and daughter are gathered to hear the reading of their beloved father's last will and testament. The lawyer begins to read. His low monotone drones on for what seems to be hours, until he pauses and readies himself: "…to my beloved son, I leave my entire estate, cash, equities, real estate, and personal property…"

A solemn daughter looks down as her heart drops.

The lawyer continues, "…except for the cloud that I used to build my expansive fortune. This I leave to my daughter, who I trust will use it to build a better world."

"See sis, I told you dad liked you best…"

Far-fetched? What great change hasn't been? It's only as unlikely as the degree to which you discount the ability we have to take on new challenges by reinventing ourselves, our society, businesses, and economies in dramatic new ways, which embrace an image of the globe leveraging the power of its connected humanity toward a world that is living and thriving in the cloud.

Endnotes

Chapter 1

1. Jerry Hirsch, "GM Plans a Short-Term Rental Service Involving Owners of Its Autos," *Los Angeles Times*, October 4, 2011, http://www.latimes.com/business/la-fi-gm-onstar-20111005,0,4636787.story.

2. Casey B. Mulligan, "The More the Merrier: Population Growth Promotes Innovation," *New York Times Economix blog*, September 23, 2009, http://economix.blogs.nytimes.com/2009/09/23/the-more-the-merrier-population-growth-promotes-innovation/.

Chapter 2

1. John Markoff, "An Internet Critic Who Is Not Shy About Ruffling the Big Names in High Technology," *New York Times*, April 9, 2001, http://www.nytimes.com/2001/04/09/technology/09HAIL.html?ex=1230872400&en=5d156fc75d409335&ei=5070.

2. "Conversation with Eric Schmidt hosted by Danny Sullivan," *Search Engine Strategies Conference*, news release, Google Press Center, August 9, 2006, http://www.google.com/press/podium/ses2006.html.

3. corbett3000, "Facebook Demographics and Statistics Report 2010 – 145% Growth in 1 Year," iStrategyLabs, January 4, 2010, http://www.istrategylabs.com/2010/01/facebook-demographics-and-statistics-report-2010-145-growth-in-1-year/.

4. "Daily Media Use Among Children and Teens Up Dramatically from Five Years Ago," *The Henry J. Kaiser Family Foundation Media & Health*, news release, January 20, 2010, http://www.kff.org/entmedia/entmedia012010nr.cfm.

5. Gordon E. Moore, "Cramming More Components onto Integrated Circuits," *Electronics*, April 19, 1965, 114–117, accessed August 22, 2011, http://cseweb .ucsd.edu/classes/wi09/cse240c/Slides/02_MooresLawAnd8080.pdf "Although originally calculated as a doubling every year,[1] Moore later refined the period to two years.[2] In this second source Moore also suggests that the version that is often quoted as "18 months" is due to David House, an Intel executive, who predicted that period for a doubling in chip performance (being a combination of the effect of more transistors and them being faster).[3]" (Source: http:// en.wikipedia.org/wiki/Moore%27s_law#cite_note-18months-3).

Chapter 4

1. At the time of this writing, Facebook had just introduced a function to do this, called Timeline®.

2. Firewalls are technologies used by many organizations to prevent unwanted or unauthorized intrusion into their network and information systems.

3. Misha Glenny, "Cybercrime: Is it Out of Control?" *Guardian News and Media Limited*, September 21, 2011, http://www.guardian.co.uk/technology/2011/ sep/21/cybercrime-spam-phishing-viruses-malware.

4. Neil J. Rubenking, "Reputation.com Protects Online Reputations," *PC Magazine Digital Edition*, February 16, 2011, http://www.pcmag.com/article2/ 0,2817,2380463,00.asp.

5. "Identity Fraud Fell 28 Percent in 2010 According to New Javelin Strategy & Research Report," *Javelin Strategy & Research Report*, February 8, 2011, https://www.javelinstrategy.com/news/1170/92/1.

6. Danah Boyd, "Managing Representation in a Digital World" (master's thesis, MIT Media Lab), Chapter 5, http://smg.media.mit.edu/people/danah/thesis/ thesis/idmgmt.html.

7. Hasan M. Elahi, "You Want to Track Me? Here You Go, F.B.I.," *New York Times*, October 29, 2011, http://www.nytimes.com/2011/10/30/opinion/sunday/ giving-the-fbi-what-it-wants.html.

8. Seema Sinha, "Live Forever, Virtually," *The Times of India*, November 7, 2011, http://articles.timesofindia.indiatimes.com/2011-10-09/man-woman/30260014_1_online-presence-cyber-world-facebook.

9. Angence France-Presse, "After Death, Web 'Assets' Often Tangled in Cloud," *Inquirer*, September 14, 2011, http://technology.inquirer.net/4179/after-death-web-assets-often-tangled-in-cloud/.

Chapter 7

1. "Small Businesses, Job Creation and Growth: Facts, Obstacles and Best Practices," Organisation for Economic Co-operation and Development, http://www.oecd.org/dataoecd/10/59/2090740.pdf.

2. Scott Thill, "Bitcoin: A New Kind of Money That's Beyond the Reach of Bankers, Wall St. and Regulators?" *AlterNet*, July 28, 2011, http://www.alternet.org/news/151822/bitcoin:_a_new_kind_of_money_that%27s_beyond_the_reach_of_bankers,_wall_st._and_regulators/.

3. Cassie Marketos, "Kickstarter Awards: By the Numbers," *Kickstarter Blog*, January 10, 2011, http://www.kickstarter.com/blog/kickstarter-awards-by-the-numbers.

4. "The Help Center," *Kickstarter FAQ*, www.kickstarter.com/help/faq.

5. Ibid.

6. Evan Ackerman, "Official NASA MMO offering up swag for Kickstarter funding (Update: It's a go!)," *DVICE*, August 26, 2011, http://dvice.com/archives/2011/08/official-nasa-m.php.

7. Philip Neustrom, "The Pros and Cons of Using Kickstarter to Fundraise," *PBS MediaShift Idea Lab* (weblog), November 15, 2010, http://www.pbs.org/idealab/2010/11/the-pros-and-cons-of-using-kickstarter-to-fundraise316.html.

Chapter 8

1. The answer to the riddle is a baseball diamond, (which, of course, you've figured out by now)!

2. Patrick Ritter, "42 Fun and Interesting Statistics for College Students," *degreecentral.com* (blog), March 22, 2011, http://degreecentral.com/42-fun-and-interesting-statistics-for-college-students/.

3. "E-Marketplace: eLance," *Businessweek Online*, June 5, 2000, http://www .businessweek.com/2000/00_23/b3684045.htm.

4. Codi Barbierri, "Elance Report: Freelance is the New Full-time," *VentureBeat*, April 12, 2010, http://venturebeat.com/2010/04/12/elance-report-freelance -is-the-new-full-time/.

5. "What My Elance Cloud Commute Looks Like by Ted Bendixson, Freelance Writer," YouTube video, 1:04, posted by "shredbots," October 20, 2010, http:// www.youtube.com/watch?v=AWvTzs8EX7w&feature=related.

6. Richard Freeman, "What Really Ails Europe (and America): The Doubling of the Global Workforce," *the Globalist*, March 5, 2010, http://www.theglobalist .com/storyid.aspx?StoryId=4542.

Chapter 9

1. "Literacy," United Nations Educational, Scientific and Cultural Organiza-tion, http://www.unesco.org/new/en/education/themes/education-building -blocks/literacy/#topPage.

2. Chikodi Chima, "Hands On: India's $35 Aakash Android Tablet Lands in Amer-ica (exclusive)," *VentureBeat, MobileBeat*, October 26, 2011, http://venturebeat .com/2011/10/26/aakash-android-tablet-exclusive/.

3. Thomas L. Friedman, "The Last Person," *New York Times*, November 12, 2011, http://www.nytimes.com/2011/11/13/opinion/sunday/friedman-the-last -person.html.

4. Leonard Medlock and Betsy Corcoran, "YouTube U: The Power Of Stan-ford's Free Online Education," *Fast Company Co.Exist*, http://www.fastcoexist .com/1678792/youtube-u-the-power-of-stanfords-free-online-education.

5. "Moodle About," accessed November 2011, http://www.moodle.org/about/.

6. "Welcome to the Moodle Toolkit - The Ultimate Guide to Moodle for Non-Profits," University of San Francisco Department of Computer Science, accessed November 2011, http://www.cs.usfca.edu/~jreyes/Moodle/index.html.

7. "Moodle in Education," accessed November 2011, http://docs.moodle.org/20/ en/Moodle_in_education.

8. "Moodle Community Forums," last modified August 7, 2010, accessed November 2011, http://moodle.org/mod/forum/discuss.php?d=155435&parent=680798.

9. "Moodle Statistics," accessed November 2011, http://moodle.org/stats.

10. Sam Dean, "Moodle Open Source E-Learning Heads for the Cloud," *OStatic*, July 15, 2008, http://ostatic.com/blog/moodle-open-source-e-learning-heads -for-the-cloud.

11. Bridget Jones, "High School from Home," Gold Country Media Auburn Journal, August 30, 2010, http://auburnjournal.com/detail/157479.html.

12. "Springville Students Use 'Moodle' for 21st Century Learning," *The St. Clair Times*, April 2010, http://www.thestclairtimes.com/view/full_story/6899262/ article-Springville-students-use–Moodle–for-21st-century-learning.

13. Kirsty Williamson, "Great Corby School: Moodle Is an Interactive Online Environment for Pupils, Teachers and Parents," *The Guardian*, December 8, 2010, http://www.guardian.co.uk/classroom-innovation/video/great-corby-school.

14. *Ibid.*

Afterword

1. "Shapeways About Us," accessed November 2011, http://www.shapeways .com/about/.

2. George O. Mohler, Martin B. Short, P. Jeffrey Brantingham, Frederic P. Schoenberg, George E. Tita, "Self-Exciting Point Process Modeling of Crime," *Journal of the American Statistical Association* 106 (March 1, 2011): 100–108, doi: 10.1198/jasa.2011.ap09546.

References

Howe, Jeff. "Look Who's Crowdsourcing." *Wired* 14:06 (June 2006).

Koulopoulos, Thomas M. *The Innovation Zone: How Great Companies Re-Innovate for Amazing Success. Boston:* Nicholas Brealey Publishing, 2009.

Kuhn, Thomas S. *The Structure of Scientific Revolution.* Chicago: University of Chicago, 1996.

Kurzweil, Ray. *The Age of Spiritual Machines: When Computers Exceed Human Intelligence.* New York: Penguin, 2000.

Malone, Thomas W., and Robert J. Laubacher. "The Dawn of the E-lance Economy." *Harvard Business Review:* 1998 Sep-Oct;76(5):144–52, 189.

Mankiw, N. Gregory. *Principles of Economics.* Ohio: South-Western College Publishing, 2011.

Marx, Karl. *Das Kapital.* Synergy International of the Americas, Ltd, 2007.

Schumpeter, Joseph. *Capitalism, Socialism and Democracy.* New York: Harper Perennial, 1962.

Simon, Phil and Chris Brogan. *The New Small: How a New Breed of Small Businesses Is Harnessing the Power of Emerging Technologies.* Motion Publishing, 2010.

Sowell, Thomas. *The Quest for Cosmic Justice.* New York: The Free Press, 1999.

Index

What's Next?

If you have enjoyed *Cloud Surfing,* I invite you personally to keep the experience alive. There are a number of ways you can do that, and they all start with a visit to, (where else?) The Cloud, of course.

There you will find:

Your Cloud Surfing IQ
www.CloudSurfing Book.com

- Measure your cloud surfing capability and compare it with thousands of other readers who have taken a short survey to identify how well they understand and are leveraging the cloud. You'll get an instant score to rate yourself and your organization.

Join the Conversation
www.TKspeaks.com

- Check out my blog, find out my latest thoughts on The Cloud, and add your voice to the conversation.

Speaking
www.TKspeaks.com

- Much of time is spent delivering keynotes on the impact of megatrends such as The Cloud on business, government, education, and society. Visit *www.Tkspeaks.com* to see dozens of videos and find out more about how I can help with your event.

Consulting
www.DelphiGroup.com

• Delphi Group has provided consulting, advisory, and educational services for more than 20 years to nearly every major company and branch of government. In fact we even have our own Cloud-based virtual events that we can customize to meet the needs of even the largest global organizations. Find out more about Delphi Group and how we can help you navigate the future by visiting www.DelphiGroup.com.

I hope that the time you have taken to read *Cloud Surfing* is only the beginning of our relationship.

See you in The Cloud! - tk